Willa Cather and the Art of Conflict

Willa Cather and the Art of Conflict:
Re-Visioning Her
Creative Imagination

by
Patrick W. Shaw

The Whitston Publishing Company
Troy, New York
1992

Library of Congress Catalog Card Number 91-75024

ISBN 0-87875-423-7

Printed in the United States of America

Parts of Chapter 2 first appeared in *American Literature*, 56, no. 4 (Dec. 1984).

Parts of Chapter 7 first appeared in *American Imago*, 46, no. 1 (Spring 1989).

Parts of Chapter 8 first appeared in *South Central Review*, 8, no. 4 (Winter 1991).

For Erin, Allison, and Pat

Acknowledgments

I would like to thank the several readers who offered sound advice for the improvement of this study. I want also to express appreciation to the National Endowment for the Humanities for a 1989 grant which further helped me formulate my ideas concerning Willa Cather. I especially want to thank Lady Falls Brown, who patiently and with good cheer critiqued the study from its earliest stages.

Contents

Introduction:
Background and Theoretical Bases

Like many artists, Willa Cather knew personal conflict. She was a free thinker reared amidst Calvinist dogma; a materialist acutely aware of the limited worth of "things"; an optimist who wanted to retain faith; a skeptic prone to depression and despair. In her fiction, successful marriages, happy families, and satisfying personal relationships are as scarce as summer rain in the New Mexican desert. Suicide marks her pages like the Platte River cuts Nebraska. Of all her conflicts, however, none is more acute or controversial than her sexuality. There are those who maintain that Cather was not homoerotic. For instance, in an interview published in the *Omaha World-Herald* (1984), Susan J. Rosowski and Mildred Bennett advocate Cather's heterosexuality and maintain that her interest in other women was nothing more than school-girl crushes (*Cather Scholar* 4). Sharon O'Brien, first in several essays and then in *Willa Cather: The Emerging Voice,* and others elsewhere have argued rather convincingly that Cather was homosexual, though the term itself is usually avoided. O'Brien's phraseology is that Cather was "a woman whose primary intimacies were with other women" and that "her fiction reveals that she found sexuality and passion troublesome forces" (*Mothers* 267). Cather's homoerotic conflicts were resolved, O'Brien argues, after she met Sarah Orne Jewett and learned to identify with her own femaleness and "commit herself to the artist's vocation" (277). *O Pioneers!* is Cather's declaration of independence as a female artist. With it Cather "resolved the conflicts that had kept 'woman' and 'artist' apart" and afterwards her novels flowed in "a steady stream" of integrated selfhood (282). James Woodress, somewhat ill at ease with the "Contemporary frankness" that "raises the question of lesbianism" (141) is noticeably politic:

> If one defines a lesbian as a woman who has sexual re-
> lations with another woman, Cather cannot be called a
> lesbian on the basis of available records. On the other
> hand, if a lesbian is a woman whose primary emotional
> attachments are to other women, regardless of sexual
> relations, the definition adopted by some feminists,
> then Cather was most certainly a lesbian. (141)

Deborah G. Lambert states the dilemma most effectively: Cather was "a lesbian writer who could not, or did not, acknowledge her homosexuality and who, in her fiction, transformed her emotional life and experiences into acceptable, heterosexual forms and guises" (676). The sociosexual conflicts implied by Lambert's summation are crucial to my arguments. Cather's psychosexuality was abnormal—if we define "normal" (as did Freud and other Victorian evaluators) as the conventional biological attraction of a representative of one gender for a representative of the other gender, with the ultimate motive of begetting more representatives of the species Homo sapiens while experiencing some emotional satisfaction in the process, albeit such satisfaction is not to be overdone. In short, Cather was "lesbian" —a woman who was sexually unorthodox by nature, who was acutely aware that she had to answer to a distinctly heterosexual society, and who may or may not have experienced intimate sexual relationships. Whether she ever consummated her sexuality is inconsequential to my theories about Cather's creativity, but the psychological conflicts which resulted from the nonconformist eroticism are crucial to those theories. I believe that Cather's primary sexual attraction was to other females and that such attraction perplexed her throughout her life because homoeroticism clashed with her strong sense of social propriety.

I am hardly the first to recognize the conflicts that beset Cather. Sharon O'Brien's hypothesis of Cather's conflicts and how she reconciled them has already been noted. Bernice Slote in *The Kingdom of Art* (1966), introducing Cather's earliest writing, observes that from the beginning Cather "was caught in that ancient pull of the gods, torn between the Dionysian and Apollonian forces of rapture and repose, release and containment. That conflict was at the very center of her creative will" (91). Judith Fryer, in *Felicitous Space: The Imaginative Structures of Edith Wharton and Willa Cather* (1986) observes that "the divided self" is a "subject central to Cather's fiction, often presented in her early works as a conflict between woman and artist, and developed with an interest, finally, not so much in reconciliation as in creating a new context in which the force, passion and energy of the creative self can be preserved" (217). She does not elucidate the observation, yet Fryer's implied thesis is close to my own. My belief is that rather than being an obstacle which Cather had to overcome to produce her fiction, those conflicts—especially the homoerotic tensions—were the energy source for her creativity. Even more importantly, she took no action which might have significantly alleviated those conflicts. Her creative genius was fueled by psychic dissonance and protected by an intuitive awareness that the dissonance was not to be tampered with. Early in his theorizing, Freud developed a principle which Peter Gay summarizes as "psychological determinism, the view of the mind as consisting of forces in conflict, the concept of the dynamic unconscious and the concealed power of passion in all mental activity" (119). Certainly the concept parallels the one I am trying to apply to Cather, but as I perceive his idea, Freud had a somewhat narrower perspective than I have in mind for Cather, focusing his idea of conflicts mainly on what he later would define as Eros and Thanatos or the life-death struggle.

Given her motif of suicide embedded in narratives ostensibly celebratory of life, we might well conclude that the primary cause of Cather's conflicts was the Eros-Thanatos paradox. Yet Freudian theory, while helpful, never completely explains Catherean processes. *The Eros and the Id*—the essay in which Freud clarifies the Eros-Thanatos battle and which was published at the height of Cather's productivity—came late in his career (1923). It is, as Peter Gay correctly notes, "indispensable" (411) in understanding Freud, for Freud saw those "two elemental pugnacious forces in the mind" (401) at the center of all his other concepts. It is within the Id that the battle between being and not being occurs, and the fallout is neuroses. For Freud, neuroses were destructive. Cather's view, however, is more accurately reflected by Freudian revisionists such as Norman O. Brown, who in *Life Against Death* disagrees with Freud and sees neuroses with their "fixation on perversions," as positive demonstrations of "the refusal of the unconscious essence of our being to acquiesce in the duality of flesh and spirit" (31-32)—the duality otherwise expressed in Eros-Thanatos. Brown agrees with Freud that the genital or male orientation produces undesirable side effects, but he categorically rejects what he terms Freud's "rude, persistent demand for the bodily origin of spiritual things" (25).

He finds comfort in the fact that despite all "parental discipline, religious denunciation of bodily pleasure, and philosophic exaltation of the life of reason" have been able to do, the human animal remains unconvinced that its "pleasure-seeking" (or life seeking) impulses are wrong; and neuroses are the positive signs of our stubborn refusal to say good-bye to the lost paradise of childhood, the stage at which these impulses are formed (31).

Cather could not in her own life reify her subconscious desires, could not shake the dust of the Nebraskan village or free herself from "parental discipline" and "religious dununciation"; but in her fiction she sublimated the desires. Especially in her children (which are so dominant in *My Ántonia* and *Shadows on the Rock*, and which are transfigured as the uncorrupted Indians of *Death Comes for the Archbishop*) she intuitively projects both the sexual freedom inherent in the preadult stages of erotic development and the natural freedom from death awareness that ultimately constricts the adult. For Cather, the child is not only a literary symbol of innocence and exuberance, but an artistic extension of the essential design of her narratives, an image of sexual guiltlessness and the time when sexual pleasures could be pursued and enjoyed, free of what Brown terms "the tyranny of genital organization" (29). As Frederick J. Hoffman reminds us, the entire life of the individual and of the race is encapsulated in the child, and the artist naturally turns to the child for inspiration (19). From the child in her, Cather received both her artistic imagination and answers to questions arising from her own "perverse" sexuality. Projecting this child self, Cather populates her fictive world with male and female children who are free from erotic confusion and guilt and who lack conscious knowledge of their mortality. What Cather wanted to convey with her fictive children was not slavish nostalgia or escapism but an integrated attempt to reunite herself psychologically with nature, to lessen the culturally imposed strictures of sexual (and sexist) dogmas. If, somewhat mystically through an imagination drawing heavily from childhood and the past, Cather could regain or reenter a preadult stage of innocence, she could thereby free herself from the complexes that first create and then feed upon guilt and repression. Such a desire was impossible to reify, but the effort to do so is nonetheless perceptible in Cather's thinking.

The method I follow throughout in trying to "get at" the sources of Cather's imagination is essentially psychoanalytical, but not purely Freudian. Though I disagree with Sharon

O'Brien in several instances, I do agree that the "important recent development in feminist literary criticism is psychoanalytic
rather than cultural in orientation" (*Mothers* 266). Not feminist,
my own critical approach is psychoanalytic, with reservations
which will be noted. My methodology derives also from theories summarized in *A Theory of Narrative* by F. K. Stanzel, who
refers to the "deep structure" of narrative, where characters
move beyond the strict control of both author and audience and
where their purpose "can be made visible only with the help of
theoretical operations" (15-16). Stanzel, along with Kenneth
Burke (in *The Philosophy of Literary Form*) and other theorists,
assumes an experiential base of the imagination and thus to fiction. In discussing mediacy and the figure of the fictive narrator
Stanzel states that "every apprehension of reality is dependent
upon more or less accurate presuppositions or a prior understanding of this reality" (10-11). The transmogrifications which
occur between the experience and the imaginative portrayal of
that experience, however, are extremely complex; and it is that
complexity with which I try to deal, depending upon "theoretical
operations" to clarify what text and biography often leave mysterious. And while on the point of biography: I feel that Cather,
like most artists, was less than candid in personal statements relative to her biography and art. (Faulkner's outrageous distor-
tions, Katherine Anne Porter's fabricated biography, and other
similar authorial falsehoods come to mind as parallels.) So
while I quote from a number of her interviews and public statements, I do so carefully, realizing her potential for disingenuousness. Knowing her record of destroying correspondence and
having had to hurdle some of the barricades she erected against
readers of that which remains, I take anything she says about
herself with due caution. For the facts of her life, I depend most
often upon the usual sources such as Elizabeth Sergeant, E. K.
Brown, and especially James Woodress, though I may at times
disagree with conclusions they draw from those biographical
facts. At every moment, I am aware of the warning with which
Murray Kreiger begins his *Theory of Criticism*: "Literary theory
is a vain discipline" (3).

    To construct the experiential base of my own theorizing, I
want first to look briefly at Cather's noted cross-dressing and
then more carefully at her decision not to align herself with the
expatriate lesbian movement of the era—a movement which
did much to liberate other female artists from the conflicts and

tensions of Victorian strictures and which helped define modernist fiction per se.

I choose Gertrude Stein as a convenient figure of comparison because she personifies the female artist who consciously elected to associate with and find her identity in the lesbian community which flourished in Paris between the two World Wars and because she was Cather's near-exact contemporary (Stein 1874-1946, Cather 1873-1947) and was of similar background. As those familiar with Shari Benstock's *Women of the Left Bank* will immediately recognize, I am overlooking numerous other American women writers who were involved in the Left Bank life and am foregoing several differentiating factors (such as economics) which led to some subtle and not so subtle gradations in the lesbian typology. However, Stein serves more accurately than others of the Left Bank personalities as a model for some of the points I wish to sketch for Cather. The pertinent question—more rhetorical than answerable—concerning Cather and the Left Bank community (both in its actuality and in what it symbolized) is why she never became a part of the subculture, especially since her great love Isabelle McClung lived in Paris and in light of her devotion to French culture, her frequent trips to France, and considering the solution such commitment might have offered to some of her psychosexual dilemmas. In other words, why did she keep going back to Red Cloud when she could have stayed in Paris, even though, as she herself said, every time she crossed the Missouri River when returning to Nebraska she was so confused she "could not decide which was the real and which the fake 'me'" (*WC in Person* 37).

Cather's abandonment of conventional female attire and her adoption of conventional male attire are the only incontrovertible facts which link her to "inverted" or "perverted" sexuality. The details are familiar: From the time she was approximately thirteen until she entered college, Cather "cut her hair shorter than most boys" and "wore boys' clothes, a derby, and carried a cane" (Woodress, *WC* 55). Moreover, she insisted on being identified by the patronymic "William" and several times played male parts in amateur dramas. Her naturally deep, masculine voice aided her disguise. As an adult, Cather (like Stein) discontinued the radical male dress, at least publicly, but sublimated the trait into the symbolic projection of self in fictive male characters. Contrary to what we might assume, such crossdressing may be but is not necessarily an endorsement of love for others of the same gender. As Benstock notes in discussing

Stein, cross-dressing such as Cather evidenced constitutes "a simultaneous denial of the feminine and a taunting of male authority." Moreover, "Although cross-dressing was an antisocial act that called attention to societal definitions of female homosexuals as 'inverts' and 'perverts,' it nonetheless was not a sign of liberation from heterosexual norms or patriarchal domination" (181). That is, Cather's cross-dressing was the manifestation of a complex and contradictory set of responses to her femininity and to the environment in which fate placed her. On the one hand it identifies her as being ashamed of the characteristics which biological chance has granted her and marks her consequent desire to abjure femininity and assume the male persona which society has designated as dominant. On the other hand, it shows her mockery of that unjust "dominant" designation—a designation based almost entirely upon superficialities (clothes, canes, hair style).

Like Stein, who openly fulfilled the masculine role in her "marriage" to Alice B. Toklas, Cather seems to have occupied that same dominant role in her long-term relationship with Edith Lewis, with whom she lived from 1908 until her death in 1947. As Leon Edel explains in offering caveats about Lewis's biography of Cather, Lewis was so subservient that she could have written nothing but a "worshipful life" of her friend (189). However, much unlike Stein, who went public with her homoeroticism well before World War I commenced in Europe and thereby effectively "resolved the personal conflict that troubled her youth" (143), Cather never liberated herself from what Benstock calls the "modes of entrapment, betrayal, and exclusion suffered by women in the first decades of the twentieth century" in America (6). As Joanna Russ says, "the social invention of the morbid, unhealthy, criminal lesbian" had become so dominant by the late nineteenth century in America that the "innocent rightness in feelings of love for and attraction to women" which an earlier generation enjoyed was no longer possible for Cather (79). Consequently, Cather was obsessively private about her personal life. Her adolescent cross-dressing before her Nebraska friends and family was, therefore, the only time she dared publicize her homoeroticism. Once past that stage of freedom which childhood allowed her, she never felt secure enough to make public the true nature of her relationships with Lewis or any other women with whom she may have been intimate. Her secret self, she thought, was safe from the world at large—but the folks back home had more evidence than most for passing judgments.

Across the wide Missouri in Nebraska, the prairie society adhered to Freud's pronouncement that the only normal sex was heteroerotic, penis-in-vagina intercourse. Indoctrinated by that definition of normality, Cather was unwilling to modify her adult sexual ethic radically enough to rebel publicly against it. The antisocial conduct that came spontaneously in the pre-sexual days of thirteen was tolerated by a Red Cloud that, not wanting to cope with matters taboo, dismissed her cross-dressing as mere tomboyism and showing off. However, the town was not quite so willing to ignore those same traits when Cather was twenty or thirty, and she had to suppress them. After her Age of Awareness, that is, her society would not grant the latitude which it was willing to grant in her Age of Innocence. The resulting psychic tension, however, came less from Red Cloud's not continuing its moratorium on "Sin" than from Cather's not distancing herself enough from such society to grant self-immunity—as Stein and many others in the Left Bank community did to a noticeable degree. Stein, in contrast to Cather, separated literally and psychosexually from a society which she felt was "provincial, restrictive, and belonged—like Queen Victoria—to another century" (Benstock 12). Once freed, Stein wrote with comparative openness about her lesbianism (as in Q. E. D. [1903]) and institutionalized her lifestyle into one of the influential literary salons of Paris. Cather never managed such a societal break or realized such autonomy.

In analyzing Stein's place in American fiction, Cynthia Secor offers some parallels to Cather that are apropos to my thesis. (That others before me have thought of Stein and Cather in the same context is also implied by the fact that Secor's essay is juxtaposed with Sharon O'Brien's essay on Willa Cather in Fritz Fleischmann's *American Novelists Revisited: Essays in Feminist Criticism*.) We can apply to Cather many of the same points Secor clarifies for Stein. Like Cather, "How [Stein] means and what she means remain open to question" (301). In reading Stein,

> The serious reader is expected to grapple with the significance of representation, the strategies whereby meaning is generated, the nature of voice, the structure of narration, and the possibility or impossibility of ascertaining definitively what is being expressed. "What she means" is problematic for many readers be-

cause she is deliberately writing beyond the patriarchal tradition and is, therefore, difficult to grasp until
one understands that the male, as such, the masculine,
the hierarchical, the phallic, the violent, the con-
flictual, the linear, the direct, and the masterful are
not what she writes about. (301)

In other words, that Stein was lesbian did not mean she was
male or that her sensibilities were masculine. Because in large
measure she separated herself from that patriarchal dominance
and escaped the strictures of the puritan society, and freed her
psyche by writing openly of her sexuality, Stein—unlike
Cather—"created out of the fundamental female sense that the
womb, the room, the nipples, the tender buttons, are a never-
ending fount of life and nourishment" (308). Having faced
essentially the same obstacles as Cather, Stein shows in her texts
that "despite her direct personal involvement in two wars and
the loss in both of dear friends, the principal aesthetic at work is
that of abundance, pleasure, and satisfaction." Though frightened at times, she "was never torn by despair or terror" and "the
texts render unnecessary a distinction between the *texte de
plaisir* and the *texte de jouissance*" (308).

That Cather's tensions emanated less from society's rules
per se and more from her own inability (or unwillingness) to
distance herself from those rules is a significant distinction.
Quite simply put, such internal locating of responsibility effectively prevented Cather from blaming society for her conflicts.
Thus, in her fiction society is seldom indicted for whatever problems may befall her protagonists. Having no psychological
scapegoat, Cather therefore is forced back time and again into the
self for someone or something to censure. In short, unlike
Hemingway for instance or even Stein, she does not have that
external "they" to cast as villain. Consequently, her conflicts re-
act upon themselves in a kind of mental fusion chamber which
energizes, changes the forms of, and multiplies the tensions.
This refusal to hold society accountable for personal faults is also
in part what often makes us as audience and society's representatives so comfortable in the presence of Cather's fiction and what
has given her the reputation (albeit inaccurate) of a sanguine
humanitarian, almost at times a Pollyanna trapped in a cruel
world from which she wanted to flee. Because we as "society"
feel exonerated from whatever crime and punishment the narrative may demand, we tend to judge the creator of that exculpa-
tion too benignly.

No one can safely argue that had Cather followed Stein's example by first placing blame squarely upon American society and then by abandoning that society she would have avoided the disappointments that marked her life or that she would have produced consistently "better" fiction. We can only surmise what could have been from what Cather in "The Bohemian Girl" calls the record of "inverse development" (*Collected Short Fiction* 114), such as the motif of the imprisoned self which permeates her fiction. Cather remained incarcerated by the same strictures which drove Stein and other American women artists to the liberating tolerance of the Left Bank milieu, "where life was economically, psychologically, and politically easier" (Benstock 13). While for Wharton, Stein, Colette and other women associated with the Paris expatriate life writing may have been a process of sexual self-discovery and at least partial liberation, it was not so for Cather. It was instead a process by which she consciously tried to mask but unconsciously struggled to reveal her homoeroticism. She was often her own mortal enemy. In that psychic war lies both the compelling tragedy and the power of her fiction.

We have no way of knowing what psychological peace (if any) might have resulted if Cather had been more open with her homoeroticism or could have experienced the camaraderie ("matria") that the Left Bank group offered. We do know, however, that Cather did not choose to associate herself openly with the lesbian community, though that option was clearly available to her even in the earliest stages of her development as a writer. Moreover, as a result of her choosing to reside in a homophobic America and to suppress her homoeroticism, she consequently was conflicted both personally and artistically. Had she emigrated and had she become part of the Left Bank lesbian community, her fiction could well lack many of the tensions which her unresolved conflicts generated and which give it its distinctive tone and texture. Therefore, the true importance of Cather's homoeroticism—contrary to what O'Brien argues—is that Cather never totally reconciled herself to her own sexuality, never came to terms with her masculine-feminine selves, even though a well-defined and easily accessible and perhaps palliative lesbian community was available to her. Just as Stein's decision to live openly and write openly as a lesbian was the essence of her art, so on the contrary was Cather's decision to deny her homoeroticism the essence of her artistic processes. The larger realm of these artistic processes, not the homoeroticism, is what I wish to concentrate upon in the following analyses, hopefully to alter some of the traditional attitudes which have accrued to Cather's novels.

The specifics of the traditionalist view become more apparent in the discussions of the individual novels, but for the sake of introduction the view is definable as one which sees Cather as a more or less optimistic regionalist; an autobiographical writer who faithfully recorded the Nebraska prairie and the life it engendered; a woman who clung to the theological, sexual, ethical values inherited from the Victorian or pre-Freudian ethic. The tradition ties her to Henry James, notes her conflict between Old World and New World cultures, and more often than not sees her as an artist who generally revered the past and turned away in disgust from the twentieth century. Cather's most noted biographer James Woodress, for example, bases his evaluation of Cather's life and art upon "her high regard for traditional values" (WC 142) and holds that her fiction consistently offers an "affirmation of life after death" (WC 215).

Numerous texts epitomize this critical tradition which Woodress summarizes and with which I take some exception. Not wishing to duplicate work already done by others, such as Marilyn Arnold in her introduction to *Willa Cather: A Reference Guide*, I will avoid summaries or listings of these texts. Instead, I have rather arbitrarily chosen to comment on two chronologically diverse books which convey the traditional values. David Daiches's *Willa Cather: A Critical Introduction* (1951) is an early effort by an intelligent non-expert to "write a work of literary criticism and appreciation, not a work of philosophy" (v). Daiches first connects Cather to Henry James, then establishes his thesis, which he restates several times: like James, the major theme in Cather's fiction is "the relation between the Old World and the New" (16). He pursues this thesis through a discussion of her novels. His comments are balanced by a recognition of artistic weaknesses, especially in the early novels; but his final estimate is a laudatory summation which sees her transcending American themes to become universal via the multicultural scope of her narratives. He says that Cather is "civilized"; and, he warns, "if we interpret that term too narrowly that is because we have not read Willa Cather carefully enough" (189). The weakness of Daiches's introduction is that he himself seems to have read Cather carefully but not deeply enough. He argues, rightfully, that Cather deserves credit for her unique vision of "the American scene" (189); but he does not elucidate that vision. His text is predominantly plot summary and extensive quotations from Cather's own writing, and his brief analyses do not carry the reader much beyond the thesis that Cather dealt with the relations between the Old World and the New. (I find it interesting that Hemingway and Fitzgerald, for example, were not limited by similar critical theses, especially since they dealt more extensively and directly than Cather with the meeting of the Old World and the New.) In all fairness to Daiches, however, we must recall that he was writing his introduction in the late 1940s, when hardly anyone was writing anything about Cather.

The persistence of Daiches's general approach can be demonstrated in the second text I have chosen. *The Art of Willa Cather* (1974), edited by Bernice Slote and Virginia Faulkner, grew out of a 1973 seminar conducted at the University of Nebraska in celebration of Cather's hundredth birthday. It exemplifies the types of criticism which Cather's fiction has received during the past twenty years or so and which have been centered at the University of Nebraska. The text contains some notable commentaries by respected literati and is interesting on several levels. After an opening essay by Eudora Welty which is rich in praise of Cather's accomplishment but essentially noncritical, the text presents Marcus Cunliffe's view of Cather. Cunliffe, who totally ignored Cather twenty years earlier in *The Literature of the United States*, had by 1973 familiarized himself enough with her work to modify Daiches' early thesis and recognize that Cather's fiction deals with "a whole set of tensions between West and East" (24) and to note, therefore, historical parallels with Frederick Jackson Turner. Essays by James Woodress, Leon Edel, and Alfred Knopf—not surprisingly—focus on Cather's biography, while several other writers comment on Cather's relationship with foreign countries (another variation of Daiches's earlier thesis). By far the wisest analysis in the text is the essay presented by James E. Miller, Jr., "Willa Cather and the Art of Fiction." Miller offers intelligent assessments of Cather's development as a novelist—from *Alexander's Bridge* to *Death Comes for the Archbishop*. Even here, however, as the title immediately establishes, Miller is elucidating the traditional connection between James and Cather. Notable about all the essays in *The Art of Willa Cather* is the paucity of discussion or comment about Cather's sexuality or her feminism, though certainly by 1973 such issues were topical.

The best of this traditional criticism—too extensive to annotate here but summarized in Arnold's bibliography—has by no means been detrimental to Cather. Less like a tyrannical warden and more nearly like a loving parent, it kept Cather's work viable when mainstream criticism was ignoring her in its exaltation of more "modernist" fictionists such as Joyce, Lawrence, Hemingway, Fitzgerald, Faulkner, and even Katherine Anne Porter—many of whom, I might argue, were more "traditional" in structure, content, and personal ethics than Cather. The limitation of the Cather tradition is that in its zeal to promote and protect, it may have discouraged an earlier and more thorough application of contemporary critical theory and objective evaluation generally to Cather's work. Yet, the existing traditional criticism makes possible comparatively "untraditional" and unorthodox evaluations such as mine. My evaluations have no argument with, and in fact endorse, many of the traditional approaches. My points of disagreement are (1) that Cather was less a victim of circumstance and biology and more an intuitively wise manager of those factors, and (2) that there are additional steps beyond the traditional which still need to be taken in appraising Cather's novels. There are, that is, other "visions."

In constructing my own visions of Cather, I do not attempt to offer an unfailingly positive view of her fiction. Perhaps more so than many great artists Cather has major faults. For instance, in an era (roughly 1900 through the 1920s) when American fiction distinguished itself for its experimentation with and creative management of point of view, Cather was seldom able to get her own narrative perspective under control. (Very late in her career, she was still doing such things as drowning her point of view character or suddenly inserting a five-year old child in an epilogue to claim narrative responsibility for the dark tale which precedes.) Following the leads set by James, Twain, Anderson, and others, Hemingway and Fitzgerald were carrying first-person narration to new elevations, and Faulkner was making multiple narrative perspectives the raison d'être of his fiction. Cather, meanwhile, seems to have remained unaware of many of the elements involved in making that which is "not true" seem true to an audience. From *Alexander's Bridge* to *Sapphira and the Slave Girl*, her struggle with point of view is discernible, and intriguing. This problem with authorial perspective vis-à-vis audience and fictive personae arguably resulted from Cather's failure to reconcile the conflicting elements in her own psyche—a matter I will pursue later. As her own prefaces and other comments on fiction writing attest, she herself was more honestly "hard" on her work than many of her critics. She revered fiction making more than image building, and to avoid noting the bruises she took in pursuit of her art would do Cather a disservice.

I deal almost exclusively with Cather's novels—or, more precisely, with those twelve books commonly considered to be her novels. Numerous of her shorter works—both fiction and nonfiction—are mentioned, but none is discussed in detail. This limitation is attributable mostly to the pragmatic realities of time and space, but attributable more importantly to the fact that many of the elements I address in the novels would be duplicated in discussion of the short stories. Moreover, Cather was not a prolific short story writer—nor an especially effective one—and her reputation correctly rests predominantly upon her long fiction, a genre with which she was both prolific and expert. She seems often to have viewed the short story form as preparatory work for longer fiction, and her stories frequently were early versions of novels in progress. *O Pioneers!*, for example, began as two short shories, neither of which satisfied Cather until they were subsumed into the longer narrative form; and several of her stories were trial runs for tales that later became parts of novels—as with "Peter," her first published story that resurfaced in *My Ántonia*. As for her poetry, when compared to her prose fiction it is minor and does not add greatly to any appreciation of her art other than to foreshadow certain motifs that she elucidates in the novels. Cather herself had minimum interest in writing poetry after the publication of *O Pioneers!* in 1913.

My analyses of these twelve novels are not consciously "constructionist," "deconstructionist," "Deriddean," "Feminist," or any other of the critical theories that fall under the general rubric of "reader response" and which have been in vogue for the past two decades or so. Clearly, the analyses are "reader response" (as it seems any criticism must be), but they are not premeditatedly allied with any specific school. The restrictive definitions of many of these recent theories seem often to be more detrimental than the traditional approaches which they decry; and, perhaps more damning, the jargon of some of the theories obscures and confuses more than it clarifies. In this respect, elements of the theories seem premeditatedly elitist. Hemingway comes to mind with his posturing and the "aficionado" pidgin-Spanish which also sought to make the dealing with bulls seem more noble than it is. I hold with Sandra Gilbert and Susan Gubar, who in speaking of new wave criticism generally and Derrida specifically, feel that much such theory "bears a striking resemblance" to past critical "fantasies" (261) and is in some respects more reactionary than progressive. On the other hand, the demand for reevaluation which rests at the heart of these theories is truly valuable, and that essential worth hopefully informs my commentaries. More precisely, my approach for each novel is to focus upon specific textual elements which have not previously been analyzed but which simultaneously elucidate both the narrative under discussion and Cather's overall creative processes.

While my analyses of these interrelated conflicts follow the publication chronology of Cather's novels, my views of those novels were not originally determined by so convenient a sequence. In large measure the views were articulated retrospectively, after I had come to terms with the final three of her novels: *Shadows on the Rock* (1931), *Lucy Gayheart* (1935), and *Sapphira and the Slave Girl* (1940). These novels make more explicit the fear, darkness, physical and psychological isolation that are embedded in the subtexts of the previous novels and that culminate in the masterpiece *Death Comes for the Archbishop*. Therefore, I feel we might benefit more from re-visioning our own perspectives by looking at *Archbishop* and the preceding novels through the lenses Cather offers in her final three narratives, thereby to realize that the earlier novels (especially *Archbishop*) are not as bright and affirmative as much traditional criticism presents them—or, more precisely, as we might wish them. Thus, though I follow publication dates for clarity and to promote a sense of Cather's artistic development in other respects, this retrospective view colors much of my critical attitude toward her work and informs my analyses.

One half of Cather's novels were published between the end of World War I and the beginning of the Depression in 1930. More precisely, they were published between 1918 and 1927. These six include and are bracketed by the publication of Cather's two consensus masterpieces: *My Ántonia* (1918) and *Death Comes for the Archbishop* (1927). Between these two are three novels which are not as consistent in tone, narrative focus, or characterization but which are nonetheless impressive narratives: *One of Ours* (1922), *A Lost Lady* (1923), and *The Professor's House* (1925). *My Mortal Enemy* (1926), perhaps the least articulate of Cather's novels, belongs to the grouping. Apropos to my point, *My Ántonia* was also revised moderately in 1926. By any standards of measurement, therefore, the greatest of Cather's work—both numerically and artistically—occurred in the Twenties. This chronology is noteworthy not only because few novelists can match Cather's output for any similar period, but also because it puts her head to head with those novelists of the Twenties who are commonly regarded as the phenomena of American fiction—Lewis, Fitzgerald, Hemingway, Dos Passos, Wolfe, and Faulkner.

While Cather's novels sold consistently well after *O Pioneers!*, she did not outdo the male writers in cash-register popularity. Just as an example, *One of Ours*, while far from her best effort artistically, was a best-seller. It sold more than 54,000 copies its first year and secured Cather financially. Fitzgerald's *The Beautiful and Damned*, published the same year (1922), sold approximately the same number, but both were far behind Sinclair Lewis's *Main Street*, which sold 295,000 copies in 1921. Insofar as critical attention was concerned, in the first five or six decades of the century she never came close to receiving the range of analysis afforded the male writers of the Twenties. As Marilyn Arnold notes, Cather was "virtually ignored by the writers of some important studies in twentieth-century American literature" (xvi), their attitude being that for any woman "to write at all is remarkable" (xvii). For example, Marcus Cunliffe in his 1954 survey of American literature does not even include Cather among his list of novelists whom he must exclude because of space limitations; and his criteria for inclusion are "current fashions in American literary history" (*Lit.* 11). Alfred Kazin in *On Native Grounds* (1942) does devote several pages to Cather, though his critique is purely traditional. He links her with Ellen Glasgow—a common and somewhat misleading pairing—and calls her a "conscious traditionalist." He then places himself within the tradition of Cather criticism by interpreting her as being nostalgic and regretting the loss of the "primary values" of the past (185). Her work, he suggests, parallels "the decline and fall of her own great tradition" (187).

These facts of juxtaposition and relative inattention hold true despite the additional fact that none of the other writers challenged Cather in the quantity of fiction produced or in the quality of that fiction. (Only Hemingway, with his two masterpieces of the Twenties, comes close quantitatively. Faulkner's "big" decade would come later, 1929-1939.) The ironies of Cather's comparative lack of acclaim relative to the quantity and quality of her output during the 1920s bear remembering. My appreciation of Cather developed out of my appreciation of the Twenties in general and of those "famous" male writers more specifically; and it was in context of my interest in them that I first became aware of Cather's less flamboyant, more persistent genius. Although I do not directly address the topic of Cather as an artist of the Twenties, my comments about her novels are made with an awareness that she contributed to and was influenced by the dynamics of the "Jazz" age.

Though her creativity declined in volume and quality with the three post-Twenties novels, those written after *Death Comes for the Archbishop*, these twilight-year narratives are equally revealing of Cather's art and mind. The lights they cast may flicker, but they nonetheless illuminate various elements of the earlier fiction, especially Cather's struggle with authorial perspective and her controversial psychosexuality. Moreover, they have been slighted by critics, who even after the revival of interest in Cather, have continued to concentrate on the pre-Thirties novels. O'Brien, for instance, in what is otherwise a significant analysis of Cather's work, chooses to de-emphasize the works after 1913 on the theory that Cather found her feminine voice at that point and little else remains to be scrutinized. I find the final three novels more informative and interesting than such dismissal implies, while recognizing that as a group they are not on the artistic level of the Twenties novels. As for the three novels written prior to 1918, *Alexander's Bridge, O Pioneers!* and *The Song of the Lark,* I believe them to be works in which Cather is trying to find her style and purpose, and I discuss them collectively in Chapter One.

Finally, to end the introduction, I need briefly to explain the book's title. The "conflict" I have already explained. Aside from echoes of Prufrock's visions and revisions, the subtitle comes from *Prairie Women: Images in American and Canadian Fiction.* Therein Carol Fairbanks borrows a term from Adrienne Rich: "re-visioning." Re-visioning means to look back on yesterday's literature in order to break tradition's hold upon it. Though directed by some preconceived notions, which I have stated, my analyses are predicated mostly upon the general concept of re-visioning suggested by Fairbanks's study. The re-visioning is needed for Cather because despite some recent criticism that is innovative and intelligent, she still has failed to receive the type of scrutiny her fiction requires and deserves. Early in her career as a novelist, which did not commence until she was thirty eight, some of that failure was attributable to willful neglect. As Cather herself suggested, critics did not "care a damn what happens in Nebraska" (*On Writing*, 94). Later, however, it was not the dearth of criticism per se but the relatively limited perspectives of the criticism that hampered appreciation of Cather's art. With relatively few critics attending her, as I have already noted, several preferred views developed regarding Cather. These views are the "traditional" Cather criticism which is outlined above.

The re-visioning of Cather reveals that Cather is an immensely complex artist, quite capable of encompassing or even upholding "tradition" while simultaneously using it in the most ironic of ways. As we will see, for example, her apparently praiseworthy portraits of bishops Latour and Vaillant, in *Death Comes for the Archbishop*, turn out to be just as condemnatory as they are laudatory. And, if her portrait of Ántonia Shimerda is seen traditionally as a heartwarming account of what Woodress calls the "Madonna of the Wheat Fields" (*WC* 293), in the revisionist view Ántonia is a woman trapped in and nearly destroyed by the traditional patriarchal values which victimize her. Ántonia herself may be too naive or too conditioned to compromise to recognize her plight, but the audience need not share Ántonia's myopia. From her earliest days of writing as a journalist, Cather revealed herself as an acerbic commentator on the life about her and as adept satirist. Her ironic comments on puritanical Pittsburgh, for example, rival Mark Twain in their sharpness. Her portrait of Ántonia is but a more sophisticated example of that early ironic bent, and serves to demonstrate that Cather is an ironist who challenges the reader to be aware of the potential of that irony, though Cather herself may at times be unaware of her own ironic complexity.

One final note about editions. As we know, Cather altered several of her novels in editions subsequent to first publication. Some indications of these changes can be readily obtained—at least for the early novels—from the "Notes on the Texts" pages of *Willa Cather: Early Novels and Stories* (1987). Such alterations are a writer's prerogative and a critic's dilemma; but since my study is not textually oriented, and since Cather's emendations are not extensive, the dilemma is lessened. I use the best conveniently available texts for citations. In the few instances when differences between the original text and subsequent revisions might present interpretation problems, the textual distinctions are discussed as they occur.

Works Cited

Arnold, Marilyn. *Willa Cather: A Reference Guide*. Boston: Hall, 1986.

Benstock, Shari. *Women of the Left Bank: Paris 1900-1940*. Austin: U of Texas P, 1986.

"Cather Scholar Disagrees with Lesbian Conclusion." *Omaha World-Herald*, 3 Nov. 1984: 4.

Cather, Willa. *Alexander's Bridge* (1912). Boston: Houghton Mifflin, 1922.

—. *Death Comes for the Archbishop* (1927). New York: Vintage, 1971.

—. *The World and the Parish: Willa Cather's Articles and Reviews*. 2 vols. Ed. William M. Curtin. Lincoln: U of Nebraska P, 1970.

—. *Willa Cather's Collected Short Fiction: 1892-1912*. Ed. Virginia Faulkner. Lincoln: U of Nebraska P, 1970.

—. *Willa Cather: Early Novels and Stories*. [Selected and annotated by Sharon O'Brien]. New York: The Library of America, 1987.

—. *Willa Cather in Person: Interviews, Speeches, and Letters*. Ed. L. Brent Bohlke. Lincoln: U of Nebraska P, 1986.

—. *Willa Cather on Writing: Critical Studies in Writing as an Art*. New York: Knopf, 1949.

Cunliffe, Marcus. *The Literature of the United States*. 3rd ed. Harmondsworth, England: Penguin, 1967.

—. "The Two or More Worlds of Willa Cather" in *The Art of Willa Cather*. Ed. Bernice Slote and Virginia Faulkner. Lincoln: U of Nebraska P, 1974. 21-42.

Daiches, David. *Willa Cather: A Critical Introduction*. Ithaca: Cornell U P, 1951.

Edel, Leon. "Homage to Willa Cather" in *The Art of Willa Cather*. Ed. Bernice Slote and Virginia Faulkner. Lincoln: U of Nebraska P, 1974. 185-204.

Fairbanks, Carol. *Prairie Women: Images in American and Canadian Fiction*. New Haven: Yale U P, 1986.

Fryer, Judith. *Felicitous Space: The Imaginative Structures of Edith Wharton and Willa Cather*. Chapel Hill: U of NC P, 1986.

Gilbert, Sandra M. and Susan Gubar. *No Man's Land: The Place of the Woman Writer in the Twentieth Century*. New Haven: Yale U P, 1988.

Kazin, Alfred. *On Native Grounds*, 1942. Garden City: Doubleday, 1956.

Krieger, Murray. *Theory of Criticism: A Tradition and Its System.* Baltimore: Johns Hopkins U P, 1976.

O'Brien, Sharon. "Mothers, Daughters, and the 'Art of Necessity': Willa Cather and the Creative Process" in *American Novelists Revisited: Essays in Feminist Criticism.* Ed. Fritz Fleischmann. Boston: Hall, 1982. 265-298.

—. *Willa Cather: The Emerging Voice.* New York: Oxford U P, 1986.

Secor, Cynthia. "The Question of Gertrude Stein" in *American Novelists Revisited: Essays in Feminist Criticism.* Ed. Fritz Fleischmann. Boston: Hall, 1982. 299-310.

Woodress, James. "Cather and Her Friends" in *Critical Essays on Willa Cather.* Ed. John J. Murphy. Boston: G. K. Hall, 1984. 81-95.

—. *Willa Cather: A Literary Life.* Lincoln: U of Nebraska P, 1987.

1
The First Three Novels: To Be Not Female

While hardly juvenilia, Cather's first three novels are definitely fiction in which the artist has not yet found her mature artistic voice. They range from the artificiality of *Alexander's Bridge* to the artiness of *Song of the Lark*. Especially in *Alexander's Bridge* Cather is working with a dilemma which Judith Fetterley articulates in *The Resisting Reader: A Feminist Approach to American Fiction* (1978). "American literature is male" (xii), Fetterley emphasizes; then goes on to explain the resultant female quandary:

> To be excluded from a literature that claims to define one's identity is to experience a peculiar form of powerlessness—not simply the powerlessness which derives from not seeing one's experience articulated, clarified, and legitimized in art, but more significantly the powerlessness which results from the endless division of self against self, the consequence of the invocation to identify as male while being reminded that to be male—to be universal, to be American—is to be *not female*. (xiii)

Cather later disowned *Alexander's Bridge* and explained in the 1922 preface that *O Pioneers!* marked the spot where her "life line" and her line of "personal endeavor" intersected (*AB* vi). Though partially obscured by connotations of palmistry, Cather's meaning is not hard to ascertain if we recall that she wrote *Alexander's Bridge* intentionally to break into that male domain of the American novel which Fetterley notes and that both Winifred Alexander and Hilda Burgoyne subordinate everything in their lives (career, fortune, self respect) to satisfying Bartley Alexander's smallest whim, to making sure that he has "all the things that a great man ought to have" (107). Their

groveling parallels the "sexual nausea" that Fetterley recognizes
in Catherine Barkley's attitude toward Frederic Henry in Hemingway's *A Farewell to Arms* (69). Cather realized—apparently
before her contemporary readers realized—that Alexander was
not The Great and that the Brahminical Boston milieu was foreign to her "life line." As Judith Fryer observes, "in her mature
works" Cather has "traveled a great distance from what is only
suggested in *Alexander's Bridge*." By comparison to the early
writing, her great novels exhibit "secret revelations of her garden layered with interpretation, moments of epiphany controlled, if not repressed, in presentation to the reader" (226).

After *Alexander's Bridge*, Cather began plumbing her own
psyche to discover the potential of a woman who quietly rebels
against patriarchal restraints to find financial independence and
a modicum of personal happiness within the prairie environment that has shaped her. She discovered in *O Pioneers!* and
Alexandra Bergson the physical place and the associated realities
that lay "at the bottom of [her] consciousness" (*AB* vi). She discovered too that while her "place" may be tolerable for the non-
artistic soul (such as the pragmatic farm owner Alexandra), it
was a prison house for the person damned by having the soul
"strung" differently by the god of Art (*World and Parish*, 52). In
The Song of the Lark, therefore, Cather retains the prairie heart-
land for setting but moves one step further and offers her document of artistic emancipation in the guise of Thea Kronborg, an
artistically gifted, but socially restricted young woman who must
give her soul to Art and who, unlike Alexandra, divorces herself
physically—though never psychologically—from that same
geography. That *The Song of the Lark* is too strident in its advocacy of Art is but another indication of how strongly Cather was
reacting against the female subservience she felt compelled to offer in the text of *Alexander's Bridge*.

This trio of early novels, therefore, gives us separately the
narrative motifs that permeate, at times dominate, the subsequent fiction. To one degree or another, all the novels after 1915
concern the essential dilemma implied by the two motifs most
explicit in *O Pioneers!* and *The Song of the Lark* (the romance of
the prairie and the demands of art). When seen binocularly
rather than separately, the motifs may be summarized thus: The
mysterious prairie grows wheat, corn, wild flowers, and pragmatic people aplenty, but it cannot nurture artistic sensibility,
sexual unorthodoxy, philosophical diversity, or idealists. Given
that paradox, a strong, intelligent female (presented as either a

feminine or masculine persona) struggles to prove her competence; at first she remains within the milieu that is her nemesis; but ultimately she must attempt to separate herself from that milieu if she is to remain true to her own psyche or art. Either she realizes separation or she does not, but in either case she will be unfulfilled.

To be historically exact, we must note that Cather's perception of the American novel being male-dominated was not entirely accurate. As Nina Baym points out, "women's fiction" (novels written by women for women and focusing on a heroine) was the most popular type of fiction published in America during most of the nineteenth century (22); and "although the novelists of this period now considered important are all male, from 1850 until well after the Civil War (some would say until the 1920's) the novel was chiefly a form of communication among women" (32). Nonetheless, like Gertrude Stein and many other women writers of the late Victorian era, Cather "saw serious writing as a male activity" (Benstock 12), a misconception her own early reviews and denigrations of female writers attest. As James Woodress says without overstating the case by much, readers of her early anti-feminist newspaper articles probably wondered if Cather were indeed a woman (110). Her first novel was to be her passport into that powerful male domain and thus a manifestation of the masculine facets of her psyche. The ambiguous emotions underlying the creation of *Alexander's Bridge* are implicit in her submitting the manuscript under a pseudonym and in its original title: "Alexander's Masquerade." *Alexander's Bridge* received favorable contemporary reviews, and a few devout Catherophiles—such as Edith Lewis who said it spoke with "passion and authority" (78)—have tried, with limited conviction, to elevate it on the basis of its intrinsic merits. More recent critics, however, dismiss it as an interesting literary failure. Bernice Slote's introduction is about as balanced a summary of evaluations and statement of appreciation as we have. Slote succinctly notes, among other things, that Alexander's death by drowning foreshadows one of Cather's "most persistent personal images" (xx), that the "theme of double selves is pervasive in Cather's works" (xxi), and that gold or money "is associated in Cather with love and sexuality" (xix). Indeed, all these elements in *Alexander's Bridge* anticipate some of Cather's artistic techniques in the later fiction.

The value of *Alexander's Bridge* in the development of

Cather's artistic imagination is less in the literary motifs which she superimposes on the text than in the ways it serves as a prototype of the artistic mind in the making, especially insofar as it demonstrates in more rudimentary form those conflicts of self which never disappear from Cather's narratives but which become increasingly subtle in expression. Therefore, I wish to use *Alexander's Bridge* to initiate the journey which F. K. Stanzel explains as moving from narrative "surface structure" to narrative "deep structure," where with the help of some risky theorizing the real intent of the author "can be made visible" (15). My theorizing will be limited to two comparatively unexamined areas of the narrative complex: (1) the discomforting subservience Cather inflicts on both Hilda Burgoyne and Winifred Alexander in their relationships with Bartley Alexander; and (2) the irony with which Cather imbues that female subservience—an irony superficially obscured by the conventional romantic triangle defining the narrative surface. In theorizing about the Winifred/Hilda subservience and the irony, I am talking secondarily about Cather's technique as a novelist and thereby initiating a consideration that carries throughout my analyses of her narratives. With Mark Shorer, I realize that "When we speak of technique . . . we speak of nearly everything" (66). As Shorer points out, technique is the only way a writer can explore and develop her subject, her way "of conveying its meaning" and "of evaluating it" (66).

> And surely it follows that certain techniques are sharper tools than others, and will discover more; that the writer capable of the most exacting technical scrutiny of his subject matter will produce works with the most satisfying content, works with thickness and resonance, works which reverberate, works with maximum meaning. (66)

It is technique which is lacking in *Alexander's Bridge* (and to a less degree in the subsequent two novels); and it is Cather's movement toward developing a technique which conveys "resonance" and "maximum meaning" that I analyze.

Bernice Slote labels Bartley Alexander "the great conqueror" (xvii) and associates him with Paris and the *Iliad*. If we are to identify *Alexander's Bridge* as being mythic, it is wise to recall a pattern of progression in the mythic novel. As Philip Stevick notes in his introduction to *The Theory of the Novel*, Northrop Frye some years ago "arranged mythic patterns according to the power of the hero." At the top were those heroes who were not men but gods; then heroes who were men but super mortals; then men who are like the reader in capability; and finally men who are inferior to the reader—"the fools and clowns" (5). Accepting Frye's categories, it is difficult to determine where Bartley Alexander fits into the pattern. Elizabeth Ammons tries to clarify the question in "The Engineer as Cultural Hero and Willa Cather's First Novel, *Alexander's Bridge*" by trying to familiarize us with the engineer's turn-of-the-century status and explaining some of Cather's thinking in selecting her protagonist. Ammons, however, is in fact demythologizing the engineer. Under any circumstances, the bridge builder remains unconvincing as a cultural hero, primarily because the epic hero in general simply was not Cather's type and secondarily because the engineer as hero has lost currency in modern society. No matter what his occupation, however, the superman at whose mercy Cather places Hilda and Winifred is self-serving, self-pitying, and self-destructive, and we cannot precisely locate him on Frye's mythic scale between god and fool.

Nor, it seems, can Cather. Far from acting as the stuff of legend, Alexander is essentially cowardly—as his association with Paris suggests. When his faulty bridge dumps him and his workmen into the river, his thoughts are not upon saving the men for whom he is directly responsible, but upon saving himself. He first tries to swim away from the drowning men, but does not have the epic strength for such a feat; and once they grab him he then hopes they might quickly drown and release him (159-160). These are not the altruistic thoughts of the legendary hero, but the thoughts we assume would be common to an ordinary mortal, biologically prone to self-preservation, who is about to die. Indeed the very predictability of such thinking reveals how mundane Alexander really is and suggests the "masquerade" Cather may have had in mind when she created the story. Far from courageous, he is instead an ordinary engineer, with a modicum of imagination and a propensity for exploiting women to further himself. The start of his success is directly related to old Mrs. Pemberton's finding in him someone who shares his interest "in the army and in politics" and who reflects her "great contempt for music and art and philosophy" (24). Moreover, Cather implies that had not her aunt Mrs. Pemberton approved of Alexander, Winifred would never have married a simple bridge builder who was at that time "a wild, ill-governed youth" (24). Cather herself referred to him as "a pa-

gan, a crude force" (Slote x). Alexander is more opportunist than
hero; and Lucius Wilson is correct in seeing in him "a big crack
zigzagging from top to bottom" (15). If he is meant to be a Colos-
sus, he is one made of clay and ultimately shattered.

Hilda Burgoyne and Winifred Alexander, on the other
hand, are credible to contemporary audiences because unlike
bridge builders actresses and housewives remain universal
types.   More importantly, they are not the stereotypical fin de
siécle women.   Though they both subjugate themselves to
Alexander (an irony which gives thesis to my discussion), both
are themselves strong, successful females.   Hilda, a beautiful,
charismatic actress sought after by playwrights and producers,
possesses powerful economic value stemming directly from her
appeal to audiences. In a word, she is famous.   More significantly, her success commenced as soon as Alexander left her to
marry Winifred, and she has achieved her fame specifically during the decade of Alexander's absence. Winifred too is a woman
not only of wealth, social status, and great dignity but also of
near epic physical stature—she is the tallest woman some of the
bridge workmen have ever seen (164).   Upon first glance of her
in the narrative, we are told that an observer "immediately took
for granted the costly privileges and fine spaces that must lie in
the background from which such a figure could emerge" (3).
Like Hilda, neither her social nor economic status depends upon
Alexander (nor upon any other man).   Moreover, again like
Hilda, she is an artist: she plays the piano "brilliantly and with
great musical feeling" (18).   Unlike Hilda, however, whose art
flourishes in inverse ratio to her contact with Alexander, Winifred has forsaken art for marriage to Alexander—a woman's
mistake Cather will try to rectify in her third novel *Song of the
Lark* and an emblem of what she feared domestic tranquility
might do to her own art.

The conundrum which *Alexander's Bridge* offers is why
Cather places these two brilliant women in the humiliating circumstances in which we encounter them. Hilda's humiliation
is most graphically demonstrated in the love scenes between her
and Alexander. If we wished to rekindle the debate as to
whether Cather ever consummated a heterosexual relationship,
these scenarios would favor those who argue her celibacy. Only
Henry James with his famous unexplained incapacitation rivals
the scenes for insipid passion. The anemic erotica of *Alexander's Bridge* may have been adequate for an audience geared to
James's bloodless lusts and intrigues, but from a modern per-

spective such love scenes are one of the most prevalent of numerous weak elements in the narrative structure. Yet, once again it is what the love scenes convey to us extratextually rather than how unconvincingly Cather manages them that is important. They emphasize and focus the humiliation of Hilda specifically and females generally.

For example, just past mid-point in the novel (Chapter VI), appears what is meant to be the emotional, erotic zenith of the Alexander-Hilda affair. Alexander arrives unexpectedly at Hilda's apartment in London, and though Hilda is delighted at his surprise visit, Alexander immediately establishes that the heaviest luggage he has brought with him from Boston is his Calvinist conscience. Voicing no concern for any emotional stress Hilda may have suffered in the months since their affair resumed, he announces that he is "not a man who can live two lives" and complains of the "misery" he has been enduring (104). After listening to Alexander's lamentations, Hilda "crept across to him" (105), assuring him that she cares only that a great man such as he must "always be happy and handsome and successful" (107). Alexander, however, cannot be cajoled out of his self pity so quickly. Not yet having pacified him, Hilda has to then "slid[e] to the floor beside him" (110). Cather concludes this facsimile of a passionate episode with the kisses and embraces of reconciliation, having Hilda exclaim "Ah, your dear arms!" (110).

Few other scenes in twentieth-century American fiction (except perhaps for Catherine Barkley's obsequious catering to Frederic Henry, as Judith Fetterley has observed) depict a woman doing so much creeping and sliding before a man in the name of love. And before exonerating Cather too quickly on the basis of It-Was-The-Era defense, we might recall that three years prior to *Alexander's Bridge*, Gertrude Stein published *Three Lives*, a work about women in which she not only stepped outside the bounds of conventional literary standards in regard to male-female relationships, but, as John Malcolm Brinnin says, "stepped beyond the pull of literary gravity" (124). No doubt Cather wanted to write a novel acceptable to prevailing patriarchal hegemony, but that hegemony had already been breached, and Cather's understandable desire for acceptance cannot adequately explain or exonerate Hilda's groveling. Whatever response the scene may have elicited from audiences of 1912, it is disconcerting for audiences today—not only for the melodrama which renders it comic but more importantly for the degrading subservience Cather unconsciously inflicts upon Hilda.

Nor can we blame Hilda's behavior on her precarious position as the "other woman," for Cather also depicts Winifred
Alexander displaying a similar acquiescence. One brief scene
emblematizes her servility. Though she dislikes earrings and
has told her husband she does not ordinarily wear them,
Alexander gives her a pair of "Flemish gold" ones for Christmas.
Winifred may well think such jewelry inappropriate for a Victorian lady of her breeding and status, but at his insistence and to
please him, she dutifully puts on the earrings (86-87). More significantly, after his death, she lives almost exclusively for his
memory, in what Wilson ironically calls "the most beautiful and
dignified sorrow I've ever known" (171)—ironic because such
"sorrow" is in actuality morbid and pathetic, the detritus of
Winifred's wasted life. Added to the fact that Alexander has betrayed her in his adulterous affair with Hilda, these passages
demonstrate that Winifred also shares Hilda's degradation.

Hilda, Alexander, and Winifred to a less degree, all represent fictive projections of Cather's divided self. Sharon O'Brien,
in her analysis of the masculine-feminine ambivalence in *Alexander's Bridge*, designates Alexander as the artist-figure (387).
She makes this designation in support of her overall thesis that
Cather said farewell to the "masculine aesthetic" (388) in writing
her first novel and immediately thereafter "reconciled the
woman and the artist" (5) in *O Pioneers!* Yet, O'Brien overstates
the case for Alexander in order to support a thesis which is itself
inadequately grounded on textual evidence. As his treatment of
Hilda and Winifred indicates, Alexander is not an artist at all,
but a mechanic, a man in whom the "machinery was always
pounding" (16). Cather is careful to make the distinction when
she has her ficelle Lucius Wilson immediately tell us (and
Winifred) that Alexander "was never introspective" but simply
has a "tremendous response to stimuli" (9). Wilson, as a matter
of fact, does not enjoy being around a man so lacking in the
"reflective habit of mind" (16). As Cather will soon show us
when she sends her artist-self Thea Kronborg to dwell alone in
the ancient cliff ruins of Colorado, the artist obviously must respond to stimuli; but without introspection there simply is no
art. It is, in fact, amidst the isolation of the Anasazi ruins that
Thea discovers what Judith Fryer calls "the ritual of creativity"
("Desert" 30)—though as we will see, the discovery does not save
Thea from marrying a dominating male similar to Alexander.

Hilda Burgoyne, not Bartley Alexander, is the persona

with whom Cather most identifies as the artist-self. Hilda is based upon one or more female singers/actresses whom Cather saw perform in London. Despite the fact that Cather herself had no musical talent (Woodress 54), she consistently portrays her artist-self not as a writer but as the singer-musician we see in Hilda and later in Thea. From childhood she was fascinated by singers/actresses and identified closely with them—both artistically and erotically. Not surprisingly, she first met Isabelle Mc-Clung (the enduring love of her life) backstage in the dressing room of Lizzie Hudson Collier, an actress they both admired (Woodress 138-139). Edith Lewis explains that during her visit of 1909 Cather saw the Irish players frequently in London and was "vividly impressed" by the "beauty and engaging personality" of one young woman, probably Marie O'Neill. From her, Lewis says, Cather drew Hilda Burgoyne (68). Taking a clue from the fact that Cather names the town nearest Alexander's fated bridge "Allway," we might surmise that the actress to whom Cather was so attracted was more likely Sara Allgood. The exact identity, however, is secondary in importance to the fact that Hilda is the primary artist figure in the novel, the female with whom Cather most closely identifies, and the fictionalized version of a young woman to whom in reality Cather was erotically attracted. By merging her fictive self with the real woman, Cather accomplishes a symbolic homoerotic union which consciously she felt to be taboo but which unconsciously she was compelled to explore. This exploration becomes an identifiable trait in her subsequent novels, and one I will analyze more fully later. Cather was never comfortable in the "lesbian literary tradition" into which Sandra M. Gilbert and Susan Gubar place her (xii), but indeed her homoeroticism dictated much of the text and subtext of her fiction.

The unanswered question which remains at this juncture is why Cather chose to subjugate her projected artistic/erotic self to a man such as Bartley Alexander. In trying to answer that question, we first should recall that despite whatever other shortcomings Alexander displays, he is powerful, influential, and physically attractive. Newspaper photographers love him, and in a later era he probably would be a matinee or TV idol or successful politician. The characteristics that attract Winifred to him are "his good looks and his fine color" (20). In short, he personifies the individual type which Cather's society marked as successful and dominant and a type which Cather presents throughout her fiction as the objective epitome of masculinity.

We see him in such figures as Frederick Ottenburg (*Song of the Lark*), Harry Gordon (*Lucy Gayheart*), and Henry Colbert (*Sapphira and the Slave Girl*). Moreover, he is the type of male who possesses traits with which she identified and into which she projected herself during her years of cross-dressing. Not at that time envisioning herself as a writer, she saw herself instead as a successful physician, war hero, "man" of command and action. Though lacking the androgyny and feminine sensitivities with which she characterizes the male personae of her projected artist self (such as Jim Burden), this socially idealized male we see in Alexander shares characteristics with "William," the name she gave her male alter ego. Enthralled by the "ideal" of such a man, Cather is consequently not objective about his faults and is desensitized to how his treatment of women may strike an audience less enamored of him. This deep seated, unconscious commitment to such a male does not rule out the possibility that Cather was intellectually or intuitively aware of his misogyny. The point is that even if such awareness were operative, emotions clouded that rational perception. In fact the tensions created by just such an emotional-rational conflict help explain why the highly ironic, nearly satirical tone of the love scenes permeates a novel which nearly all extratextual and most intratextual evidence shows was not intended to be ironic.

From the very beginning of her writing Cather showed herself to be a natural ironist and a conscious satirist. Her response to Presbyterian Pittsburgh near the turn of the century conveniently illustrates the point. As James Woodress notes, "Her early letters from Pittsburgh and columns sent back to the *Journal* are full of impatient astonishment and irony" (113). When she rejected *Alexander's Bridge* ten years after publication as not dealing with the kind of subject matter with which she felt "most at home" (Preface *AB* v), one of the reasons may well have been its artificially strict adherence to a prescribed formula which inhibited her innately ironic world view. She forced herself into suppressing her creative instincts in order to script a conventional tale which satisfied a certain audience and which would act as her passport into the world of male fictionists. Yet such compromise went against the grain, what she called her "inner feelings" (vi), and was therefore a threat to the artistic integrity she cherished. Thus, not only was Cather torn by socio-erotic conflicts, she was also torn by the problem of how the conflicts were to be presented to an audience. Was she to conform and hide her emotional self behind conventional forms and formulas, or was she to set her own terms, construct her own rules, and give vent to the angers and turmoils that were at least as strong in her psychological makeup as the love and placidity? Cather herself would struggle with the question throughout the rest of her artistic life.

Before closing our consideration of the love scenes and their implied humiliation of Hilda and Winifred, we need to note that after *Alexander's Bridge*, Cather resists the depiction of heterosexual love scenes. She does not merely shun the presentation of overtly erotic encounters, the kind Kate Chopin had dared in 1899 with her heroine Edna Pontellier. As Judith Fryer characterizes the style of *The Awakening*, "the sea, the sun, sky, [Edna's] naked body are all there for the reader to see, touch, feel, smell" (*Faces* 244). And Chopin's career was ruined as a result of such erotic provocation which the conventions of the period would not tolerate. Cather avoids as well any scene in which a male and female are placed alone and in which the dialogue or actions leave no doubt in the audience's mind that sexual intercourse will be the logical next act. In *My Ántonia*, Ántonia has all those children with only the vaguest hint of physical contact with a man whose great silent impregnations of his mate are one (or eleven) of the miracles of Cather's fiction; and later in *Shadows on the Rock*, Cather gives us Cecile Auclair: on one page the child virgin, and on the next page the mature mother of four sons. In the novel immediately following *Alexander's Bridge*, *O Pioneers!*, Cather makes Emil Bergson and Marie Shabata die for love, but except for the one innocent kiss they share in the dark at the church dance, the text offers no clear evidence of sexual contact. The two butterflies which flit above their gunshot bodies ambiguously suggest innocence and mating, and we are not sure if Emil and Marie die as adulterers or mere romantics. Perhaps the closest Cather comes to depicting overt fornication is in Marian Forrester's assignation in the woods with Frank Ellinger (*A Lost Lady*). Even here, however, Cather demurs and the audience is forced to draw its own conclusions as to how far things went on the buffalo robes. Such coyness is certainly not unique to Cather, but she is notably more refrained than most of her contemporaries in having her characters keep their erotica off stage.

O'Brien theorizes that because Cather is dealing in *Alexander's Bridge* with "romantic and sexual passion"—a subject she probably had been advised to avoid and which she herself had derided in an earlier review of Chopin's *The Awaken-*

ing—she opted to disguise her own female eroticism by casting it as male (385). Not only would her audience accept passion in a male more readily than in a female, but the gender transference allowed Cather to use fictive sublimation to explore the homo-eroticism which was her true interest. She could not dare portray a woman being passionate with another woman, but if she made an authorial transference and cross-dressed one of the women in man's clothing then her audience would be none the wiser and would accept the resulting ersatz-heterosexualism. Yet the scenes between this cross-dressed female and "his" paramour turned out to be so counterproductive to what she intended that she could not risk such encounters again. Such scenes might reveal to an astute reader that their creator was not attune to heterosexual passion and might therefore in fact be sexually "inverted."

Hilda Burgoyne and Bartley Alexander thus personify two factions of Cather's embattled self. Alexander is the projected masculine element, Hilda the feminine. Cross-dressing, as we recall, is paradoxical in that it implies the cross-dresser's conflicting desire for and rejection of the opposite sex. Thus we see Cather-Alexander exerting dominance over Cather-Hilda, even humiliating "her" and her close counterpart Winifred. Yet Cather-Hilda does not rest easy with that degradation, and the projected masculine self must pay dearly for his dominance. Cather kills him. In the complex realm of Cather's masculine-feminine conflicts, Alexander is both self and other, simultaneously "William" and an external intruder who serves as an erotic bridge to other women. Because he acts in that role as surrogate facilitator of the homoeroticism Cather both desired and feared, he must die. We can only imagine how perplexed Cather would have been by guilt arising from a devotion to her femininity in conflict with a biology that bestowed upon her characteristics most usually associated with masculinity. Though only sketchily developed in *Alexander's Bridge*, the transference of gender identification and the desire to destroy or subjugate the fictive persona who bears that identification are motifs which become more pronounced in Cather's subsequent novels.

The transition Cather makes between *Alexander's Bridge* and *O Pioneers!* is to move farther from the artifice of the novel and nearer to the art of the novel. Insofar as the literal elements of narrative are concerned, she tries to disassociate herself from the male persona or protagonist and to identify more definitely with a female persona, Alexandra Bergson. As in *Alexander's*

Bridge, though Cather retained the male protagonist superficially, much of her sympathy rested with the females he dominated. In her earlier stories, such as "The Willing Muse" (1907) and "On the Gull's Road" (1908), Cather had persistently relied on the first person male narrator. In part this was an effort, as Sandra M. Gilbert and Susan Gubar note in discussing Victorian women writers generally, to legitimize herself "within a literary patrilineage that denied women full creative authority" (185). It was also, for Cather, a continued and sublimated form of the cross-dressing which we have already noted. Once having abandoned the relatively simple first-person male narrative focus, Cather would have trouble getting point of view totally back under control. Trying to reassert her feminine self in *O Pioneers!*, she seeks to adopt more fully a female persona as her fictive spokesperson. Alexandra Bergson represents a definite step beyond Bartley Alexander in that progression, but she by no means embodies a complete transition. Rather than integrating the author-self, she fragmented it; and while Alexandra certainly dominates as the central female and the character of narrative focus, she does not personify all the multiple authorial perspective discernible in the narrative structure. The narrative mode is close to what Dorrit Cohn defines as "psycho-narration" (11f), wherein a third-person narrator reports another character's feelings and thoughts, usually keeping to that character's spatial and temporal perspective. The language is usually the narrator's, but the character's words and thoughts sometimes filter through.

Though graphically feminine, even overtly erotic with the long braided reddish-yellow hair that makes men exclaim suggestively when she passes them on the street (14), Alexandra Bergson retains masculine characteristics. On first sight of her, we see that she wears a "man's long ulster" and is a "tall, strong girl" [140]. Moreover, she is a female who is not artistic and who succeeds in areas usually reserved for the stereotypical dominant male we have just recognized in Bartley Alexander. That Cather is still struggling with the fictive identity is equally apparent in Carl Lindstrum. Though nominally masculine, Carl is feminine, with "a delicate pallor in his thin face" and a mouth "too sensitive for a boy's" (142). Artistically inclined, he will never fulfill his artistic desires, though he does come close as an engraver. He occupies small space in the literal narrative, being off stage for most of the two-plus decades the novel covers; but he will eventually return to merge with Alexandra in a marriage which Cather assures us will be platonic. It will be a "safe" marriage "between friends," purged of destructive eroticism, Alexandra promises Carl (290). Though Alexandra never humiliates Carl in the way that Alexander degrades Hilda and Winifred, she does dominate him (and other males), and we thus witness Cather's calculated reversal of the character alignment she has established in *Alexander's Bridge*.

The sexlessness of the Carl-Alexandra union suggests Cather's continuing inability to reconcile the conflicting erotic impulses she experienced. While she can artistically separate her male and female impulses and project them into her fiction as individualized personae, she cannot take the next logical step of reconciliation and unify those male and female personae with any kind of erotic relationship—a dilemma which we encounter late in her career with *Death Comes for the Archbishop* and which she manages much more subtly at that juncture. When faced with a similar dilemma in *My Ántonia*, Cather physically separates her two selves in the narrative, introduces a drone-husband, and does not let Jim get within sight of Ántonia for twenty years. She thereby guarantees the audience and her own psyche that Jim cannot possibly be responsible for any of those children. To unify her male-female selves would imply a kind of psychic incestuousness Cather could not tolerate. She bows to convention by giving Carl and Alexandra the protection of a wedding (people have already commenced to talk during Carl's earlier stay at Alexandra's farm), but she cannot bring herself to consummate that union. The relationship is conjugal in appearance only, a legality which stills society's tongue but not Cather's psychic turmoil.

The "safe" union which Alexandra and Carl accept is the only option left open to them. More correctly, it is the only option Cather's creative self, working through the psycho-narration, leaves available to them. Prior to the betrothal (Carl and Alexandra are in fact never married within the narrative context), Cather eradicates the passion, the eros, when she brings Frank Shabata into the garden to murder Marie and Emil. When narrative closure arrives, therefore, she has only friendship left, though if it is to thrive it will do so on the blood of the sacrificed young lovers. In the Emil/Marie subplot, she inculcates the destructiveness of erotic love—which she feared exposing in her private life but which surfaces in Alexandra as her graphically erotic and recurrent dream of wanting to be taken "very far" by the "mightiest of all lovers" (277). Cather makes certain to expunge this eroticism in its fictive manifestation, and her management of this psychic execution is revealing. The depiction of Marie's murder is one of the most brutal, gory scenes in all her fiction; and the most objectively distanced and callous, much in the style of Stephen Crane. Cather kills Emil quickly and cleanly with a bullet through the heart; but for Marie she reserves a relatively long and painful death: Shot through the lung and carotid artery, Marie lives long enough to drag herself over a sizable portion of the garden. Though Cather attributes her death to bleeding, more strictly in keeping with the pathology, Marie may well drown in her own blood. Moreover, throughout the novel Cather has referred to the girl as "Marie" —a melodious name connoting the Virgin, as in "Ave Maria" which brings rapture to Emil in church (264). Yet, suddenly in the death scene, Cather changes nomenclature and refers to Marie as "the woman" (269), introducing the harsh connotations which that phrase entails. (Willy Loman's whore, for instance, is "The Woman.")

Though Marie is presented as being Alexandra's closest female friend, and though Alexandra is otherwise portrayed as a loving, sensitive individual, her response to Marie's death is uncharacteristically heartless. After Frank Shabata has been sent to prison for the brutal slaying, Alexandra visits him, not only to vow that she will get him released but to comfort him by assuring him that Marie and Emil "were more to blame than you" (282). To emphasize Alexandra's anger, the narrator reiterates that "She blamed Marie bitterly" (283). The narrative per se never clarifies just what Alexandra blames Marie for or why she readily champions her killer. Nor does it clarify why Alexandra feels so bitterly betrayed by the girl. Certainly, Marie has been involved in the death of Alexandra's favorite brother, but Alexandra blames Emil equally and is not trying to exonerate him by displacing blame onto Marie.

Yet, if we realize that in the fictive context Cather is presenting a private psychodrama, both the graphic presentation of Marie's death and Alexandra's uncharacteristically harsh judgment are understandable. Whereas Alexandra and Carl symbolize displacement of the erotic impulses, Marie and Emil represent the potential reification of those impulses. Cather, however, cannot tolerate such an eventuality. Eroticism, whether homoeroticism or heteroeroticism and no matter how disguised or clothed, is dangerous. Thus Cather offers us Frank, the stereotypical male who despite his faults is nonetheless powerful. He is "burned a dull red down to his neckband, and there was a heavy three-days' stubble on his face." His appearance is that of a "rash and violent man" (206); and he wields the "murderous 405 Winchester" (267), with which he simultaneously punishes Marie and frustrates the dreaded erotic union. Moreover, he simultaneously speaks for the patriarchal code which governs in such matters. He is the wronged husband and many in his society support his violent reinforcement of his husbandly privileges—just as Alexandra supports him. Alexandra is an individual of property and influence, and when she vows to petition the governor in Frank's behalf, we can safely assume that she speaks for the populace of the Divide. Therefore, not only is Frank with his blazing rifle indicative of the powerful masculine figure which Cather partially identified herself as being, he serves paradoxically to execute the revenge which Cather feared would surely come to her from the patriarchal Law Makers for her carnal sins. She clearly intends to ally herself, through Alexandra and the execution of Marie, with that hegemony—just as she had tried consciously to do when she wrote *Alexander's Bridge* to enter the male domain of long prose fiction. In context of this attempted alliance, we should note that Cather is not unique among women writers of the period in expressing fear of patriarchal retaliation. Such anxiety has roots deep in the maternal-paternal struggle and in what Freud termed the masculinity complex of the homoerotic female. As Gilbert and Gubar state, "A number of turn-of-the-century texts by literary women dramatize just such fearful fantasies of male revenge and female filial humiliation" (176).

In Frank's brutal murder of Marie, therefore, and in Alexandra's subsequent approbation of that murder, we see Cather's troublesome paradox once more at work. Guilt ridden because of her socially unaccepted homoeroticism, she wants to legitimatize it symbolically by having the fictive Emil and Marie join in heteroerotic union. Were she able to permit them to consummate their love, she could commensurately placate if not totally reconcile her conflicted selves. Whether her psychosexuality is projected in opposite-sex or same-sex consummation does not technically matter. The important thing is only that it be made public, only that she acknowledge its importance as an element in her human-ness. Hawthorne offers the same psychosexual dilemma in a different symbolic frame. Projecting his divided self in male and female personae, he gives us Dimmesdale and Hester. The former is tormented literally to death by

denial of his sexuality, whereas the latter is sanctified by her ad-
mission of sexuality and her refusal to accept the guilt which a
patriarchal society tries to inflict upon her.

Cather, however, cannot bring her personae to climb the
public scaffold. Unable to break with conventional ethics and
laws, she sides with a society that narrowly defines "sin" and
then ruthlessly punishes the sinner. By killing Marie and Emil,
she tries psychologically to align herself with the dominant social forces and to convince herself that if "Right" can be preserved, then the social structure is secure and she therefore is
safe within it. After the deaths of those erotic youths, Alexandra's sexual dream of the domineering lover is exorcised; and
while her first reaction is anger and loss, she ultimately can
safely join Carl, who has shown little sign of libido. In fact, he
reassures Alexandra that women "too full of life and love" are
destructive and implies his agreement with her that Marie's
eradication was justified (288). Thus, in an ending which has little narrative integrity but which in light of Cather's sexual
dilemmas is perfectly logical, the narrator exults: "Fortunate
country, that is one day to receive hearts like Alexandra's into its
bosom . . . !" (290). Alexandra/Cather has been purged of her terrible eroticism, the villain Passion has been exorcised, and after a
psychological version of Shirley Jackson's lottery, the brothers
and fathers of the land can rest secure that the gods have been
pacified and will bring "yellow wheat" and "rustling corn" once
more (290).

So long as Cather transmitted her artistic self through the
first-person male narrator, as she did in many of her short stories, she managed her authorial perspective quite well. However, once she abandoned that restrictive point of view in an effort to exert her feminine creative authority, she encountered
difficulties she would not resolve in the longer narrative genre.
She tries in *My Ántonia* to return to the first-person format, and
though she solves some of the creative problems relative to her
masculine-feminine conflicts, she has Jim Burden tell us things
he could not possibly be privy to. Only the genius of the novel
otherwise compensates for these problems. Later still in *My
Mortal Enemy*, she returns to first-person narration to produce
the worst of her novels. Such difficulties of perspective are
manifestations of her own multiple views of self and are revealing in that context. Insofar as narrative style or technique is
concerned, however, the problems become distracting idiosyn-
crasies. The authorial perspective in *O Pioneers!* is the psycho-

narration already noted; yet from out of the fictive matrix an editorializing voice incompatible with that mode wishes to interpose itself. It has the sound of a persona who does not quite trust its audience and wants to make certain that the audience is remaining attentive and getting the right slant on narrative action—almost as if Cather the Pittsburgh school teacher were still present.

In describing Alexandra's farm, for instance, Cather writes: "Any one thereabouts would have told you that this was one of the richest farms on the Divide, and that the farmer was a woman, Alexandra Bergson" (178). The point-of-view question here is who is the "you" and who is addressing the "you"? If the "you" is the reader of the text, there is scant reason for bringing that reader inside the text, since the basic assumptions of reader-audience relationship in fiction is that there is a "real" world from which the reader operates and a fictional world of the nar-rative. The author knows that a reader will be "out there" and need not address that fact intratextually, unless there is some particular satiric or perspectivist advantage to be gained. Huck Finn demonstrates this advantage when he warns the external reader against trying to discover any plot or purpose to his story, knowing full well the reader-gull will immediately expect both. Such is not the case in *O Pioneers!*, which is neither first-person nor satiric. On the other hand, if the "you" is a designated "listener" within the text, much as we might have in confes-sional narrative such as Albert Camus's *The Fall*, or, in a differ-ent way, with Salinger's *Catcher in the Rye*, then as the "real" reading audience outside the fictive reality of the text we need to know the identity of that designated listener—especially if we are the designee. Moreover, we need to know who within the fictive context is giving that listener information. Whose judg-ment, for instance, determines that Alexandra's farm was the richest?   Admittedly, the question of who is judging might be inconsequential when applied to farmland, but when applied to ethical, psychological values such as the ones surrounding the Emil-Marie deaths, it is crucial. Also, why does the psycho-narrator depend on "any one thereabouts" to give us informa-tion? Why does he/she not tell us? If he/she must trust a stranger to convey information, then why are we to believe what we hear otherwise?

Again, Cather writes this about Frank Shabata: "Perhaps he got more satisfaction out of feeling himself abused than he would have got out of being loved" (245). If the novel is presented to us from the omniscient point of view (which psycho-narration essentially is), the "perhaps" is unnecessary. An omniscient narrator would *know* whether Frank got more satisfaction out of being abused. Unless she is emulating Stephen Crane's attempts at objectifying naturalistic experience and his refusal to assert the simplest fact, there is no satisfactory explanation for Cather's qualifiers. The Crane explanation cannot work, however, for Cather is at other places in the narrative far more judgmental than objective. Who, for instance, arbitrarily informs us about just how fortunate the country will be in having women such as Alexandra? If her portrait has been accurately painted, we should be able to determine for ourselves, without authorial prompting, how fortunate or unfortunate the country is. We need not belabor the question of Cather's point of view management here, but *O Pioneers!* does anticipate an increasingly complex series of author-art-audience relationships in Cather's novels.

The Song of the Lark is Cather's next step in the move toward dealing fictively with her artistic persona and its struggle to usurp the prominent position in her creative processes. Cather tries to make Alexandra Bergson admirable via character-istics more foreign than natural to her own personality. Unlike her creator, Alexandra possesses a mind which is "slow, truthful, steadfast" and without "the least spark of cleverness" (168). In contrast, Thea Kronborg epitomizes the Artist: she is quick, clever, inspired, and dedicated. She is willing to forsake prairie, home, family, and friends for her art. Whereas Alexandra re-mains on The Divide and pursues the provincial life of the Nebraska frontier, Thea opts for the cosmopolitan loneliness of Europe and the opera circuit. The very last we hear of her, she has just sung for the King at Buckingham Palace (580). Were it not for the unexpected traditional marriage which Cather forces on Thea, we could argue some rather distinct existential possi-bilities for the novel. Thea has an aura of the ontological drifter about her, a kind of noble fierce devotion to defining the self internally but within the context of her interaction with the external world and the comparatively mundane people who inhabit it. Fritz Oehlschlaeger has briefly applied the philosophy of R. D. Laing to explaining the ontological insecurity Cather presents in the characters of *Alexander's Bridge*, and though Laing's theorizing has fallen into disfavor, it remains inter-esting; and much of what Oehlschlaeger says could be applied to *The Song of the Lark*. Certainly the motif of the frightened, insecure self trying to find security in a world that does not ratify the self is noticeable in Thea.

Perhaps sensing that her heroine was drifting toward a metaphysics that she was as yet unwilling to define, Cather later revised *The Song of the Lark* more than any other of her novels. As she says in the Preface to the 1937 edition, she felt its chief fault "is that it describes a descending curve" from struggle to success, and that the struggle is more interesting than success (v). Insofar as our present discussion is concerned, the novel's chief fault is that once again Cather cannot bring to her narrative the absolute commitment of artist to text—or at least cannot convince the audience that such ultimate merging of artistic processes and realized form has occurred, albeit the tale itself explores that very process. Her own psyche remains repressed by the artifice of novel "making," rather than being liberated by creative free play. That is, the same consciousness of her art that led her in 1912 to produce *Alexander's Bridge* as an overt attempt to write like the prevailing male hegemony would have her write has not yet in 1915 been totally eradicated. Thus, in a brief "Epilogue" which directly contravenes the prolix account of Thea's struggle and success as an opera singer, Cather once more is compelled to force her heroine into a marriage with Frederick Ottenburg which satisfies nothing more than conventional expectations. Despite the battle of the feminine self to prevail as an artist, that self must ultimately acquiesce to the male persona, this time in the character of a dilettante whose sole entrée into the rare world of Art is predicated upon the fact that he has much money which emanates literally from a brewery. His being "wed" to this money is accurately emblematized by the maiden name of the sluttish girl he secretly marries: Miss Beers. Thea's struggle to survive as an artist while Ottenburg leads the idle life on his inherited beer money is one of Cather's more effective uses of narrative incongruity in her efforts to express the plight of the artist in a philistine's world.

Recognizing that she had undercut her narrative integrity and Thea's potential autonomy with the Thea-Ottenburg marriage, Cather significantly altered her presentation of this marriage in the 1937 edition of the novel. In both the 1915 and 1937 editions the marriage is offered as a kind of afterthought in the "Epilogue." In the first edition, however, Cather is explicit about the fact that Thea has married Ottenburg: " . . . Denver papers announced that Thea Kronborg had married Frederick Ottenburg, the head of the Brewers' Trust" (Cather, 1915 ed., 701).

However, this passage is removed altogether and the marriage is greatly deemphasized in Cather's 1937 revision. The information that Thea has wed is given only in a vague reference in context of Aunt Tillie's visit to Thea when she is performing in Kansas City: "When Thea dined in her own room, her husband went down to dinner with Tillie . . ." (578). This is the single indication in the 1937 edition that Thea and Ottenburg have wed. In neither edition does the marriage logically follow from the preceding chapters or coincide with Thea's personality; but especially in the 1937 revisions, Cather seemed to want the marriage annulled. She no doubt sensed that such union was a contradiction—even a betrayal—of Thea's and her own artistic/feminine selves as well as a serious compromise of narrative integrity. That she recognized such problems is in itself testimony to her artistic perspicacity; but she was not quite able to challenge the patriarchal hegemony and rectify the error by deigning marriage altogether—as Chopin's Edna Pontellier, for instance, had done earlier or as Emily Dickinson's created persona had done earlier still. The marriage, despite the relatively insignificant place it occupies in the text per se, is an essential manifestation of the sociosexual conflicts which continued to influence Cather's creative processes.

Such conflict is made somewhat clearer by the provenance of *The Song of the Lark*. In the same article in which she profiles Olive Fremstad, Thea's prototype, Cather discusses two other opera stars. The singer to whom she devotes the least amount of space is Louise Homer, though Homer was at the time the leading contralto at the Metropolitan opera and probably more famous than Fremstad. Cather's slighting of Homer was based on the fact that in addition to fulfilling the demands of an artistic career, Homer was also a successful wife and devoted mother to five children. Such articulation of the maternal and artistic selves disturbed Cather, who professed agreement with the third of the singers, Geraldine Farrar, that "conjugal and maternal duties" do not mix with artistic development and that the female artist must forsake all else in favor of her art (Woodress 256). Fremstad also admonished that the true artist must be "born alone" and "die alone" (Woodress 257). Rationally, Cather may have believed this All-for-Art manifesto which Farrar and Fremstad espoused; and it is this near fanatic commitment to Art that she imparts to Thea throughout the narrative. Emotionally, however, Cather was nearer to Homer than she revealed, admiring or even envious of the woman who could be both acclaimed Artist and adored mother—an ideal state certainly not precluded by Cather's homoeroticism, though perhaps made difficult by her temperament otherwise. If her writing is true witness (especially as revealed in Thea's addendum marriage to the beer prince), Cather never convinced herself that a woman could safely rebel against the conventionally defined "female" responsibility by marrying herself to Art. More importantly, the impetus for her thinking in this regard seems not only to emanate from a conditioned respect for the teachings of the Nebraska patriarchy but to emanate also from an innate doubt that total commitment to an abstraction was justified. Had Cather's "fear" of the prevailing edicts of her society been all that prevented her from creating artistic personae who damned society and espoused Art, she probably would have surmounted that fear. Her own convictions and conscience, however, were not to be compromised; and it is this intellectual, artistic integrity that keeps insisting upon attention in her narratives. Just how strong the conflict between Art and the maternal obligation was in Cather is witnessed by the fact that in *My Ántonia*, the novel immediately following *The Song of the Lark*, she discovers her most convincing heroine in a woman who sacrifices   everything to motherhood, nothing to art.

From yet another perspective, Cather's fascination with Olive Fremstad's career as the basis for *The Song of the Lark* is hardly remarkable, since the choice once again reflects her life-long identification with and homoerotic attraction for singers and actresses. Moreover, Fremstad offered another good subject for biography, a genre from which Cather had just received strong reinforcement after having ghost-written the "autobiography" of S. S. McClure—another excellent example of her sublimating herself to a public man of power and influence. She commenced to write *The Song of the Lark* before publishing McClure's autobiography and just after completing a biographical profile of Fremstad. The biographer's impulse was as fresh and strong as the fictionist's. Thus, the superficial events of Thea's operatic career parallel Fremstad's. The essential Thea persona, however, is clearly more Cather and her fantasy self than she is Fremstad. In writing her third novel, therefore, Cather sought to combine Olive Fremstad's life as a Wagnerian soprano with her own life in Nebraska—that is, she consciously grafted Fremstad's adulthood to Willa Cather's childhood. Cather was comfortable fictionalizing her own Age of Innocence, her pre-pubescence; but she could not or would not consciously confront the years of her sexual maturity. Thus, in a process that is part conscious art and part unconscious sublimation of her erotic self, Cather borrows and substitutes the career and art form of another woman. What results is an awkward paradox. On the one hand she merges the two personae into the character of "Thea," whom we are supposed to perceive as one person, an integrated fictive unit. The design is faulty, however, and what results are Siamese twins, joined but never merged. Not surprisingly, therefore, the images which Cather attaches to Thea's music and sexuality (the dominant motivations in her life) are conflicted and at times contradictory. Like Cather herself, the adolescent Thea is superficially masculine. She looks more like a boy than her rival Lily Fisher, has a boy's voice, and is cast in the role of titular hero in "The Drummer Boy of Shiloh" (86). Even her doting mother notes that Thea "wasn't pretty, exactly—her face was too broad and her nose was too big" (197). Later, one of the other music students refers to her as "the savage blonde" (224). As she matures, and paralleling her development as a musician, she becomes more superficially feminine. At her first singing audition for Mrs. Henry Nathanmeyer in Chicago, she wears a borrowed gown: "She had never sung in a low dress before, and she found it comfortable" (350). She soon develops a fascination with her breast size and is later shown marveling at her naked body, with its "long, firm lines, the smoothness of her skin" (515). Yet, despite the physical maturation and transition, she somehow retains the androgynous appearance. When rancher Henry Bitmer sees her and Ottenburg playing in Panther Canyon, his first impression is that "They looked like two boys" (384). This superficial sexual dichotomy epitomizes an essential conflict in Thea and one which transfers from Cather's own uncertainties as noted above: the conflict which results when her maternal instincts clash with her monomaniacal devotion to Art—a devotion borrowed from Fremstad and which Cather wanted to endorse, but which is incompatible with Cather's own sexuality.

The maternal image is quite strong and positive for the young Thea (who, we recall, parallels Cather herself). Thea's mother, reflecting the gentler elements of Cather's own domineering mother, is a loving, nurturing, protective woman who encourages Thea, uncomplainingly accepts her lot as the wife of an inept man, and manages to rear seven children of diverse temperaments. Thea emulates her mother in her devoted attention to her youngest brother Thor—a character drawn from

Cather's own sibling. Thea also looks so much like her mother physically that Dr. Archie is intrigued by the resemblance. Moreover, the society in which she is reared honors mother-hood, while art must be subordinated to the pragmatic needs of a frontier life. Art is honored only insofar as it enhances the prac-tical and traditional elements of prairie routine (music for wed-dings, singing for funerals, pictures for historical record) and only if it can supplement family income. Before she is twelve, for instance, Thea is teaching piano at 25 cents a lesson. By the age of fifteen she has quit school entirely and is "established as a music-teacher in Moonstone" (132). As she matures, Thea pro-gressively identifies her art with money, thereby displacing her procreative, maternal instincts with her creative and financially lucrative ones. The premature death of Ray Kennedy, who wants to marry Thea and rear children, but who ultimately sup-plies the funds which guarantee that she will wed herself to art, epitomizes this displacement.

Near this juncture in the narrative Cather displaces her own autobiography with Fremstad's biography. Thus protected behind the mask of another woman, Cather is less restrained in contemplating sexuality. In Chicago, when Thea exchanges the relatively private piano playing for the very public and literally exposed singing, Thea realizes the erotic power of her art. That is, she has sublimated into her public singing performances the sexual impulses that would ordinarily manifest themselves as children. When she hears her first symphony, her response is orgasmic: "She would have it, what the trumpets were singing! She would have it, have it—it! Under the old cape she pressed her hands upon her heaving bosom, that was a little girl's no longer" (255). Later when she returns to Moonstone, and just after her mother notes that Thea's chest "was fuller than when she went away, her breasts rounder and firmer" (282), she goes to sing for Spanish Johnny and his friends in Mexican town. The men's response to her singing is near comic in its overt eroti-cism. The men sigh, sweat, and pant; and when the song is fin-ished they "began hunting feverishly for cigarettes" (293). Though Thea recognizes the erotic power of her performance for Spanish Johnny and his friends, her singing retains an exuberant innocence. Time, however, progressively destroys that naiveté. Years afterward, made up for her part as Sieglinde, she accompa-nies Dr. Archie and Ottenburg to a New York restaurant, where she warns them that she may be mistaken for a prostitute: "With all this paint on my face, I must look like something you picked up on Second Avenue" (534). Thus we have a series of peculiar psychological alterations, confounded by the incompatible Cather-Fremstad union. Though as a girl Thea feels no conflict between her music and her motherly role and its contingent financial duties, once she leaves Moonstone she commences to dissociate art from the maternal instincts. Through some indescribable psychic chemistry, based more on the shift to the Fremstad persona than on logical narrative transitions, art now is perceived as being counter-maternal, and the money it brings is associated with prostitution. Thea therefore equates her devotion to art with betrayal of her perceived maternal obligations. The mother-to-be has sold herself, has become whore to Art.

Perhaps sensing the disharmony which such transitions create in the narrative design and the dilemma they present to the audience, Cather constructs the long Panther Canyon episode. With the Panther Canyon images she seeks to supply clarifying evidence of Thea's peculiar and contradictory dissociant processes. The contrasting bird images and the metaphor of the ancient Indian women warrant comment here. Cather first gives us the swallows, which Thea sees as a "timid, nest-building folk" (375) and which symbolize the rural domesticity she has abandoned. Such swallows, we might recall, are communal in their nesting habits, common to barns and rural areas, and identified with peace and domesticity—as the Capistrano Mission legend suggests. Shortly after the swallows Cather gives us the mighty soaring eagle which, as we are informed quite unequivocally, symbolizes the "glorious striving of human art" (399), the released soul or spirit which in turn is manifested in the creative process—and the eagle is male, as the masculine pronouns which are used to designate it attest. At this stage of her development Thea definitely identifies more positively with the lone male eagle than with the maternal and gregarious swallows. As seen in her profile of Fremstad and in her advocating that women forsake motherhood for art, Cather tried to establish her feminine right to artistic sovereignty, tried to free her creative self from the strictures of traditional male-female roles. Yet in this bifurcated imagery of the birds Cather unconsciously contradicts the implied argument of that advocacy. The nest-building swallows emblematize the domestic or female life; the eagle just as distinctly emblematizes the rarefied atmosphere of an art that Cather continued to associate with masculinity. In trying to deny the maternal obligations of her femininity, she denies as well the artistic potential of femininity, as the male eagle imagery shows. With such an impasse she seems to have fallen pray to the oversimplified idea implied by Fremstad's advocacy of female art—the idea that art itself has gender. It is the same fallacy, ironically, which marked Cather's own earlier belief that fiction was a male's domain. Erroneous though such thinking may have been, it nonetheless created very real narrative problems for Cather.

The swallow-eagle symbology is separated in the text by a contravening image cluster which illustrates how persistent the art-maternal conflict was in Cather's creative processes. The images originate in Thea's reconstruction of the ancient Indian women walking down the steep trails of Panther Canyon to bathe in the clear stream and to transport water back to their cliff houses in the handmade clay vessels (376-377). Thinking of the Indian women, Thea imagines a baby "hanging to her back" (376) while she contemplates the pottery which served as "the envelope and sheath of the precious" water (377) and which she assumes the Indian women created. She venerates these mythical Indian women because in her imagination they were able to reconcile the domestic-artistic conflict implied by the swallow-eagle symbology. Not only do the women literally have their babies, but in the "graceful jars" which they have made and decorated they recreate the artifice of the womb, with its amnion or placenta (sheath and envelope) and life-giving amniotic fluid. This image seems to come more naturally to Cather and definitely counteracts the anti-maternal philosophy which Fremstad represented and which is manifested in the swallow-eagle tensions. Moreover, the very canyon in which the ancient women lived replicates the female body and thus the birth process seen microcosmically in the jars. As Judith Fryer has noted in discussing Cather's imagistic use of landscape, land such as Panther Canyon "is a textured map of the female body, wild and gentle, rocky and fringed and smooth, seemingly inaccessible, yet sheltering life deep within its hollow center" ("Desert" 33).

There is, however, continued discordance in Cather's symbology of the Indian women. Thea says at one point that human life is hard, that the artist must know this above all else, and that the knowledge is not felt in the mind. "You have to realize it in your body," she emphasizes (554). The comment, with its undertones of gestation, locates art once again within the maternal processes. Yet, Cather is paraphrasing the anti-maternal Fremstad in these comments on art, borrowing words she used in her earlier interview with Fremstad. The contradiction may be explained by the fact that the operatic artist might well feel the artistic impulse emanating from the "body" more literally than would the fictionist, who is more prone to feel art in the abstractions of the mind than in the musculature of chest and lungs. For the fictionist, therefore, the body image doesn't seem quite precise. The point is that the grafting of autobiography, biography, and fiction leaves contradictions in the psychic or creative levels of narrative revelation which are difficult to sort out. Cather tries, for instance, to accomplish a kind of modal shift by philosophizing not about the art of fiction but about the art of singing. No matter how much she knew about opera superficially, she had no essential comprehension of it—no more, say, than Fremstad had of the art of novel writing. In this regard, Frederick Ottenburg's dilettantish fascination for opera is more indicative of Cather than is Thea's supposed innate genius. In the strictest sense, singing is not a creative but an interpretive art and does not totally interchange with writing in Cather's design. Unlike the bird for which the narrative is named, singing does not come naturally to Cather. The two modes of artistic expression—singing and writing—are distinct and are informed by different muses. Cather inevitably transfers her own subconsciousness into Thea's personality; but she cannot realize a similar transference for Fremstad's psyche. The discrepancies involved in substituting the metaphysics of one art form for another need not detain us, but they do bear witness to the narrative inconsistencies which mar *The Song of the Lark*.

Panther Canyon remains, however, an appropriate geographical setting for Thea's ruminations. Thea is imagining the Indian women in context of her personal relationship with Ottenburg, a relationship which reminds her constantly of her own eroticism and of the imminent possibility of marriage and eventual motherhood. She does not yet know of his existing marriage to Miss Beers and is anticipating a request he will later verbalize: he wants to "marry and raise a son" (559). She has quit singing while in the canyon, thereby reverting momentarily to the impulses of the earlier, less conflicted Moonstone period when, like the Indian women, the traditional life of wife and mother seemed plausible. Ottenburg's desire to father her child is not unappealing to her. For a while, Thea thinks she can be both artist and conventional woman, and though that idea does not coincide with either Cather's earlier denial of the mother-artist union or with the contradictory images of Panther Canyon, it seems to guide Cather's hand in closing the narrative with

Thea's marriage to Ottenburg. Susan Lanser proposes in *The Narrative Act* that certain elements of narrative "allow the opposition to the culture text signified in [a] story to be conveniently barred from coming to fruition in lived experience" (261). What Lanser suggests applies to Cather in this instance, for Thea's marriage conveniently offsets a demanding, total commitment to the artistic, nonconformist life.

Upon emerging from the mystic canyon, Thea returns to problems directly related to the art-motherhood tension: Ottenburg's pressuring her for a liaison with him in Mexico; his request that she enter into a common law marriage; the quandary about giving up her singing to be a "kept" woman. The Indian myth complex does not transcend the limited domain of the canyon to offer any solace in the quotidian world outside the imagined experience. The Indian women are idealized, surviving only in the canyons and arroyos of Thea's imagination. Yet she tries to duplicate their tranquility by entering into a marital relationship which Cather herself soon realized was inappropriate (thus her trying to eliminate it in the later edition). The final irony of the entire series of conflicting and perplexing images is that Cather betrays her fictive self with a conclusion that verges on the same kind of humiliation we see in *Alexander's Bridge*. Not only does Thea adhere to the pragmatic concept that art must justify itself by paying "a big contract" (555), but she marries a man who, while hardly evil, is void of true artistic genius and saturated with Teutonic arrogance. She passively listens to his condescending advice that she probably should not marry him because she would get lost "in the upholstery" of his family's "big German houses" (460), that she speaks poor English, and that she needs to be around people of her own kind—that is, peasants (464). The audience realizes at this point, if not before, that Thea would be foolish to marry Ottenburg. By so doing she simultaneously compromises her art and her maternal instinct; yet, somewhere in the void between the final chapter and the Epilogue she marries him nonetheless.

Works Cited

Ammons, Elizabeth. "The Engineer as Cultural Hero and Willa Cather's First Novel, *Alexander's Bridge*." *American Quarterly*. 38 (5) Winter 1986: 746-760.

Baym, Nina. *Woman's Fiction: A Guide to Novels by and About Women in America, 1820-1870*. Ithaca: Cornell U P, 1984.

Benstock, Shari. *Women of the Left Bank: Paris 1900-1940*. Austin: U of Texas P, 1986.

Brinnin, John Malcolm. *The Third Rose: Gertrude Stein and Her World*. Boston: Little, Brown, 1959.

Cather, Willa. *Alexander's Bridge* (with Preface). Boston: Houghton Mifflin, 1922.

—. *O Pioneers!* (1913). *Willa Cather: Early Novels and Stories*. New York: The Library of America, 1987. 132-290.

—. *The Song of the Lark* (1915). *Willa Cather: Early Novels and Stories*. New York: The Library of America, 1987. 291-706.

—. *The Song of the Lark* (1937). Boston: Houghton Mifflin, 1943.

Cohn, Dorrit. *Transparent Minds: Narrative Modes for Presenting Consciousness in Fiction*. Princeton: Princeton U P, 1978.

Edel, Leon. "Homage to Willa Cather" in *The Art of Willa Cather*. Ed. Bernice Slote and Virginia Faulkner. Lincoln: U of Nebraska P, 1974. 185-204.

Fetterley, Judith. *The Resisting Reader: A Feminist Approach to American Fiction*. Bloomington: Indiana U P, 1978.

Fryer, Judith. "Desert, Rock, Shelter, Legend: Willa Cather's Novels of the Southwest" in *The Desert Is No Lady: Southwestern Landscapes in Women's Writing and Art*. Ed. Vera Norwood and Janice Monk. New Haven: Yale U P, 1987. 27-46.

—. *The Faces of Eve: Women in the Nineteenth Century American Novel*. New York: Oxford U P, 1976.

Gilbert, Sandra M. and Susan Gubar. *No Man's Land: The Place of the Woman Writer in the Twentieth Century*. New Haven: Yale U P, 1988.

Lanser, Susan S. *The Narrative Act: Point of View in Prose Fiction*. Princeton: Princeton U P, 1981.

Lewis, Edith. *Willa Cather Living: A Personal Record*. New York: Knopf, 1953.

Miller, James E., Jr. "Willa Cather and The Art of Fiction" in *The Art of Willa Cather*. Ed. Bernice Slote and Virginia Faulkner. Lincoln: U of Nebraska P, 1974. 121-148.

O'Brien, Sharon. *Willa Cather: The Emerging Voice*. New York: Oxford U P, 1987.

Oehlschlaeger, Fritz. "Willa Cather's 'Consequences' and *Alexander's Bridge*: An Approach through R. D. Laing and Ernest Becker." *Modern Fiction Studies*, 32(2) Summer 1986: 191-202.

Schorer, Mark. "Technique as Discovery" in *The Theory of The Novel*. Ed. Philip Stevick. New York: Free Press, 1967. 65-80.

Slote, Bernice. "Introduction." *Alexander's Bridge*. Lincoln: U of Nebraska P, 1977. v-xxvi.

Stanzel, F. K. *A Theory of Narrative*. Trans. Charlotte Goedsche. London: Cambridge U P, 1984.

Stevick, Philip. "Introduction," in *The Theory of the Novel*. New York: Free Press, 1967. 2-12.

Woodress, James. *Willa Cather: A Literary Life*. Lincoln: U of Nebraska P, 1987.

2
My Ántonia: Emergence and Authorial Revelations

Retrospectively comparing her novels in 1921, Cather noted that while she enjoyed writing *The Song of the Lark*, she "care[d] less for it than any of her books" (*WC in Person* 35). The previous chapter cites a number of reasons why Cather may have reached this conclusion. She learned something about her craft from trying to manage the patterns of *The Song of the Lark*—the conjoining of her own adolescence with Fremstad's adulthood, the inarticulate symbols, the conventional plot movement from struggle to success, the traditional marriage affixed to a persona rebelling against tradition. For *My Ántonia*, as she said in 1925, she wanted to show "the other side of the rug, the pattern that is supposed not to count in a story. In it there is no love affair, no courtship, no marriage, no broken heart, no struggle for success. I knew I'd ruin my material if I put it in the usual fictional pattern" (*WC in Person* 77). Her comment is disingenuous, of course, for in the text there are marriages, broken hearts, and love affairs; but she is correct in that she deviates from her usual fictional pattern.

In offering the other side of the rug in *My Ántonia*, Cather concentrates not upon artistic struggle but upon the more primitive struggle for human survival. When seen against Ántonia's fight to endure hunger, cold, physical abuse, and the ravages of time and drudgery, Thea Kronborg's struggle to succeed as an artist pales into relative insignificance and acquires a certain irony. Only if one is guaranteed those basic human comforts which Ántonia lacks can thoughts be turned to the "higher" callings of elitist art. Only because others supply creature necessities for Thea, only because she inherits money, does she have the luxury of worrying about her artistic integrity. That Cather found the fundamental struggles more appealing than the nonessential ones accounts in large degree for the articulation between artistic purpose and achieved text in *My Ántonia* as opposed to the unresolvable points of difference in the narrative structure of *The Song of the Lark.* (Why, in short, *Ántonia* is great, *Lark* mediocre.) Moreover, Cather consciously faced the point of view difficulties which we note in her early novels. The story-within-a-story device, borrowed perhaps from Hawthorne who ironically distances himself from authorial responsibility by crediting Surveyor Pue with (or blaming him for) the tale of the scarlet letter, alleviates for Cather some of the difficulties of facing head-on the homoerotic implications of the subtext. The fictitious, assumed narrator—while not a totally successful device, as we will see—nonetheless gives to Cather a projected masculine self through which to offer her own tale of the love, fall, and redemption of an adulterous outcast. Thus, though the homoerotic conflicts are subtextually discernible, they are at least absent from the text per se, thereby presenting a creative field in which Cather was more comfortable than she was in those narratives in which she had to assume more direct point of view responsibility, as with the psycho-narration technique. Indeed, Cather's "rug" metaphor is apropos, for the differentiation in narrative quality between her third and fourth novels is a matter of clever and fortuitous creative adjustments rather than radical departures.

In *My Ántonia*, Cather retains the biographical-autobiographical technique she attempted in *The Song of the Lark*, but she puts more psychological distance between herself and the text than she does in the earlier novel. She avoids the difficult effort to combine adult-other and child-self which interfered with creative process and realized text and subsequently caused difficulties with symbology, authorial intent, and narrative control when she grafted Olive Fremstad's life to her own Nebraska childhood. Rather than incorporating selves in *My Ántonia*, Cather diversifies, splitting her own psyche into two fictive personae: she translates her childhood through the personae of actual Bohemian girls with whom she had been reared and with whom she could imaginatively identify. She spoke several times of the "Bohemian girl" who more than any other suggested Ántonia to her. She said in 1921, for instance, that the prototype "was good to me when I was a child. I saw a great deal of her from the time I was eight until I was twelve. She was bighearted and essentially romantic" (*WC in Person* 22). The girl is identified elsewhere as Annie Sadilek (Woodress 41). Having settled on the source for Ántonia, Cather then translates her adult self through the fictive male narrator who is a successful business man first and a writer only in passing—certainly no artistic monomaniac like Thea Kronborg. Cather thereby unifies a creative self she had de-articulated in *The Song of the Lark* and simultaneously brings into harmony many of the sociosexual tensions noticeable in that novel. By separating rather than attempting to singularize psychological elements which are incompatible, Cather manages to coalesce factors in her imagination and thereby realize the creative paradox that unity can result from polarity. She discovers, in other words, that conflict—emblematized textually by Jim and Ántonia's polar existences—can be the source of equilibrium if correctly translated through the imagination.

To have Thea Kronborg succeed as an artist, Cather must wrench her away from the prairie homeland and make her a stranger in a strange land. Yet, in *My Ántonia*, Cather bifurcates her psyche in the dual personae of Jim and Ántonia, and thus alleviates the psychological trauma induced by such separation from home. Through this bifurcation device, Ántonia-Cather may remain in Nebraska, be dutiful wife and helpmeet, and fulfill her maternal obligations a dozen fold; while Jim-Cather may wander to exotic lands, become wealthy, successful, and cosmopolitan. Moreover, the two selves can be reintegrated because Jim returns home, reacquaints himself with Ántonia, and anticipates (albeit somewhat illogically) a future with her and her family. That such closure is hardly "realistic" is beside the point, since Cather was not intent upon producing a realistic/ naturalistic narrative. David Stouck notes in speaking of Cather's earlier stories that "Eventually her best fiction was to be written out of an emotion and developed largely in terms of setting and character" (76); and on this point, especially for *My Ántonia*, Stouck is correct, though Cather seems here to be working from a cluster of emotions rather than from a singular emotional impulse. The point, however, is that she is guided by her emotions, not by a preconceived notion of what a novel should be or do. More importantly, such bifurcation symbolizes not only the articulated self but offers also a solution to the maternal quandary evident in *The Song of the Lark*. In a manner of speaking, since the type did not come innately to her, Cather psychologically adopts a maternal self in Ántonia. By solving the dilemma of how to fulfill the feminine "obligations" and yet remain creatively unfettered, Cather also avoids such problems of narrative design as the deux ex machina marriage which compromises the textual integrity of *The Song of the Lark*.

However, because Cather manages to articulate the creative self and to lessen the psychosexual difficulties evident in *The Song of the Lark* does not mean that all is placid in *My Ántonia*. On the contrary, the light emerges from but does not permanently brighten darkness. Borrowing Cather's own "rug" metaphor, we may view Ántonia as the obverse of Thea Kronborg—a portrait of what might have been if Ray Kennedy's death had not granted Thea the insurance money to finance her music studies or if she had succumbed early to the prairie conventions of marriage, work, and children. Ántonia begins with as many attributes for potential success as Thea. She has physical beauty, a dynamic personality, drive, and enough inherited musical talent to be something other than the haggard prairie wife she becomes. Fate, however, does not permit Ántonia's escape from the harsh life of the prairie to the bright lights of fame and fortune. Cather herself explained Thea's success as "the play of blind chance, the way in which commonplace occurrences fell together to liberate her from commonness" ("Preface" *SL* vi). In *My Ántonia*, she shows how fate casts commonplace occurrences into an entirely different design—a design motivated in large measure by altruism but one not completely optimistic in its manifestation.

The positivist argument is that Ántonia with her troupe of loving children and her adoring husband transcends the superficial limits of worldly acclaim which Thea epitomizes and therefore represents a success that cannot be gauged by the mundane values of wealth, fame, or physical attractiveness. Thea has her $1000-a-night contract, but Ántonia (no matter how haggard or uneducated) has Cuzak, kids, and contentment. Randolph Bourne's effusive review of *My Ántonia* in the December 1918 *Dial* is typical of the positivist view. He sees Ántonia as a "free and warm and glorious girl" who "marries to a simple Bohemian farmer, strong, and good like herself," to live happily thereafter as a paragon of contentment (145-146). More recently, James Woodress eulogizes Ántonia as "the Madonna of the Wheat Fields and the symbol for the American westering myth" (293). This argument of inverted values has a modicum of plausibility, as we shall soon see. Yet, remembering Cather's devotion to art, her propensity to wealth and easy living, and her persistent anti-marriage motifs, we should recognize also the potential irony inherent in her making one of her fictive selves

(Ántonia) into a toothless, ugly slattern. (At the time of writing *My Ántonia*, Cather was living comfortably at 5 Bank Street in New York's Greenwich Village, socializing with the literary elite such as Elinor Wylie, Henry Canby, Zoë Akins, Dorothy Canfield Fisher, and Elizabeth Sergeant and enjoying considerable fame and popularity, though not necessarily the psychological peace of mind such creature comforts might suggest [Woodress 276f].) A similar potential irony underlies her bringing Jim home to encounter his past in such a vision as Ántonia personifies and to romanticize (against all logic) a happy future for himself as part of Ántonia's life. Such a scenario contradicts the major motifs we have seen in Cather's fiction before *My Ántonia* and those we shall see in it after *My Ántonia*. Moreover, Cather's own attitudes during the time she was writing the novel do not support the quaint romanticism the Jim/Ántonia situation might superficially imply. Among other disappointments in Cather's life, Isabelle McClung had recently wed Jan Hambourg, entering a marriage that devastated Cather. As she said in a letter to W. H. Boynton, "the winter [of 1916] has been full of changes and troubles, the loss of old friends by death and even by marriage" and she wanted to write something "hard and dry." She would write her next novel, perhaps, "for the same reasons that violinists play Bach after they have been working hard on very romantic modern things" (Woodress 277). Recent events, especially Isabelle's union with Hambourg, suggested to her "that the pursuit of happiness was not the reality it was supposed to be; the pursuit of pain seemed to be just as irradicable a human instinct" (277). A trip west in mid-1916 eliminated some of the writer's block she was experiencing and cheered her somewhat, but did not essentially alter her feelings; and such pessimism may well account for the horror that is a significant factor in Ántonia's life.

The greatness of *My Ántonia* therefore lies not in any idealistic view of the primitive life amidst nature's bounty but in the delicate balance Cather creates from the psychological opposition personified in the Jim-Ántonia bifurcation of her creative psyche. The narrative design operates as a paradigm of Cather's own life at the time of World War I. It serves as a momentary stay against confusion, to borrow Robert Frost's term for another genre of literature. Subsequent analyses of *One of Ours* and the other post-Ántonia novels will show that the stay against confusion was temporary, that Cather moved—if not in a straight line at least progressively—away from the articulated self. The world fell apart. Yet, for a few moments the very dynamics of conflict created balance, like a child's gyroscopic toy on the edge of an abyss; and Cather found equilibrium in the contraries that tormented her. The resulting psychic articulation is reflected in the design and realization of *My Ántonia*.

The truism is still valid, of course, that no theory really explains the phenomenon of the creative mind. We have to work with product more than process. As Murray Krieger warns, literary theorizing "is a vain discipline" for "each attempt at theoretical completeness is rendered fruitless by the teasing elusiveness of the entities and experiences for which it is to account" (3). And no text is more teasing and elusive than *My Ántonia*. Thus, in analyzing the narrative techniques that coalesce to form *My Ántonia*, I make no claim to explaining fully how Cather's imagination distilled the raw material of experience into her most complex and subtly wrought novel. My focus instead is upon an analyses of several motifs and images which have not previously been scrutinized and which offer some insight into Cather's creative imagination. Perhaps appropriately, the analysis commences in a void.

In one of the saner efforts to discover *My Ántonia*, Terence Martin comments on the twenty-year gap between Books IV and V. He does not elucidate the hiatus, but he does inadvertently touch upon its importance when he states that Jim Burden's absence from Nebraska and the intervening life "afford little but material for conjecture and inference" (308). Indeed we do conjecture and infer when faced with the missing decades, for the narrative blank space is a kind of fictive black hole into which most of the meaning of *My Ántonia* has fallen. Primarily, we as audience ponder the superficially simple but ultimately complex question of what exactly is the progress Jim undergoes, and consequently, what does the entire novel "mean"? We watch Ántonia change substantially—see her experience times of searching calm, bitchy hoydenism, sexual debauchery, physical and psychic pain, and maternal tranquility. Her emotional range is greater and considerably more convincingly authentic than any previous Cather "heroine" and in fact will not be matched by subsequent ones. These changes in Ántonia are graphic in the narrative design: Ántonia's maniacal attack on Jim in chapter XVIII, Book I; her dehumanizing labors in chapter III, Book IV; and her serenity which seems to transcend physical beauty throughout Book V. In contrast, Jim is static. We notice little commensurate growth or change for him. Viewed against

Ántonia's near epic struggles, what David Daiches calls her "vast symbolic progress" (44), Jim is strangely flat, peculiarly immutable. Since his place in the narrative is at least equal to hers and since Cather does not typically offer contrastive characters without giving each adequate stature (as with Hilda and Alexander in *Alexander's Bridge* or later Latour and Vaillant in *Death Comes for the Archbishop*), Jim's apparent lack of development does perplex.

Others have tried to solve the riddle of how Jim's stasis coincides with Cather's narrative intent. Evelyn Helmick looks for a solution by tracing Jim's personality back to "primordial matriarchal mysteries" (178). She explains *My Ántonia* generally and the pivotal Cuzak section particularly in terms of these ancient Greek rites and locates Jim's gradual movement toward self-awareness in the realm of Ántonia's matriarchy. Helmick is correct in implying the matriarchal context, for as I have noted, the matriarchal-patriarchal conflict permeates Cather's first three novels and easily transfers to the fourth. Helmick is also correct in recognizing the presence of myth in the novel, and her offering of the Eleusinian Mysteries to account for questions raised by Jim's befuddling personality is ingenious and a useful balance to the more psychoanalytical approaches I offer. Cather, however, does not force us quite so far afield in search of answers as the Eleusinian association implies, because her entire narrative is replete with light sources of its own. The familiar story is that she once belittled her own art with the comment that she wished she had a thousand dollars for each of the faults in *My Ántonia* (*WC in Person* 79); but such self-deprecation suggests the effort she made to mask how careful she was in composing the novel and how close it was to her own psyche. Ultimately we discover that her myths are domestic and that her mysteries are solvable from intertextual clues.

In novels before and after *My Ántonia* Cather relies on a rather simple chronological device, the temporal void. That is, she transposes or transfers narrative action from one point in time to another point years beyond, with no transitional explanation for the missing years. For example, she "voids" sixteen years in *O Pioneers!*, fifteen years in *Shadows on the Rock*, and twenty five years in *Lucy Gayheart*. This chronological device reiterates the earlier point that Cather's success with *My Ántonia* is a matter of subtle adjustments rather than radical departures, but she manages it most effectively in *My Ántonia*. The essential change which Jim undergoes, his moral or psychological growth, occurs during the apparent vacuum of the lost twenty years. He reaches no final goals or absolute conclusions, for Cather's narrative is not predicated upon linear progressions and terminal events. Jim does, however, experience a definite quest. It begins literally when he leaves Virginia as a child and it enters the metaphysical or transcendent stage when he returns to Ántonia after twenty years. Because his psychic changes are indeed ultimately mysterious, as Helmick suggests, Cather wisely chooses to let the metamorphoses occur out of sight, off stage; and only by examining the varied symbolic and thematic elements Cather meticulously gives us on stage can we by indirection come to understand just what Jim seeks, how he changes, what precipitates the changes, and finally how he begins to arrive at the peace and apperception that have long evaded him. By examining the subtlety of Cather's design, both dramatically and metaphysically, we realize that the twenty-year lacuna contains a spatiotemporal reality which engulfs, alters, and finally helps explain *My Ántonia* and, by extension, the conflicts which fueled Cather's creative processes.

The objects of first focus are the concrete, internal clues which Cather offers on the narrative surface. She uses a number of motifs, but lying at the heart of her design is the theme of submergence-emergence—an artistic manifestation of her personal conflicts and contradictions. She names this central motif early when she marks the "subterranean habit" (30) of the owls and prairie dogs. Thereafter she develops the subterranean concept along all levels of conceptualization, from the simply visual to the transcendent. As expected, the subterranean motif is first discernible in the realistic, seemingly trivial details of the narrative surface: the black and white badger that lives in grandmother Burden's garden and that requires an occasional chicken sacrifice (17); the prairie dogs and "brown earth-owls" that share the underground (29); and the rattlesnake "monstrosity" that descends the burrows and fattens on the rodents (45). These and similar animals appear so frequently that they soon become a subliminal part of the narrative background against which we view Jim and Ántonia. Conventionally, these animals could easily be interpreted in terms of the dualistic cosmology, the good-evil dichotomy, as readily suggested by the black-white badger; but the symbolism and imagery in *My Ántonia* are not conventional and do not invite the audience to rely on conventional expectations.

From the animals we move to a more subtle but still literal aspect of the motif: the subterranean life of the people. Most apparent on this level is the dugout where we first encounter the Shimerdas. Grandmother Burden sets the tone for our response when she says she hates to think of the Shimerdas "spending the winter in that cave of Krajiek's" (30). Reality proves even harsher than grandmother's cave image implies, for we soon discover that the Shimerdas' first American home is nothing but "a door and a window sunk deep in the drawbank" (22) and that the family survives in less comfort than the animals from which the concept of the buried life derives. The animals submerge and emerge in natural cycles, but the Shimerdas' predicament suggests darkness and the buried life or death-in-life.

Ironically the Burdens themselves are temporally not far removed from such troglodytic existence. The residue of the Burdens' past life still shows in the basement kitchen, painted "as it used to be in the dugouts" (9) and in the adjoining long cellar which Jim explores but tentatively. The subterranean motif continues even more graphically when the blizzard strikes and the men have to dig a "tunnel through the snow . . . with walls so solid that grandmother and I could walk back and forth in it" (93). Juxtaposed with the digging of the tunnel is Mr. Shimerda's suicide, which culminates in the ever present grave that stands like "a little island" on the prairie and that is the "spot most dear" to Jim (119). His fascination with the grave suggests also that at this stage of his life Jim relates more to submergence than emergence. His own impulses remain buried for many years, and the crossroads location of the grave implies the choices lying before him.

The literal placing of Mr. Shimerda into the earth (planting, as the old cowboy Otto Fuchs might say) begins our entrance into the metaphysical or unconscious realm of Cather's motif. On this level the most pervasive element is the prairie itself and the plants it nurtures. We note that though Jim originally feels that the prairie is "nothing but land" (7), the earth roundabout is in fact very productive. Wasteland images occur in the "muddy little pond" and "rusty willow bushes" (14), but the pages are dominated by emblems of natural growth: the cornfield, the sorghum patch, the box-elder, and the red grass that dyes the landscape the eucharistic "colour of wine-stains" (15). And within the controlled growth of grandmother's garden are the "big yellow pumpkins" (16), which in retrospect stand as an early emblem of Jim's own emergence or transcendence in that the pumpkins initiate for him the desire to "float off" into the sky with the sun which produces them (16). Finally we see the fruit cave of Book V, the cellar from which Ántonia's children tumble with glee—"a veritable explosion of life out of the dark cave into the sunlight" (339) and a positive counterpoint to the depressing hole in which we first meet Ántonia. Here the emergence and symbolic rebirth are so startling that even stolid Jim becomes dizzy. Terence Martin sees this particular image as being strained, which it certainly is. The strain is an integral part of the dynamics of conflict which Cather develops. She consistently places images under stress and tension, and the strain here seems no less intentional. By this stage of the narrative Cather wants to place tension upon the image to emphasize the literal-metaphysical associations, the animate-inanimate relationships. Just as badgers and pumpkins spring from the secret permutations of the earth, so spring children and self-realization. So spring creativity and the imagination.

The type of emergence most emphasized is the movement from darkness to light, a point Cather makes via reiterated light images. Beginning in the very first lines of the Introduction, where the train "flashed" through "bright-flowered pastures," the imagery continues in grandfather Burden's "snow-white beard" (12), in the "shining white bark" of the cottonwoods (21), and in the "sunflower-bordered roads" (28). Indeed, light symbols permeate the novel. We are here most concerned, however, with the light which Cather casts upon Ántonia, since Jim emerges from his darkness into the brightness of her humanism. This spiritual emergence is foreshadowed by the first description Cather gives of Ántonia's eyes, which are "big and warm and full of light, like the sun shining on brown pools in the wood" (23). The eye/sun image repeats in the major symbol concluding Book IV. Near father Shimerda's grave, Jim and Ántonia are saying good-bye for what they think may be the last time, just prior to the twenty-year hiatus. They linger on the prairie until tears appear in Ántonia's "bright, believing eyes" (321) and the sun begins to set. Simultaneously, the "moon rose in the east," and for several minutes "the two luminaries confronted each other across the level land, resting on opposite edges of the world" (322). The luminaries symbolize Jim and Ántonia, with Cather's ironic reversal of conventional sun-moon symbolism. As poetry such as Sylvia Plath's and studies such as Judith Kroll's *Chapters in a Mythology* demonstrate, the passive moon is usually feminine in symbology and the dominant sun masculine. More specifically, as Anne Stevenson notes in discussing Plath's "The Moon and the Yew Tree," the "mother-moon" (229) was part of Plath's personal mythology. Here in Cather, however, the sun is Ántonia, with her powerful, warming light, and the moon is Jim, who reflects but does not yet emit light. At this moment on the prairie, as in the two decades immediately following, Jim and Ántonia are physically worlds apart, though spiritually unified. The entire eye/sun image is the light which Cather gives to help us illuminate the darkness of the missing twenty years. As with the cave image, the symbolism is purposely conflicted to make it convey the psychological complexity of the Jim/Ántonia union.

Cather's intent with the "luminaries" passage is perhaps further appreciated if we realize that the lines present not an isolated piece of symbolism but are a continuation of a motif she inaugurates at the outset of Jim and Ántonia's life together. Literally within minutes of their first meeting, Ántonia offers Jim "a little chased silver ring she wore on her middle finger" (26). Typical of his submerged personality at this stage and of Cather's consistent hesitancy in depicting erotic unions and matrimonial commitments, Jim refuses the ring because he is subconsciously aware of what it emblematizes. "I didn't want her ring," he says emphatically, and goes on to chide Ántonia's reckless behavior in wanting to betroth herself "to a boy she had never seen before" (27). (Ántonia's incipient sexuality is later reified in her multitude of children.) Even at this early age Jim exhibits fear of commitment, not only to the pubescent Ántonia but more so to life's natural forces, which she so graphically represents. Ironically, while she lives destitute in the dark cave and Jim dwells in the reflected light of Burden wealth, he is the one who inhabits the darkness of his own doubts and timidity. Though intelligent and educated, and though he is appointed her tutor immediately after the ring episode, Jim and not Ántonia dwells in subterranean ignorance. He does not emerge until near the end of the novel, when as a middle-aged knight of American industry he makes his pilgrimage back to Ántonia, the source of his true enlightenment.

Thus the silver ring episode culminates in the sun-moon image of Book IV. We recall that during the latter passage Jim finally confesses his love for Ántonia—or at least comes as close to confessing as Cather can permit. Even if he cannot utter the word "love" to the Bohemian girl he has been warned against, he does admit that he would like to have her "for a sweetheart, or a wife, or my mother or my sister—anything that a woman can be to a man" (321). These disparate roles indicate not only Jim's (and Cather's) emotional confusion but also the multiplicity of Ántonia's character, the cosmic femininity she symbolizes, and probably the reason Cather was so drawn to her as a fictive persona. At the moment of Jim's confession, the "pale silver" moon rises, with Cather's choice of adjectives echoing the silver ring which Ántonia has previously offered. Whereas Jim rejected the symbolic union she proposed so long ago, here he notes that the sun and moon join to form a "singular light" (322) that emblematizes the spiritual union which has taken place over the years. Jim, at the end of Book IV, is not yet conscious of the union, but the mysterious forces of the union sustain him through the silent twenty years and carry him back to Ántonia in the very next book. Of note also is that in this instance Cather displaces her masculine-feminine selves by joining her bifurcated personae symbolically via the sun-moon singularity, rather than attempting psychosexual union literally as she does in *The Song of the Lark* with the unsuccessful Fremstad-Cather combination.

In "The Forgotten Reaping Hook: Sex in *My Ántonia*," Blanche H. Gelfant emphasizes various sexual symbols and concludes that Jim is a pusillanimous character fearful of sexual encounters, one who sublimates or represses his sexual drives so that they ultimately find expression in his penetrating the virgin prairie with his railroad. Gelfant believes that Jim's sexual fear makes of him "a wasteland figure who finds in the present nothing to compensate him for the loss of the past, and in the outer world nothing to violate the inner sanctum of memory" (63-64). Aside from the unfortunate train/penetration metaphor, Gelfant's argument is persuasive; but she seems finally to oversimplify both his character and Cather's narrative design and to apply Eliot's terminology too hastily. Freudian sex theory elucidates but does not fully explain the creative processes underlying *My Ántonia*.

What the text indicates is not that heterosexual love is some horror to be avoided via escape into the past but that certain forms of love (be they homo- or heterosexual) transcend lust or carnality and, for that matter, time. Typical of Jim, he does not fully comprehend this transcendent love at its instant of manifestation; but during the twenty years he is physically separated from Ántonia the love develops as inexorably as the other natural processes which permeate and inform the narrative. We are reminded, perhaps, of Andrew Marvell's' term "vegetable love" from another context, though with Jim and Ántonia the love is anything but carnal. In fact, it must not be carnal, for since Jim and Ántonia emblematize divisions of Cather's creative self, they cannot unite sexually—a point I will elucidate shortly. Thus, when Jim subsequently returns to her, his emergence from darkness is commencing, for he begins to accept and understand this magical, mysterious love. The love emanates indeed from "the precious, the incommunicable past" (372), but it does not suggest that Jim wishes to retrogress or that his life is circumscribed by yesterdays. The love comes from the past literally in that it began as a biologically earlier stage in his growth, but it exists in a contiuum. It sustains him permanently, even if at the time he is almost totally ignorant of its existence. Here we might recall that one of Jim's final observations in the novel concerns the future: his promise to himself to "tramp along a few miles of lighted streets with Cuzak" (370). The literal trail to the past—"a bit of the first road that went from Black Hawk out to the north country" (370)—is still discernible, but the streets of the future are lighted, and they are the byways that Jim anticipates with some enthusiasm.

In Book V the images and motifs of the earlier books are extended to emphasize Jim's realization of the "miracle" (331) that has been gestating for twenty years. Light images once again characterize Ántonia: white cats, light kitchen, shining range, white aprons, and the recurring yellow pumpkins. She has completed her emergence physically from the dugout and psychologically from the dependence that previously mired her in darkness. Throughout the early parts of the novel she has been in thrall to her father, her sullen brother Ambrosch, the scoundrel Larry Donovan, and even to Jim himself. But in Book V, she has worked herself free, has risen toward the light like one of the rugged prairie sunflowers that are so frequently mentioned. No longer dependent, she is the one upon whom others depend, and in that ironic freedom she attains a transcendent beauty as difficult for the superficial view to reveal as is the beauty of the snakes, owls and other natural prairie life. Despite her many batterings and her physical unattractiveness, she retains the mysterious "fire of life" (336) which has for so long beckoned to Jim. In the closing lines of Book IV, Jim departs from Ántonia in "intrusive darkness," but in Book V he emerges into the light that she emits, there to become aware of his own purpose, his own self. He is abiding by natural laws as inexorable as those which determine that the sun will generate light and energy and that the moon will be illuminated out of darkness by that light.   In this context, the Ántonia-Jim union represents an expression of Cather's most optimistic impulses.

The fact that at the conclusion of the novel we are still uncertain what Jim has realized about himself and that his personality still remains tantalizingly imprecise is in keeping with Cather's utlimate uncertainty about her own social, sexual attitudes.   The uncertainty coincides also with the overall design and with the specifics of the twenty-year break.   As E. K. Brown says, "Everything in the book is there to convey a feeling, not to tell a story" (206), and indeed the entire narrative operates on a delicate balance between realism and surrealism, with the prairie forming a solid background but with the personalities of the foreground actors being far more nebulous.   Like the prairie flowers that bloom a day and are gone, our understanding of the characters's psyches is ephemeral.   Ultimately and ironically, this element of Cather's design is also "realistic," for such vagueness is the best we can expect when analyzing human personalities. Percy Lubbock fixes the truism for us by noting that in reading a novel, all we can hope to attain is "a cluster of impressions, some clear points emerging from a mist of uncertainty" (1).   So it is with Cather's narrator.   Jim himself does not fully understand the mysterious transformations that have occurred during these silent years in which natural processes change him.   For Jim it is the cocoon time, and he can no more explain it to the reader than the prairie can explain its grasses or the moon its light— thereby revealing his ultimate unreliability as a narrator.   What Jim can do, however, is to create the "feeling" Brown notes and trust that the patient reader can share it.   We can appreciate the subtlety of Cather's design even more, perhaps, if we remember something that William Carlos Williams liked to point out about the reader of literature: the reader can comfortably perceive the past and future, but "he never knows and never dares to know . . . what he is at the exact moment that he is" (89).   It is this poetic conundrum of the ephemerality of our own mortal perceptions and the ironic transference between reader and fictive character that *My Ántonia* conveys so well and that makes some readers uncomfortable with it.

Clearly, then, an understanding of Cather's adeptness with symbols and motifs yields an appreciation of her artistic sophistication.   Equally important, by realizing how clever and subtle Cather can be with literary devices, we in turn gain insights into the artistic psychology which generates the technique, for Cather herself is a study in submerged and emergent elements. Such insights can best be organized in terms of several persistent questions about Cather: (1) why does she use the male persona as spokesperson; (2) why does she emphasize the child in *My Ántonia* when children are noticeably absent in previous novels and her denial of maternal obligations is notable; and (3) why does she seemingly worship the past?

To answer the first of these questions—and ultimately the remaining two—I must commence by reiterating the psychosexual conflicts which underlie Cather's previous novels and which are implicit in *My Ántonia*. Concerning Cather's homoeroticism, Deborah G. Lambert states the situation well when she characterizes Cather as "a lesbian writer who could not, or did not, acknowledge her homosexuality and who, in her fiction, transformed her emotional life and experiences into acceptable, heterosexual forms and guises" (676). The resulting bifurcation of the artistic self is evident in *My Ántonia*, for in the Jim-Ántonia juxtaposition we see the twin selves that were suppressed within Cather. Jim Burden and Ántonia Shimerda are externalizations of Cather herself, emerged from the depths of her very private personality. This point is hardly revolutionary, since we have clarified it in discussing the first three novels and since Leon Edel (for one) showed years ago in his psychoanalysis of *The Professor's House* that Cather, more protective of her private self than most writers, exposed her suppressed fears and doubts in her fiction. (A summary of Edel's analyses of *The Professor's House* appears in my discussion of that novel.) But the point is important enough to restate. Through the chemistry of her art Cather tries to separate Jim and Ántonia, but ultimately she cannot do so and the male-female personae appear as a literary Janus—or, to adopt Mark Twain's terminology, extraordinary twins. By projecting those inseparable twins from the depths of her psyche, Cather thereby tells us more than she knew.

Jim is but nominally masculine, a condition which Cather unconsciously emphasizes by surrounding him with stereotypical males such as Jesse James, whose biography so impresses the young Jim; Otto Fuchs, himself a character who could have "stepped" from the pages of that same biography (6); and the lustful Wick Cutter, who literally tries to rape Jim/Ántonia and whose name so appropriately connotes both emasculation and defloration. "Wick" is a common euphemism for the penis, and the vulgarism "dipping the wick" equally common for sexual intercourse. The pun on "cutter" seems self explanatory, both in the sense in which it is used to express the male's fear of aggressive females and the more specific contextual sense of "wick cutter," implying castration. Even when compared to meek Anton Cuzak, the great impregnator, childless Jim is conventionally lacking. He shields his feminine sensitivity, however, with the armor of success in the masculine world of law and high finance. He makes a lot of money. Thus protected from fault and accusation, he is transformed into Cather the artist—careful, premeditative, and safe. On the other hand, Ántonia presents the conventional male traits in feminine disguise. She is the quintessential but paradoxically masculine woman, the Bohemian secret-self Cather longed to express. Lambert correctly notes that Ántonia reveals "the consequences of Cather's dilemma as a lesbian writer in a patriarchal society" (677). In her roles of cook, gardener, mother, and wife she conforms to the code of the stereotypical frontier woman, thereby masking the mannish qualities which she has exhibited throughout the first four books of the narrative. Just as no one can get at Jim through his Big Business shield, no one can possibly fault Ántonia in her Earth Mother guise. Even her sins are sins of love and motherhood, and in her astonishing fecundity she fulfills not only her assumed female purpose but compensates for her one premarital misstep. With each new baby she legitimizes and re-legitimizes the bastardy of her firstborn. Like Hester Prynne, she pays her dues, and by Book V she has long since moved into able and absolution out of adultery—though the physiological costs have been high. It is not difficult to see the childless, husbandless, doubtful Cather seeking her own salvation via Ántonia, trying to appease the prairie society which intellectually and geographically she could reject but which psychologically was always with her.

We need look no further than Sinclair Lewis' *Main Street* (1922) to be reminded of the village virus that was so epidemic and to which intelligent young women such as Cather were especially susceptible. Never able to free herself completely of the virus, Cather nevertheless could create a healthy fictive persona which vicariously assuaged her guilt over unfulfilled maternal obligations and proved to the world that she could be the good girl, the prairie female personified—a bit rebellious and unlucky but in the final accounting bathed in the redeeming light of motherhood and heterosexual legitimacy. Moreover, by juxtaposing this idealized frontier female with Jim, the successful capitalist who incidentally is articulate enough to write a book, Cather managed the extralegal, truly spiritual marriage, the integration of selves that was in fact impossible. In *Freudianism and the Literary Mind*, Frederick J. Hoffman borrows a term from Freud and refers to exogamy, the galvanizing fear of incest we inherit from our most primitive ancestors (18). The term conveniently explains the taboo with which Cather struggled in the Jim-Ántonia characterizations. Because they represent the dual halves of Cather's psyche, the brother-sister of her unconscious, she could not allow them any physical intimacy. They had to remain pure of each other, else she unconsciously sanctioned the most forbidden of sexual "crimes." Hoffman goes on to point out that James Joyce, her contemporary, was able to write openly about incest and homosexuality because he was "not enchained or imprisoned by the power of his unconscious life" (149). Cather was not exactly imprisoned by her unconscious life either, but above all else she remained a daughter of the Nebraska village and was more prudent than Joyce in exposing the painful dichotomy between the private self and the social self. Her art, consequently, is both syntonic and asyntonic, a paradox we see manifested in her intermingling of narrator and heroine.

As for the question of Cather's preoccupation with children, we cannot deny that they do dominate *My Ántonia* as they dominate no other of Cather's novels. Jim, Ántonia, and her sibling initiate the action, and the outpouring of Cuzaks concludes it. The children, however, are more than simple embodiments of authorial sentimentality or escapism. They are central to the subterranean-emergence motif we have discussed and are another key to understanding Cather's own psychic perceptions.

Freud's theory that children are innately and naturally "perverse" in their refusal to conform to what society defines as proper behavior casts some light on Cather's use of children (and for that matter on Cather's own early cross-dressing). In discussing infantile sexuality Freud elucidates the child's innate perversity, a quality brought about by the fact that "the psychic dams against sexual transgressions, such as shame, loathing and morality" have not yet been formed (592). For the artist this quality makes the child an ideally suitable emblem of the guiltless exploration of all erotic possibilities. Unconsciously sensing that eroticism should express itself in various forms, not just genitally or heterosexually, the child develops naturally through oral, anal, and genital stages of eroticism, a process Hoffman refers to as "the blessed anarchy of childhood" (99). Particularly apropos to our immediate purposes is Freud's note that the pre-genital phases cannot be "designated masculine and feminine" since the gender distinctions form only later in the genital stage (597). Unfortunately, the individual enters adulthood during the genital stage of development, and what was once an inno-cent "perversity" becomes a destructive genital fixation with def-inite male-female gender differentiations. In short, selfish plea-sure must surrender to the demands of reproduction in order to guarantee the species, and reproduction is unavoidably a hetero-sexual-genital demand. Freud sees the resulting conflict between natural erotic pleasures and social prerequisites as the major cause of neuroses; and for Freud, neuroses were conflictive and destructive. In passing, I might note that Peter Gay offers a help-ful, clarifying definition of Freud's concept of neuroses: "For Freud . . . a neurosis is not some outlandish and exotic disease, but rather the all too common consequence of incomplete de-velopment, which is to say, of unmastered childhood conflicts. Neurosis is a condition in which the sufferer has regressed to early confrontations; he is, in short, trying to dispose of unfin-ished business" (146).

As noted in the Introduction, however, Cather disagrees with Freudian theory, especially on the point of neuroses being destructive. Her view coincides more with the theories of Norman O. Brown, who in *Life Against Death* argues that neu-roses are an expression of our unconscious refusal to acquiesce to the incompatibility of the flesh and the spirit and to accede to the teachings that our "pleasure-seeking" childhood impulses are evil. In short, neuroses are a positive expression of our finest natural impulses. In her fictive children Cather intuitively projects both the sexual freedom inherent in the pre-adult stages of erotic development and the natural freedom from death awareness that ultimately constricts the adult. Significantly, though Ántonia truly loves the apron-clad and dutifully atten-dant girls of her brood, her favorite child is Leo the faun, a child epitomizing the sexually free, uninhibited spirit—the "perverse" and socially rebellious soul. For Cather, therefore, the child personifies both innocence and the "image of inviolability" that Blanche H. Gelfant recognizes in "The Forgotten Reaping Hook" (76). Childhood is not a stage to which Cather simplemindedly wishes to return, like a badger retreating into the dark burrow. It is instead a perpetual element of the human psyche which helps make the rigors of life bearable and from which the artist-as-child can draw.

For Cather, therefore, childhood and the psychosexual conflicts common to it were neither perverse nor undesirable, as Freud defines them in his discussions of neuroses. Instead, such neuroses are the positive remaining signs of a natural rebellion against social norms and restrictive conformity to those arbitrary edicts. As a product of a patriarchal and conformist society, and as a person of "reason," Cather felt the pressure to abide by the rules; but in her imagination (which is first and foremost the sanctuary of the child-self), she refused to renounce the conflicts which emanated from her childhood. To resolve such conflicts (even if such resolution were possible) would effectively destroy the very source of her creativity. She shows in the children of *My Ántonia* that the child-self must continue to emerge from the depths of the unconscious, guiltless and free to pursue whatever paths it must.

Shifting from Cather's children to her concept of time is more a matter of nuance than of substantive distinction, for just as childhood's natural and innocent perversity is lost to adulthood's demand for sexual organization and species continuity, so commensurately is the child's freedom in time sacrificed to the adult's imposition of chronological schemes—with similar adverse consequences. As Karl Malkoff phrases it, using Freudian-Brownian theories in his analysis of contemporary verse, "Instead of experiencing unending nowness, we locate ourselves at some specific point along a continuing line" (5). Unlike Freud and many of the other novelists of her era (such as Katherine Anne Porter and Scott Fitzgerald, who saw moral debts, like monetary ones, rolling out of the vaults of the past with ruinous surcharges having accrued) Cather intuitively rejected the linear perspective. She could not readily conceive of the "me" of the present forever fleeing some "me" of the past down an inescapable track of time. Untypically, her view of the past was neither Freudian nor puritan. It was—and the term seems more apropos than hazardous—childlike in its positive and benign trustfulness.

Again Norman O. Brown assists me with my point. Until recently we had little choice about temporal theories. Historical-linear time seemed the sine qua non of existence. Freud subscribed to this view and concluded that our desire to retain the past means that we consequently search for the past in the future, thereby enmeshing ourselves in neuroses. However, Einsteinian physics and other post-Freudian developments have forced reexamination of the historical time concept. Brown borrows from these new theories to hypothesize the existence of a consciousness emancipated from the historical-linear idea and therefore freed of the learned complexes that frustrate and repress us. If we can be set loose from the birth-life-death syndrome, which demands conformity and biological reproduction, then the individual is subsequently free to exist "not in time but in eternity" (94). Such an articulation of time is precisely what the child enjoys innately, before socialization squelches the natural, harmonious impulses. With no awareness of mortality and no fear of death, and thus blissfully ignorant of the compulsion to reproduce its kind, the child is released into eternity.

Earlier I stated that Cather is not a conventional symbolist in *My Ántonia*, citing the example of her refusal to adopt the black-white badger as an easy emblem of good and evil. That point needs to be elucidated. The comments about Freud and Brown make the statement easier to explain. Overall, Cather uses animals organically in her narrative design, not as isolated instances of symbolic devices. The big rattlesnake, for instance, no matter how convenient the explanation may seem, is not simply phallic. Such an interpretation leaves us holding the troublesome shovel, the instrument of death which Jim wields so fortuitously. The badger, the snake, even the Russian wolves who devour the bride on her wedding night, merge to form Cather's overall statement that such beasts, no matter how frightening or horrifying they may seem to the human observer, are integrated with nature, just as are children. Unaware of their own mortality, they are unconcerned with the mortality of other living things. The animals, in fact, stand in contrast to the adult human characters who have divorced themselves from nature and who suffer the pangs of the life-death dichotomy. Peter and Pavel, the exiled Russians who toss the bride to the hungry wolves, epitomize this separation. Not only are they ultimately cut off from the "normal" sexual relationships that the marriage scene suggests, but they are tormented to death for an act which guaranteed their survival, their biological continuation. The Russians make a blood sacrifice to survival just as grandmother Burden sacrifices the chickens to the badger. The difference is that grandmother in her innate harmony with nature and from her years of experience realizes that the smaller sacrifices are a form of primitive ritual, a way of staying from her own door the unspeakable horror. Cut off from the mainstream of human intercourse, people are individually and collectively open to disaster, a fact illustrated not only by the Russians but by Mr. Shimerda, Wick Cutter, the farmhand who plunges into the threshing machine, and—more importantly—with Jim before his final emergence into Ántonia's natural life force, her light. Only through retaining or reacquiring the harmony suggested by the wild beasts, only by somehow reconciling the life-death conflict can people endure. If the animals sometime appear horrific, bloodthirsty, and evil, it is but another of the ironic paradoxes upon which Cather's artistic design rests, for her wild animals and innocent children share the same innate guiltlessness and freedom from historical time and moral dogma.

My Ántonia explores the numerous battles humans fight each day, year after year, in the war of attrition against self and external circumstance. In her next novel, Cather shows what happens when homo sapiens, the most "reasonable" of animals, get entangled in historical time and lose the natural harmony which children and wild animals innately possess. In *One of Ours* Cather continues the battle motif, but depends upon a much more graphic form of conflict for her central metaphor: war. That she knew nothing of World War I from personal experience no doubt accounts in part for the lack of creative intensity and the noticeable artistic decline from *My Ántonia*; but that lack of experiential awareness matters little insofar as how Cather uses the war as part of her narrative design. The Great War is simply, and somewhat rudimentarily a tropic device which parallels other tropic devices she also uses to promote the ironic tensions of *One of Ours*.

Works Cited

Bourne, Randolph. "[Review of *My Antonia*]," *Dial*, 65 (14 December 1918): 557. Rpt in *Critical Essays on Willa Cather*, ed. John J. Murphy. Boston: Hall, 1984. 185-186.

Brown, E. K. *Willa Cather: A Critical Biography*. New York: Knopf, 1953.

Brown, Norman O. *Life Against Death*. New York: Vintage Books, 1959.

Cather, Willa. *My Ántonia*. (1918; revised 1926). Boston: Houghton Mifflin, 1954.

—. *The Song of the Lark*. (1915; revised 1937). Boston: Houghton Mifflin, 1943.

—. *Willa Cather in Person: Interviews, Speeches, and Letters*. Ed. L. Brent Bohlke. Lincoln: U of Nebraska P, 1986.

Daiches, David. *Willa Cather: A Critical Introduction*. Ithaca: Cornell U P, 1951.

Edel, Leon. *Stuff of Sleep and Dreams: Experiments in Literary Psychology*. New York: Harper & Row, 1959. Excerpted in *Critical Essays on Willa Cather*. Ed. John J. Murphy. Boston: Hall, 1984. 198-217.

Freud, Sigmund. *The Basic Writings of Sigmund Freud*. (1938). Ed. and trans. A. A. Brill. New York: Modern Library, 1966.

Gay, Peter. *Freud: A Life for Our Time*. New York: Norton, 1988.

Gelfant, Blanche. "The Forgotten Reaping Hook: Sex in *My Ántonia*," *American Literature*, 43 (1971): 60-82.

Helmick, Evelyn. "The Mysteries of Ántonia." *Midwest Quarterly*, 17 (1976): 176-85.

Hoffman, Frederick J. *Freudinism and the Literary Mind*, 2nd. Baton Rouge: LSU P, 1957.

Krieger, Murray. *Theory of Criticism: A Tradition and Its System*. Baltimore; Johns Hopkins U P, 1976.

Kroll, Judith. *Chapters in a Mythology*. New York: Harper & Row, 1976.

Lambert, Deborah G. "The Defeat of a Hero: Autonomy and Sexuality in *My Ántonia*." *American Literature*, 53 (1982): 676-690.

Lubbock, Percy. *The Craft of Fiction*. New York: Viking, 1957.

Malkoff, Karl. *Escape from the Self*. New York: Columbia U P, 1977.

Martin, Terence. "The Drama of Memory in *My Ántonia*," *PMLA* 84 (1969), 308-319.

Stevenson, Anne. *Bitter Fame: A Life of Sylvia Plath*. Boston: Houghton Mifflin, 1989.

Stouck, David. *Willa Cather's Imagination*. Lincoln: U of Nebraska P, 1975.

Williams, William Carlos. *Imaginations*. New York: New Directions, 1971.

Woodress, James. *Willa Cather: A Literary Life*. U of Nebraska P, 1987.

3
One of Ours: Stress and Narrative De-Articulation

In 1925 Cather tacitly dismissed *My Ántonia* as a masterpiece when she claimed that *One of Ours* (1922) was the novel she liked "best" of all her novels because it "has more of value in it than any of the others" (*WC in Person* 78). She may have had her tongue firmly in cheek, of course, since *One of Ours* was the novel that made her independently wealthy and won the Pulitzer Prize, thus clearly possessing considerable market-place value. If meant as a serious literary evaluation of the novel, however, Cather's observation has few supporters. Marilyn Arnold speaks for the traditional wisdom concerning *One of Ours* when she terms it "Cather's losing battle" and discusses the narrative problems which resulted from Cather's innate dislike of her protagonist Claude Wheeler (259f). Even Susan Rosowski—one of Cather's most determined admirers—admits that *One of Ours* contains writing that is "sometimes embarrassingly" bad (110). Indeed, Cather's fifth novel continues to be—as Cather said in defending it—"one that all the high-brow critics knock" (*WC in Person* 78).

I will concede the faults of *One of Ours* so that I might then continue to analyze it within the broad perspective of the psychosocial, psychosexual tensions already established as my controlling vision of Cather's fiction and which keep us in the realm of subtextuality and authorial revelations (conscious and unconscious). More specifically, I would like to concentrate on an identifying stylistic element of *One of Ours*: the way in which Cather distorts or de-articulates the narrative in order to emphasize certain motifs she is intent upon exploring. Some argue that Cather was a conscious experimentalist, but evidence seems more to suggest that she was a pragmatic stylist, doing whatever she had to do with narrative form to make it "say" what she wanted it to say. Cather spoke of "style" quite often. One of her more telling comments relative to her pragmatic attitude is: "Style is how you write, and you write well when you are interested" (*WC in Person* 78). Certainly a better known comment in the same vein is in "The Novel Démeublé": "The novelist must learn to write, and then he must unlearn it; just as the modern painter learns to draw, and then learns when utterly to disregard his accomplishment, when to subordinate it to a higher and truer effect" (*Not Under Forty* 49). *One of Ours* is a good example of this stylistic attitude. Deciding that previously applied techniques would not answer all the problems she encountered in writing her war novel and would not attain the "higher and truer effect," Cather "de-articulates" the conventional narrative, just as war de-articulates human routine. I use the term "de-articulation" to distinguish variations in the previously-noted technique of narrative stress and tension. The term implies a negation of "articulate" in both the verb and adjective forms, suggesting that Cather neither utters her meanings distinctly nor offers a narrative that has all its segments conventionally connected.

In discussing *My Ántonia,* I analyze the stress which Cather places upon the root cellar/emerging children image and the strained quality of the image. That the de-articulation of *One of Ours* is part of the overall narrative stress and conflict we have already noted suggests an artistic continuity; yet the technique differs in *One of Ours* in that it seems a premeditated authorial effort to place both form and content of the entire novel under unusual strain, rather than to stress one or two strategically situated images. In *Tradition and Counter Tradition: Love and the Form of Fiction,* Joseph Boone, discussing the novel of marriage (which to a considerable degree *One of Ours* is), offers the thesis that the appeal of the conventional love story lies in the formulaic structure which contains the traditional dogma of romance. Novels intent on breaking with such tradition, however, rebel against both the thematic limitations and the narrative strictures which help define those limitations. With *One of Ours,* Cather joins this counter tradition of unusual form and function associations. As Frederick T. Griffiths recognizes while discussing Cather in a context dissimilar to Boone's, what at first appears to be a "harmless bit of flag waving" turns out to be "a much more troubling book of revelation" (270).

Falling as it does between *My Ántonia* and *A Lost Lady,* two of Cather's most subtle narrative accomplishments, *One of*

Ours seems an atavistic—almost primitive—narrative form. That is, after *My Ántonia* with its complex ironies and super-subtle narrative techniques, *One of Ours* appears elemental and noticeably more self-conscious in design. Not that *One of Ours* is lacking in "furniture," to borrow Cather's own much polished metaphor. Far from being "unfurnished," it has furniture enough for a rooming house; but the furniture itself is rough hewn. This simplicity results partially from Cather's efforts to transform into fiction the literal exploits of her war-hero cousin, a technique which affords us another instance of the biographical-fictional grafting seen in *The Song of the Lark* and which once again is discordant. *One of Ours* was precipitated by the death of G. P. Cather, who was killed at Cantigny on the Western Front in W. W. I. His death left Cather befuddled that "anything so exalted could have happened to someone so disinherited of hope" (Woodress 304). Cather never overcame her initial disgust for the ignorant, pedestrian individual her cousin personified, and her posthumous admiration never quite convinces. Too, we have another indication of Cather's reluctance to break free from the prairie hegemony.

Yet, the biographical elements alone do not account for the narrative awkwardness of *One of Ours*. Instead, there is a fundamental stress or tension upon the creative process itself as the raw material of experience is processed into fiction. Cather admitted that in writing *One of Ours* she tried to "cut out all analysis, observation, description, even the picture-making quality, in order to make things and people tell their own story simply by juxtaposition" (*WC in Person* 24). Such elements as "picture-making" distinguished her previous narrative style (or at least she thought they did), and excising them suggests that she was consciously trying to attain the narrative stress or conflict which simple "juxtaposition" of inarticulate characters might accomplish. She envisioned Claude as being "just a red-headed prairie boy," incapable of seeing "pictures" (39)—that is, unable to visualize scenarios beyond his literal experience, as creative writers must do. Cather admitted that the turning away from her tried and true style was "hard" (39). It was a premeditated imposition of stress on her creative processes.

This conscious de-articulation of her narrative style manifests itself in functional, conventional literary devices which first set up certain expectations for the audience but which then fail to deliver conventional results or permit us to rest comfortable in familiar, conventional responses. The resulting stress dislocates us from authorial intent and thereby requires a series of audience shifts relative to narrative action. We are constantly unsure of whose side the implied author supports in the various wars that are being fought; who it is that is one of ours; who that "we" implied in "ours" is; how we are meant to respond to fighting men who spend more time dawdling in French houses than paying the price for glory. Once we realize that Cather de-articulates both form and function and often makes superficially simple devices perform in unorthodox fashion, the uncertainty is not totally removed but it is at least more easily accepted as a notable element of Cather's authorial intentions. An analysis of her management of three literary conventions will demonstrate the point: the Oedipus complex, her allusions to *Paradise Lost*, and her use of bird imagery.

After both utilizing and then transcending Freudian sexual theory in *My Ántonia*, Cather selectively reimposes those limitations on *One of Ours*—goes against "the things I do best" (*WC in Person* 39). She thereby (either consciously or unconsciously) ensures that the audience shares her narrative perspective. Borrowing Freud for her narrative skeleton was a tactical and intelligent maneuver. The "new" Freudianism was at its zenith of popularity in the early Twenties, and though Cather claimed to distrust Freudianism she certainly was commonsensical enough to take advantage of its literary value. That she had Freud on her mind when she wrote *One of Ours* is witnessed by an interview she gave in 1923. She has just won the Pulitzer Prize for the novel and expresses pleasant surprise. She goes on to say that the "new American novel . . . is better than the old-fashioned conventional one" and that she prefers "the modern novelist, even if he does become a little ridiculous when he carries too far the process of chopping up his character on the Freudian psycho-analytical plan" (*WC in Person* 58). We should note that she does not reject Freudian psychoanalysis as a source of fiction, but is only leery of its being carried "too far." She had toyed with Freudianism even in her first novel, *Alexander's Bridge*, when she has Professor Lucius Wilson, a philosopher, visit Boston to spend a "long morning with the psychologists" (16) and attend talks given by an eminent psychologist, possibly Freud, who visited and lectured in Worcester, Massachusetts, in late 1909. As Peter Gay states, by World War I, Freud "had become a savant with an international reputation" (379)—and one that a philosopher would travel far to hear. That *One of Ours* became her first best seller, made her wealthy, and won the

Pulitzer Prize attests to Cather's literary astuteness (and business acumen) in utilizing Freud more fully. The Freudianism appears in several narrative contexts but is most obvious in a classical, almost clinical case of the Oedipus complex: the mutual devotion of Claude Wheeler and his mother Evangeline, which forms the sexual relationship of central focus. Once Freud articulated his idea of the Oedipus complex in *Totem and Taboo*, it would remain not only the most popularly known (and thus perhaps most distorted) of his theories of human behavior but the theory he kept central in his own thinking. In that complex, predicated upon the primitive act of the son's trying to usurp and thus destroy the father, lay the explanation of "the same great event with which culture began and which ever since has not let mankind come to rest" (*Basic Writings* 918). In light of subsequent research in genetics and related fields, however, Freud seems to have extended his Oedipus theory too far, and its current usefulness is more in its mythological rather than scientific value. (For further discussion, see Gay, 323f). Cather, too, was of course ignorant of later genetic research that would compromise Freud's extensive application of the Oedipus concept; but such subsequent revisions of Freud's basic formulation do not alter the literary purpose to which she applies it.

Cather, perhaps being even more Freudian with her ravishment imagery than she knew, tells us that Evangeline Wheeler has built psychological walls so that "rash and violent men could not break in upon" her; but for Claude she lives "on another plane" and pulsates "with poor, blind, passionate human feelings" (990). With her husband gone to Colorado, she thinks it is "almost like being a bride, keeping house" for Claude (1005). Claude, reciprocating her emotions, feels "disloyal to her" for being "so happy with Mrs. Erlich" (1010). He quickly returns to his mother when his wife Enid leaves for China, and Evangeline is the only woman we ever see him embracing—actually clinging to (1012). As we would expect with a traditional Oedipus complex, the psychosexual impetus for this son-mother bonding is readily found in the father-husband.

Nat Wheeler is among the best of Cather's ironically ambiguous minor portraits. Superficially a florid faced, good-natured, rich Nebraska farmer who indiscriminately likes "every sort of human creature" (948), he is essentially sadistic. Giving us an example of the "juxtaposition" which she stated was part of her conscious narrative purpose, Cather introduces Nat Wheeler in conjunction with her depiction of the overtly

"savage mountaineer" (959) to whom the housekeeper old Mahailey was once married and who daily brutalized her. Lest we
miss the purpose of this ironic juxtaposition of characters,
Cather substantiates it with metaphorical clues to Mr. Wheeler's
sublimated cruelty. Early in the novel he spends much time going about the countryside in an uncomfortable buckboard rather
than in his car, because he knows Evangeline will not want to
ride in the "rickety" buckboard with him (947). Moreover, when
Evangeline is deluded by his superficial kindness and asks him
to help pick the cherries from her favorite tree because she cannot reach the top, he chops the tree down. He "humorously"
tells her that she and Claude can now "run along and pick 'em
as easy as can be" (963). The felling of the erotically emblematic
cherry tree symbolizes both Nat Wheeler's meanness and the
loss of sexuality between him and his wife. Alone, rejected,
trapped in a marriage that demands her subservience but offers
no affection or sex, Evangeline Wheeler has little choice but to
bond to the only son who remains at home—and the only son
with a modicum of sensitivity and sensibility and who has been
the constant target of his father's painful humor. She does not
become the archetypal mother as love goddess which A. C.
Hoffman suggests in surveying the "Archetypal Women in the
Novels of 1922" (62f), but Evangeline's attraction to Claude is as
much the result of repressed eroticism as of genuine maternal
affection.

   Claude in turn is receptive to his mother's ambiguous affections because he has been psychologically de-sexed, intratextually by his father's mental cruelty and extratextually by Cather's
erotic ambiguity. Isolated and immature, he does not form successful erotic relationships with females of his own generation,
though he does relate consistently to older maternal females. He
feels safe only in his mother's figurative and literal embrace. He
is, for instance, dumb to Gladys Farmer, the young teacher who
desires him and tries with all the guile permitted a prairie lady
to prevent his marrying the frigid Enid. At college he is naively
drawn to one Miss Peachy Millmore (certainly one of the most
allegorically erotic names in Cather) until he hears that she had
"subdued a pale cousin in Atlanta" and has thus been exiled to
Nebraska (988). Though Peachy is ripe for sexual conquest,
Claude rejects her and proudly contemplates his "sharp disgust
for sensuality" (988) like a red badge of prudery.

   We understand the denying of sensuality as Claude's
method for keeping himself pure for his mother; but such self-

righteousness also makes him vulnerable to Enid Royce. Enid is herself a Freudian cliché of repressed sexuality, with her frigidity, her coy sublimated eroticism that emerges as fanatic religiosity, and her do-gooderism that harms as many as it helps. The popular interpretation of Enid would probably be that she is working her way through a castration complex, having been born sans penis, and is retaliating against males whom she envies. As Gay notes, "By the early 1920s, Freud seemed to have adopted the position that the little girl is a failed boy, the grown woman a kind of castrated man" (515)—subsequently (and fortunately) one of the least accepted of his theories relative to psychosexuality. In Enid Claude marries a woman who personifies his own disgust for sex and with whom he can cohabit with the least degree of betraying his mother, who shares many of Enid's personality traits. For that matter, Claude may not cohabit with Enid at all. Maidenhood still intact, she expels him from the Pullman berth on their honeymoon night, and insofar as the reader can prove, he never convinces her to let him have a second try. All we know is what we surmise when we see him guiltily fondling "one little lace" undergarment which she has left—perhaps accidentally—in the yard (1084). As the narrator tells us emphatically, "Everything about a man's embrace was distasteful to Enid" (1102). If we couple that distaste with Claude's "disgust for sensuality" we have evidence enough of the sterility of their marriage. We understand too why Claude returns straightway to his mother and her welcoming arms as soon as Enid walks out the door.

Various elements of the Oedipal complex relative to *One of Ours* have been outlined elsewhere by others (Stanley Cooperman, for example, in *World War I and the American Novel* [129-137]), and at this juncture it serves best as a demarcation point for the discussion of related narrative elements and Cather's de-articulation technique. The Oedipus myth is a clue to the complexity which results from Cather's switching the gender of her artistic persona. No matter who the literal prototype for Claude was, we may feasibly assume that his invented psyche is in large measure Cather's. As she herself admitted, the fictive "Claude" took "complete possession" of her, and even though the "expensive boy" cost her a lot, he was worth it because of the "excitement and pleasure" she derived from him (Woodress 304-305). Claude is another variation of her "crossdressed" projected self, as is Jim Burden. Thus the bonding between Claude and his mother escapes the bounds of the

traditional Oedipus story with its heterosexual incest and acquires modernist, multisexual implications.   That is, Cather
de-articulates the classic tale.   If Claude is Cather's artistic self,
the "boy" who took "possession" of her, then it is plausible to
conclude that the authorial impulse underlying the creation of
his fictive relationship with Evangeline is homoerotic; and
the Claude-Evangeline bonding therefore serves as another
indication of Cather's same-sex predilections.   But just as she is
subconsciously drawn to attempting fulfillment of that homoeroticism via sublimated relationships such as Claude-
Evangeline, Cather is equally compelled by her social consciousness to frustrate the homoeroticism.   In general Freudian
terminology, Cather's dilemma could be cast as a conflict
between the Id and the Superego, as Freud came to define those
still imprecise terms in *The Ego and the Id* (1923).   Consequently,
to forestall public revelation of that homoeroticism, Cather
carefully inserts the machinery which prevents the sexual consummation she must not tolerate: she preempts the homoerotic
impulse with the more powerful taboo of incest which the
Oedipus story dramatizes and which we see foreshadowed in
Miss Peachy Millmore's being ostracized for the sexual liaison
with her cousin.   In other words, Cather utilizes the conventional literary device of the heterosexually incestuous Oedipus
story as a deterrent or "screening" metaphor against the homoerotic metaphor underlying the Claude-Evangeline relationship.
Consciously aware of her homoeroticism and equally sensitive
to society's refusal to condone it, Cather therefore sublimates
both those pieces of knowledge into her creative imagination,
where they are distilled and from which they emerge as
"warring" tropes, thereby giving us another example of the
technique of narrative stress.
        In light of this incest motif, the Oedipus allusion which is
otherwise rather transparent as a literary device within the narrative, acquires a complex of shadows and shadings.   In its original Sophoclean form, the classic incest tale allowed Oedipus to
consummate the forbidden affair with his mother and to produce children.   That literal, physical transgression, however, has
with time been transformed into poetic metaphor—or, for our
present purposes, Jungian archetype, removed from its literal
base into the collective racial unconscious.   We should note that
Totem and Taboo, in which Freud first articulated the Oedipus
complex, was composed in part as a response to Jung, who by
1913 had begun the break with Freud, his intellectual "father."

In *Totem and Taboo*, as Peter Gay says, "Freud was displaying in his own struggles an aspect of the oedipal wars often scanted— the father's efforts to best the son" (326). As stated, Freud's Oedipus concept has proven more useful as myth than as science. That is, Jung's view is more nearly "correct" for the applications of the Oedipus complex I am making here. In the collective racial unconscious, it functions as a perpetual reminder of the horrors of incest. Because Oedipus committed the crime of crimes and suffered horribly, we know that we must avoid the same actions. In that poetic or metaphysical form, the incest taboo serves Cather first as a reminder of what potentially may occur and second as a barrier against what literally must not occur in civilized sexual practices. Therefore, when Cather connects the incest taboo to her own disguised homoeroticism as manifested in the Claude-Evangeline relationship, she accomplishes an ironic paradox. She permits herself (and us as audience) a "safe" examination of the homoerotic act itself while at the same instant she guarantees avoidance of the act.

Moreover, she takes advantage of a literary, social quirk: her audience will tolerate the fictive exploitation of mother-son incest because the precedent of classical literature has validated such a relationship in *Oedipus Rex*. In short, the process of fictionalization and the distancing which time has allowed defuse the topic and render it safe. Cather knows, however, that that same audience will probably not tolerate fictive exploitation of overtly homosexual relationships and that literature had not in 1922 validated such relationships, no matter what Gertrude Stein and others of the Left Bank lesbian community might have attempted. (As previously noted, the Paris Left Bank lesbian community flourished at the time Cather was facing her own dilemmas as a homoerotic female in a male-dominated, staunchly heterosexual American society. She could have chosen to emigrate, as Stein and others had done, but chose not to. For details, see Shari Benstock, *Women of the Left Bank: Paris 1900-1940*. Austin: U of Texas P, 1986.) In other words, amidst the milieu in which Cather wrote, the incest motif was commonplace; the homosexual still forbidden. Thus, to vent her doubts and fears in the public forum (to confess as it were), she cleverly offers the forbidden in the guise of the commonplace.

Cather's adaptation of the Oedipus metaphor further suggests her need to identify with the maternal female and her contradictory refusal to allow herself to commit to that identification—a conflict already noted in *The Song of the Lark* and to appear again in *Death Comes for the Archbishop*. Cather has limited sympathy for the traditional figure. Mrs. Jason Royce, for example, is an inconsequential mother with a "deep pre-occupation about her health" and a consequent "insensibility" (1038). Even Augusta Erlich, generally a positive albeit passing influence on Claude, may be motivated by more than maternal concern for him. She pretends surprise, but sighs wistfully when the lustful Madame Wilhelmina Schroeder-Schatz suggests she take Claude for a lover (991). Cather's maternal antipathy is also suggested by how often Evangeline stands aside and permits her favorite child to be mortified by his father's cruel humor and how passively she allows Claude to fall prey to the patriotic gore of World War I. Neither Evangeline speci-fically nor the mother figure in general is Cather's artistic self or alter ego. Yet, despite the peculiar form in which it is offered to us, we can perceive in the Claude-Evangeline relationship the biological and social imperatives which drove Cather to con-template the issue of motherhood at all.

These imperatives are most apparent in two instances: Cather's joining Claude to Enid in a superficially traditional marriage from which offspring ordinarily would result; and her allowing him to establish an erotic relationship with the mater-nal female, Evangeline. Because Claude is Cather's artist-self, the implications of that relationship are such that we can as-sume the existence of a procreative instinct, albeit the instinct is here given masculine figuration. The actual cohabiting cannot occur, however, as we have already discussed; and because no real children can result, Cather is faced with a question of com-pensation: how to satisfy the maternal drive without having to resort to biological motherhood? Her answer is to usurp the ma-ternal instincts that seem sorely lacking in both Enid and Evan-geline and safely outfit them in the uniform of the brave soldier. Thus we have Claude's concern for the hungry quails, his nurs-ing of his men during the flu epidemic, his persistent desire to help the refugee children. The persona of Claude is therefore simultaneously the child Cather cannot literally produce and the maternal instinct safely exercising itself in male attire.

For that maternal masquerade, however, Claude-Cather must pay a rather dear price. He has to die, much as Bartley Alexander has to die in *Alexander's Bridge*. Such death is neces-sary not only because the biological imperative cannot condone such ersatz maternal displays lest the race disappear but also be-

cause Cather herself is apparently perplexed by the multiple ramifications of Claude's persona. We observe how viciously she
kills off the German officer who dares deviate from conventional mores and publicize his homosexuality with the locket
containing his lover's photograph. By killing this German
"deviate" she foretells what she must do to Claude; and by
killing Claude and making him a posthumous Hero she punishes herself for the socially taboo homoerotic impulses, removes the "mother" imago, and glorifies the male society which
she wanted to placate. Having purged herself via Claude's
death, Cather lets the subservient female Evangeline survive,
albeit in circumstances which Cather may well have viewed as
rightful punishment—exiled on the Nebraska prairie, left with
only an illiterate housekeeper, depending on religious dogma
for comfort. But she is at least alive. Society approves the type
of woman personified by Evangeline: the obedient female who
bears children, gives them up to the patriarchal jingoism of battle, then quietly mourns their demise. Evangeline is almost
archetypal, sharing personality traits with such women as Henry
Fleming's mother in *Red Badge of Courage*, a novel which
Cather echoes in several ways. Cather does not hesitate to send
the childless Enid Royce to far off China, never to be seen again;
but she cannot eliminate Evangeline Wheeler. Despite her
weaknesses, she is still "mother" and has society's sympathy.
She must not be eradicated.

One other relatively long episode illustrates Cather's specific borrowing from Freudian theory. Since it is apropos to
Cather's homoeroticism and the Oedipus motif, and since it represents another good example of the de-articulated narrative, it
warrants brief examination. In Book Five Claude visits the hospital and encounters the wry-necked boy who has lost an arm,
been shot in the neck, and has become guinea pig to an early
Freudian psychoanalyst who terms him "a psychopathic case"
(1200). The episode comes late in the narrative, following
Claude's fiasco with Enid and all the events relative to his personal contact with Evangeline. As the doctor points out to
Claude, the bullet has created a peculiar type of amnesia in the
boy: he has absolutely no recollection of women. Upon hearing
that females are "clear wiped out" of the boy's memory, Claude
replies: "Maybe he's fortunate in that" (1201). Soon thereafter he
continues to contemplate the phenomenon: "He wished he
could do something to help that boy; help him get away from the
doctor who was writing a book about him, and the girl who

wanted him to make the most of himself; get away and be lost altogether in what he had been lucky enough to find" (1201). Though traumatized by the war, the wounded youth has been compensated by having awareness of the evil female eliminated from his consciousness. With thoughts of Enid, Evangeline, and his other contacts with dangerous females still raw in his memory, Claude wistfully envies the boy. The irony of a boy in such physical condition being considered "lucky" is itself striking; but even more noticeable is Claude's thinking that the boy whose intersexual relationships closely parallel his own has found the ideal state. To Claude, regardless of the physical pain and suffering which purchase it, a psyche free of libido, a santuary which no woman can compromise is paradise. With thoughts such as these as precedent, Claude's overtly heroic but unconsciously suicidal facing of the German machine guns seems a predictable rather than a radical action.

Claude is perceptibly attracted to the wry-necked boy and spends all day looking "among the crowds for that young face, so compassionate and tender" (1201). His quest compelled by vaguely understood impulses both maternal and homoerotic, Claude thinks how blissful it would be to have such troublesome erotic thoughts eliminated entirely from his mind. Claude personifies Cather's own desire to purge herself of the concern for females—mother, sister, fiancee. She wants not only the erotic attraction eliminated but all possible feminine relationships, for as we have glimpsed with the Claude-Evangeline pairing, even the maternal association is fraught with danger. Jim Burden asks of Ántonia that she be to him mother, wife, sweetheart or any and all things that a woman can possibly be. Here, however, Claude—and by extension Cather—wishes for just the opposite. He wants the total removal of all feminine associations.

The episode thus suggests that Cather is perplexed not only by the homoerotic potential of her relationship with women but by female relationships in general. It implies throughout that if she could lose the female self and enter into a state of pure nonsexual, non-gender innocence, then she could return to the pre-sexual innocence which the wry-necked boy has regained—the same innocence which we have seen her explore in Ántonia's children and which she herself had in her days prior to cross-dressing, just before biological and social imperatives overtook her and she had to accept the reality of sexual polarities. The boy makes his own reality out of the books he has read, a reality "better than his own life" (1201). That too appears to be what Cather would desire: to construct herself from the pure clay of imagination, free of the sexual impulses that torment and betray. Yet, as she shows with the boy's being arrested for "quit[ting] his uniform" (1201) and taking up life as the son of French farmers, Cather knows she cannot go AWOL from biological fact and sociohistorical commands. The body can hide in any uniform, but the psyche is always naked.

These several examples of the various levels and facets of the male-female identity question which Cather contemplates in *One of Ours* make the point of how complex the matter is, and such complexity accounts for a significant portion of the narrative stress. Joseph Boone, in *Tradition and Counter Tradition: Love and the Form of Fiction*, argues intelligently that Anglo-American fiction has the tradition of conventional love/marriage relationships at its heart. As we might suspect, the tradition is most noticeable in the novels of the Victorian era, with its exaggerated patriarchal hegemony. Much of the "idealizing appeal" of the love/marriage tradition lies in the "manipulation of form" (19) which traditional authors resort to in order to present the conventional dogma in attractive packages. There are, as we have already noted, counter traditional texts which rebel against that tradition both in its thematic limitations and its narrative strictures. Boone does not discuss Cather, but the essence of his thesis parallels the points I made previously concerning Cather's early attempt to enter the male domain of fiction by conforming to traditional expectations.

By the time of *One of Ours*, however, she was challenging the limitations of that tradition. Thus, she alters the conventional narrative form as well as conventional themes to convey her doubts about the love/marriage tradition. For her, sex generally is a torment and marriage specifically a guaranteed torture—the polar opposite of the romance credo. This counter-traditional thought is more clearly demonstrated in the fractured construction of *The Professor's House*, a novel in which Cather confronts directly the conventional marriage syndrome; but it is also perceptible in *One of Ours*. Thus, though we as audience may not consciously be aware of expecting a novel to conform to a conventional device such as the Oedipus story or to a larger tradition such as the romance genre, the novel's failure to conform may well be what imparts the sense of stress or fracturing we experience with *One of Ours*.

As the "wry-necked boy" episode with its return to a state

of lost innocence shows, Cather not only incorporates the Oedipus concept but also the "paradise lost" motif. She is even more self-conscious in her *Paradise Lost* allusions than she is with those pertaining to Oedipus. In fact Cather is *too* obvious with the Miltonic allusions. In addition to numerous garden images, she tells us that Enid hates sex and childbirth and views it as something inflicted upon her for "Eve's transgression" (1102); that Gerhardt, the violinist, is fighting for "the sins of our fathers" (1257); that Claude dreams he must hide his nakedness from Enid "like Adam in the garden" (1065); and, lest the point be missed, that Evangeline reads to Claude from *Paradise Lost* (1011). Such conscious overemphasis is a key to the de-articulated way she is using the conventional references. Seen superficially, the exaggeration may well appear to be evidence of awkward narrative management. Considered in context of her "de-articulation" methodology, however, it becomes more a sign that Cather expects her audience to experience a series of perspectivist shifts and follow her through some rather sophisticated narrative maneuvers.

Cather's tale extends into the realm of the theodicy which *Paradise Lost* exemplifies, but with distinctly modernist trappings. Claude tells his mother that Milton "couldn't have got along without the wicked" (1011), a truism which is then transferred to and reified on the battlefields of France. Yet the audience is seldom as intrigued by Cather's evil as by Milton's Satan, nor as inspired by the hope of reattainment, primarily because in the twentieth century (especially with Freud's redefinitions) the traditional lines between good and evil have blurred to indistinctness. Thus the struggle between Satan and God which Cather gives is almost grotesquely comic in its exaggeration— similar to a cubist distortion of reality. "You swine," one Satanic German officer snarls in perfect English after shooting an innocent American boy through the eye, "go back to Chicago!" (1275). As Frederick T. Griffiths and others have noted, *One of Ours* is a form of the "crusade myth" (263). The Americans therefore are supposed to be Christian crusaders, though we see them do little in Nebraska or elsewhere that bears witness to why God would prefer them. In France they spend more time devouring cheese, selecting concubines, and overrunning private homes than they do fighting the Satanic Huns. One French woman wisely perceives that there is little distinction between the two invaders. The Germans, she says, "destroyed material possessions," but the Americans threaten "everybody's integrity" (1192). Against this somber assessment we hear another French woman—who has obvious ulterior motives in that she has benefited greatly from the American invasion and has a hoard of American foodstuff in her store room—exult over the American soldier: "*That is a new man!*" (1242). Indeed, the Dough Boy may be the New Adam, but given the context in which Cather places him and her hyperbolic depiction of him, the entire presentation hints of burlesque.

In the trench scenes Cather shifts away from the burlesque and moves more toward a broad parody of Milton's lines. We are shown the consequences of our dispossession from the Garden, and digest once more "the fruit / Of that forbidden tree whose mortal taste / Brought death into the World, and all our woe. . . ." The horrible noises of the "gases, swelling in the liquefying entrails of the dead" (1286) are purposely hyperbolic and straight from Hell, as are the vignettes in which we see the soldiers bathing amidst the decaying corpses, the dead hand protruding sickeningly from the trench side, the mines that erupt like a "volcano" and obliterate the soldiers. Pandemonium is recreated. Yet, unlike the prototype from which Cather borrows, there is no hope of Paradise regained here. Evil proves forever devious. The diabolic Germans premeditatedly rig the trenches to blow the crusading Americans literally to bits; and Claude's theatrical heroics are but a momentary stay against chaos. That one of their officers is named Walter Scott is a clue to how ridiculously quixotic the Americans' romantic quest is. Despair, not hope, dominates. The foreshadowing objective correlative of this truth is the statue of the Virgin which we see in the French churchyard and from which the infant Jesus has been blasted (1236).

Ironically, the actual verbalizing of the theodicy comes from Evangeline Wheeler, not from Claude-Cather. She is the one who tries to justify God's ways to man, and it is indeed a paradoxical justification she offers. With Claude's death "She feels as if God had saved him from some horrible suffering, some horrible end" (1297), for she knows if God had not taken him, he would have committed suicide. He hoped too extravagantly, and could not possibly have survived amidst the reality of postwar America. Such logic is a peculiar twisting of grace. It combines predestination and free will in that it states the belief that God chooses and takes whom He pleases but that the individual can unilaterally and at any moment choose not to be, thereby preempting God's prerogatives. By anticipating Claude's suicide, Evangeline implies, God purposely intercedes to permit a consecrated death. Such reasoning entails a kind of blackmailing of or an admonition to God: take me now or I shall kill myself later, and thus place myself at Satan's mercy and remove myself from your salvation. Not surprisingly, the logic is a modification of ideas Cather had previously entertained. In late 1915, for instance, she published "Consequences," a short story concerning a young man who glimpses his future and then shoots himself to death. In discussing this tale, Fritz Oehlschlaeger applies R. D. Laing's concept of "ontological insecurity" (191), a state in which an individual feels more dead than alive and seeks to protect the "inner or true self" (191) by depending upon others for identity. As Claude shows in seeking identity through Enid, his mother, his fellow soldiers, and finally war, the world outside the self engulfs but does not define self. This engulfment is emblematized by the corpses literally buried in trenches, by the hands protruding grotesquely, the detached skulls. Such engulfment of the individual by incomprehensible forces leads to thoughts of suicide, a motif which runs throughout Cather's novels.

In this text, however, Cather inserts the thoughts of God and suicide into the mind of Evangeline Wheeler, a woman who has previously shown in the narrative that she is incapable of articulating sophisticated theology. She confronts wickedness (personified by her husband) with hand-wringing ineptitude and she turns to fundamentalist gospel with blind faith, just as Enid Royce has done. They accept the parasitic Reverend Arthur Weldon unquestioningly, dumb to the fact that his shysterism is a manifestation of their distinctly nontheological erotic suppressions. As Claude naively rationalizes, they project their sexuality into "holy thoughts about mysterious things far away" (1041). The question is why Cather gives this narrative responsibility to Evangeline. She does so in part because she wants the irony of having a woman (bereft of sons, husband, father, and alone with an illiterate maid servant on the prairie) uttering the final words after all the fire and brimstone of the War in distant Europe. She does it more so, however, because at the closure of narrative she has killed off her central intelligence, the voice of artist-self—both as personified in Claude and in David Gerhardt, the violinist she introduces late in the narrative to supplement Claude's inarticulateness as the artist-self. She consequently has no one left who is actually qualified to convey the theological subtleties she wants to impart. Claude would be the logical choice for such narrative responsibility. Never exceptionally cerebral himself, he has at least been sensitized to some forms of ontological possibilities via French culture, music, death itself, and a smattering of formal education; and he has been the major narrative intelligence throughout. Moreover, since the tale is essentially a *Bildungsroman*, we expect Claude to attain some modicum of self-awareness perhaps similar to that expressed in Evangeline's closing lines. Yet, because of the troublesome sexual ambiguities his persona implies, Cather must destroy him, thereby leaving herself inadequately voiced for the theodicy she feels obligated to offer in closure—and, we might add, leaving the audience with an unqualified informer. Evangeline is a figure deserving of sympathy, but we do not have adequate guideposts showing us how she got from the inane platitudes of Brother Weldon to the refined thoughts on being or not being, divine intervention, and general cosmology which are expressed in her final words.

Seemingly in sardonic dismissal of the entire problem, Cather finally transfers her allegiance—or more correctly the sympathies of the implied author—to old Mahailey. Mahailey "is not troubled by any knowledge of interstellar spaces," (1297), nor of Milton, nor of philosophical complexity. The cosmic inscrutability is mirrored in her own unquestioning brain. She locates her God within range of her ability to conceptualize: just "above the kitchen stove" (1297). Mahailey's deity is not from an era which thinks in terms of cosmology but from a simpler, more primitive time of Lares and Penates. She speaks for the theanthropic past, when gods of the hearth were reassuringly palpable. In her lack of intellectual sophistication Mahailey intuits what the entire complex of author-text-audience tries to elucidate: nobody justifies the ways of God to man, nor perhaps of author to audience.

Nor must we as audience look far to see that in Milton's classic depiction of the struggle between Adam and Eve, Satan and God, lies a metaphorical source of the psychosexual battles described by modern psychoanalysis. Explaining the ways of God to man may have been Milton's intent, but he seems also to have wanted to attribute evil to a male or female source, to give it some kind of gender identity. He readily gave that dubious honor to the female Eve; but in retrospect we may argue he reserved his most bitter blame for the gullible Adam and the dreadful choice he made to forsake paradise for such a mate. Adam's decision (metaphorically binding on us all) was either to return to a state without sexual identity such as prevailed when Adam was alone and when gender therefore had not been created (Freud's pre-oedipal phase), or to desert that sexual unity for sexual bifurcation, male and female. His choice in favor of division rather than integration was psychologically devastating (Freud's neuroses). The subsequent human quest has been to merge the male and female selves into that lost Shangrila which Milton tropically offers—a state which never had reality or biological precedent and which is therefore impossible to reacquire, but which attracts all the more because of its inaccessibility.

Unconsciously perhaps, this psychosexual metaphor of the battle between the feminine and masculine selves is what most intrigued Cather about *Paradise Lost*. Moreover, the psychosexuality of the poem is the link to the Oedipus metaphor which she also develops. Her utilizing the two literary classics, which may in some respects appear as seeking disparate anchor points for a narrative that superficially is drifting without chart, may prove instead that her creative processes were fueled most often by a kind of psychic fission: the tension resulting from her striving to understand her own eroticism in conflict with existing moral codes.

The third of the conventional references (the bird imagery) exemplifies the natural as opposed to the allusive or literary source of metaphor. Cather was more comfortable with the natural images, as *My Ántonia* with its emergence motif illustrates, and she later uses bird imagery throughout her novels. Yet, even with the birds in *One of Ours*, she does not carry the imagery through to a predictable conclusion and in several respects disrupts the natural or usual perceptions which the audience may have formed concerning birds as literary symbols.

One of the most prominent occurrences of the bird coincides with Claude's building of the house in which he thinks he and Enid Royce will spend their years. Claude is sitting on the "skeleton" of the unfinished porch: "One night a bird flew in and fluttered wildly about among the partitions, shrieking with fright before it darted out into the dusk through one of the upper windows and found its way to freedom" (1078). Shortly after this, Claude discovers a covey of quails in the timber near the new house. He is protective of them and worries that they will leave the sanctuary of his own woods and be shot (1081). Then, on the troop ship, Claude shares a cabin with a Lieutenant Bird. Contrary to what his name suggests, Bird does not soar but is among the first to die in the influenza epidemic aboard ship:

"Lieutenant Bird died late in the afternoon and was buried at sunrise the next day, sewed up in a tarpaulin, with an eighteen pound shell at his feet" (1166). And in Book Five, ironically entitled "Bidding the Eagles of the West Fly On" after Vachel Lindsay's patriotic poem, the bird metaphor is extended to all the American soldiers. There are other instances of the imagery, but these will serve our purposes.

The overall bird symbology which Cather develops derives from the same conflicting impulses noted earlier: the tension that prevails when the desire for freedom is in opposition to the various forces that seek to imprison. Though Cather locates the image in the sociohistoric context of World War I and the international ramifications of that event, her focus is upon Claude as an individual. In both perspectives, the image emerges as a statement about the desire to escape the biological restrictions of the body and the environmental restrictions of place and to find release in death. There is, Cather shows, a death worse than literal death—the kind of death Gladys Farmer means when she worries that Claude "would become one of those dead people that moved about the streets of Frankfort; everything that was Claude would perish, and the shell of him would come and go and eat and sleep for fifty years" (1062-63). It is such intellectual and spiritual somnambulance that one must avoid at any cost. Thus, in the image of the bird flying into the uncompleted house, we have both the instinctive will to be free and the life-to-death movement which the bird's passage through the house suggests. The paralleling of life to the passing of a "sparrow" through a building which represents human artifice is not unique to Cather, and she may well be giving us another literary allusion; but the image is so natural to the setting that it seems endemic to the prairie. In any event, Claude's viewing of the frightened bird seeking to escape the "skeleton" of the house is an objective epitome of his own condition. He too will be temporarily trapped in the house which signifies marriage and conventional morality. Moreover, the house suggests his own physical self, the body Claude has in mind when he ruminates that inside each living person "there were captives dwelling in darkness" (1100). That captive self will soon fly clear of the body's prison. Claude will escape the confines of both types of houses—although not of his own volition; first geographically to Europe and then spiritually into death.

Cather extends the image but alters it slightly with the quails. Quails are a game bird and are thus hunted, just as

Claude soon will be the target of someone who wishes to kill him. The quails also suggest Claude's idealism—his feminine sensibilities that lie more toward nurturing and saving than toward violence and destruction. His instincts are to feed and shelter the quails rather than hunt them. We do not know precisely what happens to the quails, but we can surmise: when Claude abandons the new house after Enid's departure, he abandons also the woods in which he found the quails. Left unfed, they will seek food in Leonard Dawson's field and he will indeed shoot them, as Claude feared. The quails, therefore, represent in one respect Claude's innate kindness and the freedom from domestic control with which he instinctively identifies (thus his spending of more and more time in the timber with them). Commensurately, however, the quails suggest the destruction of innocence and of the instinct to be free. Leonard Dawson's perfunctory killing of the birds emanates from the same violent instinct which underlies the battles in Europe, his innate fear of anything which does not fall under his control. Claude's casual and inconclusive forgetting of the birds is the factor which disrupts the overall image. Either Cather simply did not care to carry through on this particular image or she intends to suggest that Claude has no real devotion to saving the quails. In any event, she makes the audience supply its own finale, which either consciously or unconsciously is that Claude abandons the quails, just as he ultimately abandons himself. He turns them over to the shotgun just as he turns himself over to the German machine guns, thereby conceding a fatalistic inevitability. Unlike the bird which enters the house and passes through to freedom, the implied fate of the quails suggests the destruction of natural freedom, not its attainment.

The bird image as it applies to Lieutenant Bird continues the destruction motif and also transfers from the abstract to the literal. "Bird" moves us from metaphor generally to allegory specifically. That is, with Bird's death we are no longer seeing death in imagistic terms but in very concrete, manifested form. The war, previously abstracted in newspaper rhetoric, is made real by the eighteen-pound shell which is used as weight to sink Bird's body. We cannot theorize much about how his death relates to freed souls, suicide, or incarcerated selves, for Cather simply does not give us material enough; but even in its brevity, the image of Bird's body being destroyed by an enemy larger than the war itself (in this case influenza) is a powerful reminder of the various kinds of "war" that Cather wishes to include in her narrative. Moreover, his death serves to set up the irony of the title of the ensuing chapter, for Bird's burial at sea shows poignantly that American "Birds" die ingloriously and are sunk to the ocean's bottom, in graphic contrast to the patriotic idealism of American "Eagles" flying on.

To make the irony more pronounced, Cather gives us a specific example of a flying eagle in Victor Morse, another of Claude's cabin mates from the *Anchises*. Morse is superfically a heroic flyer, but he also suffers from venereal disease (1179), keeps an aging whore back in England, and is ultimately shot down by the hated Germans (1230). His name mocks him, for he has no chance of being the victor. For Morse, it is simply a matter of which of several factors will kill him first. (The name suggests the Latin *mors*, meaning "death.") As James Woodress notes, Morse is one of Milton's fallen angels (328), transformed from literary allusion to a character in a realistic novel. In reality's harsh light he is seen as syphilitic, lustful, doomed. Though it is debatable that Claude is a romantic, except in the most ironic of ways, Susan Rosowski is essentially correct when she concludes that in *One of Ours* Cather is "telling the story of a romantic caught in a nightmarish world of realism" (97), a condition made tangible by Victor Morse and the bird imagery of which he is a part.

Published in the year in which she said the world broke apart (1922), *One of Ours* marked a significant point in Cather's life. With it she switched publishers, became wealthy, and won the Pulitzer Prize. It took her four years to write, and, like *Paradise Lost*, we would not wish it any longer. Her friend Dorothy Canfield Fisher published an effusive promotional review (for Book of the Month Club) which sounds almost as if she had actually read the novel. Hemingway scoffed at its war scenes, Cather herself felt it was doomed before she ever published it, and—if the bibliographies are reliable—it has more often than not been treated as a detour critics must take to get from Ántonia to a lost lady. Yet the de-articulated technique which Cather uses to convey a de-articulated self caught in a de-articulated world offers an oxymoronic harmonious disharmony. None of Cather's fictive artist-selves is more trapped by the dogma of his society and none more devoted to self destruction than Claude Wheeler. Overall, therefore, what Cather continues to reveal in *One of Ours* is that she was an artist growing increasingly leery of the conventional institutions of her society, that she was progressively disturbed by her own sexual contradictions, and that self destruction was becoming more fixed as a part of her psychological matrix. Her own de-articulation became part and parcel of her text.

Works Cited

Aichinger, Peter. *The American Soldier in Fiction, 1880-1963: A History of Attitudes Toward Warfare and the Military Establishment.* Ames: Iowa U P, 1975.

Arnold, Marilyn. "*One of Ours*: Willa Cather's Losing Battle." *Western American Literature* 13 (Nov) 1978: 259-66.

Boone, Joseph Allen. *Tradition and Counter Tradition: Love and the Form of Fiction.* Chicago: U of Chicago P, 1987.

Cather, Willa. *Alexander's Bridge* (1912). Lincoln: U of Nebraska P, 1977.

—. *One of Ours* (1922). In *Willa Cather: Early Novels and Stories.* New York: The Library of America, 1987.

—. *Not Under Forty* (1936). Lincoln: U of Nebraska P, 1988.

—. *Willa Cather in Person: Interviews, Speeches, and Letters.* Ed. L. Brent Bohlke. Lincoln: U of Nebraska P, 1986.

Cooperman, Stanley. *World War I and the American Novel.* Baltimore: Johns Hopkins U P, 1967.

Freud, Sigmund. *The Basic Writings of Sigmund Freud.* Trans. and ed. A. A. Brill. New York: The Modern Library, 1938.

Gay, Peter. *Freud: A Life for Our Time.* New York: Norton, 1988.

Griffiths, Frederick T. "The Woman Warrior: Willa Cather and *One of Ours*." *Women's Studies*, 2 (Dec. 1984): 261-285.

Hoffman, C., and A. C. Hoffman. "Re-Echoes of the Jazz Age: Archetypal Women in the Novels of 1922." *Journal of Modern Literature* 7 (Feb 1979): 62-86.

Oehlschlager, Fritz. "Willa Cather's 'Consequences' and *Alexander's Bridge*: An Approach through R. D. Laing and Ernest Becker." *Modern Fiction Studies* 32 (2) Summer 1986: 191-202.

Rosowski, Susan J. *The Voyage Perilous: Willa Cather's Romanticism.* Lincoln: U of Nebraska P, 1986.

Woodress, James. *Willa Cather: A Literary Life.* Lincoln: U of Nebraska P, 1987.

4
A Lost Lady: The Prostitute as Secret Self

With *One of Ours* Cather partially extricated herself psychologically from the Nebraskan prairie and what it symbolized for her. Once she had liberated Claude Wheeler from the Divide and allowed him to die his (vain) glorious death in France, thus freeing himself from any possibilities of returning to the puritanical strictures he had left behind, Cather would not locate her fictive personae again in Nebraska, with one disastrous exception. As we will see, that one exception (*Lucy Gayheart*) serves to illustrate how deadly the prairie hegemony could be for the artist and how Cather personally was never able to break completely from her Nebraskan roots, no matter how much she may have yearned to do so or how much she demonstrated that desire subconsciously and subtextually in her narratives.

The five novels between *One of Ours* and *Lucy Gayheart* all avoid the Nebraska setting, *A Lost Lady* only nominally but the others with progressive distance. Bernice Slote separates the three novels between *One of Ours* and *Death Comes for the Archbishop* and groups them under the rubric "the three problem or conflict novels of the 1920's" (*Kingdom of Art* 110). My own thesis is that all Cather's novels are "conflict" narratives, but Slote is correct in recognizing that several factors mark *A Lost Lady* (1923), *The Professor's House* (1925), and *My Mortal Enemy* (1926) and distinguish them from those novels published before and after. First, as already noted, they all de-emphasize the concentration on the prairie landscape which dominates the previous four novels. Second, they are all set specifically in the rather infelicitous space of houses. Third, and directly related to the second, they all concentrate directly upon the phenomenon of American marriage and domesticity. None of the three is situated precisely in Nebraska, though *A Lost Lady* is vaguely located somewhere between Omaha and Denver and is the only one of the trio with a rural setting. As Carol Fairbanks has correctly noted in *Prairie Women*, the love of the prairie landscapes dominates the fiction by women writers such as Cather (35). In these novels, however, we see the lessening of that domination, as Cather tries to separate herself psychologically from the Nebraska frontier. The last two factors certainly do not make these three novels unique in Cather's fiction, since domiciles and domesticity frequently appear elsewhere in her work. We have just seen, for example, how houses and failed marriages are part of the "battles" fought in the war novel *One of Ours*. In these three novels, however, houses are not just incidental to the narrative action but central to determining that action. Moreover, the novels are comparatively short, two of them hardly more than short stories in length. More than fully realized narratives, they seem the produce of an artist most concerned with keeping her creative genius honed for shaping the second masterpiece, *Death Comes for the Archbishop*. *A Lost Lady*, *The Professor's House*, and *My Mortal Enemy*, therefore, form a distinguishable sub-unit within Cather's dozen novels.

Aside from its psychological implications, the phenomenon of the diminishing prairie is not surprising. Nearing fifty in 1923, Cather had not resided in Nebraska for more than 25 years. Moreover, she had cultivated it rather thoroughly for *O Pioneers!*, *The Song of the Lark*, *My Ántonia*, and *One of Ours*—her four longest novels. The Divide, perhaps, simply was depleted as part of her creative memory. As she said, "Using one setting all the time is very like planting a field with corn season after season. I believe in rotation of crops" (*WC in Person* 76). Also, as she grew older and as more physical ailments beset her, she turned her thoughts progressively to other places and other times where in memory she found comfort, most specifically the Southwest and Virginia—the latter the scene of her previously unexplored childhood, the former the scene of her wanderings as a young and healthy woman. When she does return to the prairie one final time for fictive inspiration, we see that it was essentially dead as part of her creative imagination. *Lucy Gayheart* (1935) has little original in it insofar as setting except that now Nebraska is shown to be a deadly place, the location of the drowning pool. *A Lost Lady* is set only in "one of those grey towns along the Burlington railroad" (9), with no state designated, while the other two are set in Michigan, Illinois, and California. They are not set in Nebraska, the Southwest, or any other locale with which Cather was familiar. In that respect they are peculiarly dislocated narratives. Once she had killed Claude Wheeler to prevent his having to return to the Nebraska milieu, Cather could not easily relocate her creative self there.

As for the house motif, it offers interesting material for speculation as to why Cather moved from the prairie to the confines of houses and domestic strife. Woodress and other biographers have discussed at length Cather's fascination for houses and certain rooms within them (see, for example, Woodress's discussion of Cather's move to her new apartment at Number 5 Bank Street in New York, p.234f). Moreover, the topic has been analyzed in conjunction with *The Professor's House*, most notably by Leon Edel in an essay I will discuss shortly. The topic has been little recognized, however, in the other two novels or collectively for all three. Judith Fryer does discuss houses in *Felicitous Space: The Imaginative Structures of Edith Wharton and Willa Cather*, but her analysis is somewhat surrealistic and gives only passing attention to the three novels I am analyzing here. Houses are especially important in *A Lost Lady*, since Niel Herbert is an architect and the "house" in that novel serves a particularly striking function in the narrative design. The motif in *My Mortal Enemy* is less pronounced but nonetheless interesting. As for the marriage motif, little needs to be said by way of introduction other than that all three novels specifically analyze heterosexual marriages and all three conclude that traditional marriage and its conventional accoutrements are deadly—not a particularly surprising conclusion in light of the multitude of sociosexual uncertainties which we have already recognized in Cather and which continue in her later novels. In no novel before or after these three does Cather directly concern herself so extensively with such matrimonial relationships, though in *Sapphira and the Slave Girl* the long dead marriage of Sapphira and Henry Colbert serves as the background against which the other actions transpire. The topic is also sublimated and serves an important role in the subtext of *Death Comes for the Archbishop*.

These elements of lost prairies, marriage, and houses are the comparatively obvious factors which connect the three "problem" novels or make them "common" to each other; but they are not necessarily the factors which need elucidation. Each of the novels is distinct and individually purposeful, and it is their elements of individuality on which I want to focus in this and the next two chapters.

Kathleen L. Nichols summarizes *A Lost Lady* as "the story of a sexually-repressed young man's inability to accept change, growth, and adult sexuality as the waning frontier era of his childhood consciousness ushers in the 'fallen' twentieth-century world of adult awareness" (188); and Diane Cousineau gives a Freudian analysis "of Niel's initiation into patriarchal culture" (307). Nichols' and Cousineau's comments witness the fact that the psychosexuality of Cather's sixth novel is a topic frequently recognized and discussed. In fact, Cather emphasizes sexuality in *A Lost Lady* probably more overtly than in any other of her novels. Certainly the adultery of Hilda Burgoyne and Bartley Alexander of *Alexander's Bridge* is tame compared to Marian Forrester's lusty eroticism. The more we ponder Marian, the more we suspect Cather of intentional *over*-emphasis, much in the same way she exaggerated the obviousness of the Oedipus motif and *Paradise Lost* in *One of Ours*. Like the Trojan horse, the sexuality is too conspicuous—and ultimately full of surprises. It is less the psychosexuality itself and more the dynamic irony which Cather puts into the psychosexuality that needs attention.

Cather herself explained that Marian Forrester is based on "a woman I loved very much in my childhood" and that everything else in the novel is "subordinate" to the portrait she wished to paint of this lady. The literal, historical "lady" is usually identified as Mrs. Lyra Anderson, formerly Mrs. Silas Garber, wife of a Nebraskan governor. Mrs. Anderson died in 1921, while Cather was working on *One of Ours*, thus giving her the idea for her next novel. Cather follows historical fact rather closely in presenting the lady's life, with two significant additions: Frank Ellinger, the lover Marian takes to satisfy her lust; and Ivy Peters, the lover she takes out of economic expediency. These fictive men—so polar in most characteristics but joined in that both epitomize male chauvinism and both share Marian's bed—emanate wholly from Cather's imagination and thus offer revealing glimpses into her creative processes, a point which will be elucidated in a moment. Niel Herbert, who is another projection of Cather's own persona, "isn't a character at all" according to Cather; "he is just a peephole into [Mrs Forrester's] world." He is "only a point of view" (*WC in Person* 77). Though the comment must be taken with some reservation, since Niel (then named Duncan) was the first-person narrative voice of the first version of the story and remains more complex in the narrative structure than Cather's evaluation suggests, the "peephole" concept is interesting in that it implies that very little of Marian Forrester's personality is obvious to the viewer. Like the rest of the room unrevealed to the peephole view, the remainder of Marian's character must be surmised or extrapolated from the evidence at hand. The audience (and Niel) must envision what vision does not give. Moreover, that Cather once again originally planned to project her authorial self in the guise of a first-person male narrator trying to explicate a strong feminine personality, as she had done in *My Ántonia*, shows that the feminine-masculine conflict was an essential element in her imagination. As David Stouck accurately notes, it is significant that "In *A Lost Lady* . . . Willa Cather once again looks at her past through the eyes of a sensitive boy" (58). Niel is the youthful Cather who loved Marian's prototype "very much"—an idealism which the mature Cather recognized as naive. The narrative tension resulting from the naive/experience views shows once more Cather's premeditated use of psychological conflicts for artistic gain. She revised the novel in a conscious effort to eliminate the first-person male narrator, thus de-emphasizing the masculine presence and reasserting the conflicted perspective made possible by the psycho-narrator technique. (Her unconscious or imagination, however, reasserts the male in the personae of Ellinger and Peters.) Much of the resulting narrative perspective remains Niel's, however, and the subtextual complexity of the novel originates in the conflict between what appears to be Niel's limited understanding and Marian Forrester's subtle, mature sexuality.

While Cather seems on the narrative surface to be ironic in her depiction of Niel's priggish condemnation of Marian Forrester, a closer analysis of the narrative shows that she manages a kind of ironic double cross. Viewing the novel from the perspective of the first level of irony, we see Niel as being prudish, judgmental, and wrongheaded about the immoral lady. From this perspective, Marian appears to be superficially flighty but essentially more substantial and adaptive to change than others in the tale, especially the callow Niel; at first condemned by him, she proves him wrong and is ultimately admirable. Niel, therefore, converts to Cather's true attitude toward Marian and is made to appreciate the woman whose moral standards are so different from his. Susan J. Rosowski in "Willa Cather's *A Lost Lady*: The Paradoxes of Change," espouses and surveys this view quite thoroughly. She argues, among other things, that Niel at first gives his allegiance to old Captain Forrester but gradually learns to appreciate Marian's capacity for adaptability.   Beth Burch follows the same argument in *Notes on Contemporary Literature* and says Marian ultimately triumphs and the novel ends optimistically.   Dalma H. Brunauer (in *Renascence*) agrees that Cather's sympathies are with Marian and old Captain Forrester and that Niel does not appreciate women.

Valid as such a view is, however, it acknowledges only half the ironic process and does not completely jibe with textual evidence. The dual ironic switch or double cross comes from the fact that Niel in all his puritanical, conventional morality is more flexible and less destructive than Marian and may well personify more of Cather's own ethical values than first glance reveals.   We know, for instance, that she thoroughly read Hawthorne and Bunyan when she was a child and that as an adult she maintained that *Pilgrim's Progress* "was essential to a child's library" (Woodress 51).   Such attitudes as Niel displays may appear prudish and judgmental, especially to a 1990s audience, but in truth they help make him a productive member of his 1890s society.   His chastity ultimately saves him from the ostracism and humiliation which Marian experiences.   By minimizing the prurient, he develops a sense of self-worth, a respect for law and order (both morally and legally), and a loyalty to friends and relatives—an "old fashioned" ethic which Cather upheld personally.   Especially in the Twenties, she deplored "the relaxation of moral standards, the deterioration of taste, the scramble for money" (Woodress 476)—an attitude which reaches its artistic apogee via the celibate archbishop Latour and Vaillant in *Death Comes for the Archbishop*.

The desire to believe that Cather favors Marian the lusty female over Niel the pusillanimous male is understandable, but such an attitude reflects more the wishful thinking of the post-1960s audience and less the intent which Cather's text supports. Niel may be sexless, priggish, and conventional, but he is also happy.   Or at least nothing in the narrative construct suggests that he has been irreparably damaged by his years in Sweet Water, or that he has not gone on to MIT and success as an architect, and made peace with himself and his society in the process. He has no scars from Mrs. Forrester, retaining her only as "a bright, impersonal memory" (171) which parallels Cather's own epiphanic "flood of memories" (Woodress 340) that precipitated the novel; and Niel may even have given up the celibate life, for he "has known pretty women and clever ones" since his days in Sweet Water (171). If he has any great torments of soul and society, they do not appear in narrative closure. We might even conjecture that Niel's complacent, peace-of-mind social adjustment is a major reason why he appears so unexciting and why many readers are now reluctant to accept him as anything other than a self-righteous prude.

On the contrary, however, Marian Forrester who seems so dynamic and so emblematic of enlightened modern morality is a paradigm of what not to do with one's life—especially a life judged in the context of turn-of-the-century prairie mores or against Cather's own conservative, independent, financially secure life. Inept at economic management, unable to control her sexuality, Marian is driven from Sweet Water to California and from California to final exile in Argentina. She fails to uphold the biological imperative to produce children, has no productive job or avocation, and is generally parasitic. She is married finally to a "cranky," "quarrelsome," and "stingy" old man to whom she is little more than the most recent of several female companions (173). Their living in Argentina, the land of no extradition and a haven for the world's renegades, suggests the illegality of their life and the extent to which Cather feared ostracism, whether through voluntary emigration or otherwise. Her natural beauty gone, Marian must dye her hair, paint her lips, and put on a cosmetic face to meet the faces that she meets. She ends her days like Blanche Dubois, her morality seriously compromised and trusting to the kindness of strangers—or at least to foreigners in a strange land.

Compassion Cather obviously has for such a wasted life, but she just as clearly is not advocating it as a model. Nor does she blame the society of Sweet Water or elsewhere for Marian's tragedy, though in other instances she does not avoid placing blame on society if such blame is justified—as she does, for instance, in cases such as Thea Kronborg's or, more tragically, as with Paul in "Paul's Case." In fact, for the fin de siècle period in which the novel is set, the small town morality seems quite flexible—more so in some respects than the cosmopolitan ethics we see in the stories of Edith Wharton or Henry James which concern the same period. Cather epitomizes this untypical village tolerance when she has the boy Adolph Blum accidentally witness Marian's and Frank Ellinger's assignation in the woods. Adolph sees her emotionally and perhaps literally unclothed: "He had never seen her before when her mocking eyes and lively manner were not between her and all the world" (68). Adolph is so astounded by what he has witnessed that he can only sit for hours "under the cedars, his gun on his knee" (67). Just as he is incapable of perceiving the phallic pun Cather makes at his expense, he is also incapable of passing moral judgments. Mrs. Forrester's high place in prairie society exonerates her from the rules that direct the lower classes.   Others might judge her, but

> with Adolph Blum her secrets were safe. His mind was feudal; the rich and fortunate were also the privileged. These warm-blooded, quick-breathing people took chances,—followed impulses only dimly understandable to a boy who was wet and weather-chapped all the year. (68)

Even Niel, who when seen only from the first level of irony is supposed to be so condemning and insensitive to Marian's rage to live, takes pains to protect her from her own uncontrollable emotions: the audience overhears Marian's indiscreet, sexually oriented telephone call to her honeymooning lover Frank Ellinger, but Niel cuts the telephone wire to make certain that the town gossip operator does not hear the outburst (134). Also, Orville Ogden (Ellinger's father-in-law) visits Niel in Sweet Water to offer his assistance in getting a larger pension for Captain Forrester's widow; but Marian has already betrayed her loyalty for Niel and his uncle to cast her lot with the despicable Ivy Peters, and Mr. Ogden can be of no help (149).   Ultimately Marian's own poor judgment, her inability to be discreet, her failure to direct her life socially, emotionally, and economically prove to be her downfall. She cannot logically use society as a scapegoat.

The first paragraph offers Cather's initial clue to the ironic dual perspective and to an explanation of why she does not side with Marian, a woman who despite her adulteries (or, for a modern audience, perhaps because of them) has admirable traits which evoke our sympathies. From paragraph one to the narrative's end Marian Forrester is rhetorically and symbolically linked to prostitution, a motif that then transfers from Marian to permeate the entire narrative construct. Compared to the obvious use of the Oedipus myth, the birds, and *Paradise Lost* that we discussed relative to *One of Ours*, the prostitution motif in *A Lost Lady* is distinctly understated.   It therefore needs to be tracked through the narrative with some degree of patience in order to facilitate the surface-to-theory transitions we have already established as part of methodology.

In the opening sentence, Cather emphasizes the Victorian-era time setting of the 1890s and tells us that in a "grey" town on the Burlington railroad "there was a house well known from Omaha to Denver for its hospitality" (9). In that house lives a woman identified at this stage only as "Mrs Forrester," who is consciously aware that she "was attractive in dishabille" and who therefore wears only a dressing-gown to welcome railroad men at her door (12). After considerable reiterations about "the house," and a seemingly unimportant aside that Mrs. Forrester wears obvious "jewels" (40), Cather then introduces Frank Ellinger, Mrs. Forrester's paramour (though the audience does not yet know this). Ellinger is described as a bachelor of forty, six feet two, who looks as if he "could bite an iron rod in two with a snap of his jaws" (46). From Denver, he is infamous for a past association with one Nell Emerald, a prostitute and madam of a "house" (50). Ellinger is the one who lets the audience know that the woman known formally as "Mrs. Forrester" has a more familiar name: "Marian" (65). His familiarity is soon explained, for we learn they have been involved in an adulterous affair for some years. Mrs. Forrester's prurience becomes more overt from this point onward. In a thinly veiled double entendre, she tells Ellinger that "When I'm off in the country for a whole winter, alone, and growing older, I like to . . . to be reminded of pleasanter things" (65). Two pages later Cather depicts the urchin Adolph Blum while he watches "soft shivers" go through Mrs. Forrester's body as she recalls a liaison in the woods. In another double entendre, she exclaims of her maid, Bohemian Mary, that "she makes it worth his while" for her sweetheart to visit regularly on Sunday nights (76). Shortly thereafter Niel Herbert, visiting unannounced at the "house," listens outside the window to Mrs. Forrester's "soft laughter; impatient, indulgent, teasing, eager" (86) as she participates in erotic foreplay with Ellinger. Niel thinks at this point that the brilliancy of beautiful women is "always fed by something coarse and concealed" (87). The dominant item inside the "house" is a statue of "a scantily draped figure, an Arab or Egyptian slave girl, holding in her hands a large flat shell from the California coast" (115). The last time Niel sees Mrs. Forrester is again through the window of the "house." Ivy Peters is fondling her breasts, and Niel leaves, thinking that the "house" is now a place "where common fellows behaved after their kind and knew a common woman when they saw her" (170). Then finally, years later Niel learns that Mrs. Forrester has been seen in South America, supposedly married to an old Englishman. She was "a good deal made up" with "plenty of powder, and a little red." Her black hair "looked as if she dyed it" (173).

Clustered in this fashion, the various items that compose the prostitution motif appear more distinct than they do in the text—and that is precisely the point. Any one of the items taken out of context does not convey the singular image of whoredom that they convey collectively. For instance, we pay little attention to the initial "well known" house reference until we learn that a woman inside comes to the door scantily clad to greet numerous men visitors or that the statue of an exotic concubine awaits just inside the door and that the statue holds a shell from California and that Mrs. Forrester is from California, and so forth. But the clues are incremental, and we cannot ignore the accumulating images. We note that Cather seldom refers to the Forrester domicile as a "home" but consistently as a "house," thereby reiterating the connotations of "bawdy house" or "house of ill repute" or—more harshly—"whore house." The reference to Mrs. Forrester's wearing "jewels" carries us to the name of the prostitute/madam associated with Ellinger, Nell *Emerald*, and cleverly links the two, just as the double "l's" visually connect "Nell" and "Ellinger." Soon Mrs. Forrester is associated with another scoundrel, Ivy Peters, whose name in the vernacular refers to the male genitalia. Cather uses the name much as Fitzgerald later uses "Dick Diver" for its bawdy double meaning. Too, the name of the maid who gets irritable if her boy friend does not visit to satisfy her carnal needs each Sunday (Bohemian Mary) echoes Mrs. Forrester's own name: Marian. Further, the stereotype of the Bohemian girl is that of a libertine, something Cather herself implies in her short story "The Bohemian Girl." And Mr. Forrester refers to his wife as "Maidy," perhaps being fully aware of the irony of such nomenclature and how it connects his wife to the amorous servant. The final image we have of Mrs. Forrester is distinctly whorish: dyed hair, excessive make up, living off a man much older than she, just as she lived off the aging Captain Forrester. Ed Elliott, the man who reports his chance encounter with Mrs. Forrester in South America, assumes the two are married, and though evidence supports his assumption, Mrs. Forrester is definitely more a kept woman than a conventional wife. And in passing, we note that "Ed Elliott" reiterates the double "l's" and is thus associated with Nell-Ellinger, therefore visually bringing the prostitution associations full circle for Mrs. Forrester.

The prostitute must associate sexuality as much with economics as with eroticism, which is indeed the case with Marian Forrester. Nor is she subtle about it. She tells Niel emphatically that "Money is a very important thing. Realize that in the beginning; face it, and don't be ridiculous in the end, like so many of us" (114). Not surprisingly therefore, each time we see her sexually involved, we also see signs of this monetary ethic. On the day when Captain Forrester must leave for Denver to check the failed banks which will impoverish him, Marian sends Bohemian Mary away to visit her mother so the house will be free for her tryst with Ellinger (83). When Ellinger marries the wealthy Constance Ogden, Marian telephones him on his honeymoon night and demands to know how much stock he received from marrying the girl (134), a question which indicates how readily she assumes that sexual favors must be purchased. Her affair with the horribly ugly Ivy Peters is predominantly economic: he has usurped control of her "house" and finances and has the power to foreclose on her. And we have already noted her final "marriage" to the rich old Englishman Collins. Niel's observation about this arrangement is not that she died happy but that she "was well cared for, to the very end" (174). He realizes all along that "She was one of the people who ought always to have money" (83) and senses that financial security is the appropriate thing to wish for Marian. Contemplating sexual ethics for one of her personality seems moot.

Such evidence indicates that Cather purposely fabricates this prostitution motif as another facet of the overemphasized sexuality in general. The question at this juncture is "why"? We have already touched on part of the answer: she wanted to make sure that her own attitude toward the two major characters was understood. She may at first appear to side with Marian rather than Niel, but after we recognize the Paphian imagery she associates with Marian we realize that her sympathies are slanted back again toward Niel and that we have another indication of what Woodress terms "Cather's continuing distrust of her sex"—meaning her gender (57). She does not champion either Niel or Marian, but seems instead to favor a middle ground between the two—a territory she leaves unexplored in the literal narrative. The subtextual zone suggests yet a third level of irony to Cather's treatment of Niel and Marian. Here we turn the screw one more time and theorize that Cather does after all identify with Marian in that she too fears for some reason that she has prostituted herself. Thus, because she identifies with Marian

literally, she disassociates herself from her fictively. By transfer-
ring her prostituted self emblematically to Marian and by then
denying that emblem, she hopes to distance herself from the
characteristics commonly associated with that emblem. In this
sense, Marian may seem too much like an icon in some kind of
intellectual voodoo, or a straw woman of the psyche. Yet such
transference is plausible. As we have seen in discussing her
other novels, Cather consistently tries to work through the guilts
arising from her eroticism and to fashion in her imagination a
"public" self which conforms—in Naomi Weisstein's phrase—
to "what people around her expect[ed] her to be, and what the
overall situation in which she is acting implies that she is" (395).
It is thus that Cather awards the prudish Niel, sides with him,
and gives him at least some modicum of happiness. Erotically
speaking, he is a "safe" persona—a man so flawed and essentially effeminate that no one could possibly envy him and thus
seek to do him harm, yet a man who at the same time commits
no major sins or adopts radical lifestyles and who therefore attains the security with which society awards the unintimidating
conformist. A woman of fifty, having produced no children,
unmarried, living with another female, and keeping secrets that
were probably far less reprehensible than she imagined, Cather
may have viewed her own life as unorthodox, queer by prairie
standards. For such a woman, Niel is the ideal other self. He is
the "good" self which remains after the "bad" self (Marian) has
been eradicated.

James Woodress points out that in 1922-23, when she was
writing *A Lost Lady*, Cather's attitude was becoming increasingly
"valetudinarian" (335). No longer young, she felt more acutely
the sickliness of both body and soul. *One of Ours*, though sav-
aged by many critics, brought her to the pinnacle of her fame and
fortune, yet "she felt let down" (335). Thrilled by the size of her
royalty checks, she simulataneously suspected she had prostituted her talents—just as reviewers such as Sinclair Lewis, H. L.
Mencken, and Edmond Wilson implied she had done. L. Brent
Bohlke notes that though Cather had long sought fame, "She
was embarrassed about having a Park Avenue address" and was
"never comfortable" with success (*WC in Person* xxvii). Her
great love, Isabelle McClung Hambourg, moved permanently to
Europe, and although Cather never emigrated, she was disillusioned by and alienated from postwar American society
(Woodress 336)—even if she herself was profiting considerably
from having depicted that alienation in a meretriciously bad

novel. Previously a free thinker, with a distrust of institutionalized religion, she made the religously orthodox, conformist ges-
ture of joining the Episcopal Church in Red Cloud at Christmas-
time, 1922. Several months later, she sat for a portrait by Leon
Bakst. As Woodress notes, it is not a "flattering" picture, but it
accurately captures the likeness of a "middle-aged woman going
through a profound physical, emotional, spiritual crisis" (339).

Such provenance suggests that Marian and Niel may be
viewed as opposite sides of a psychological chasm Cather was trying to bridge. With Marian Forrester Cather is trying to say
good-bye to a self-image she had flirted with for years: the rebellious, sexually inhibited, irreligious nonconformist powered
more by emotions than intellect. Even her name connotes the
forest, and Hawthorne stands as a reminder of what the wilderness symbolized to the Calvinist mind: in the woods God did not
live, Satan ruled, and sexuality was synonymous with black and
evil deeds. We see the type (minus the onomastics) in Clara
Vavrika of "The Bohemian Girl," in Hilda Burgoyne, Marie
Tovesky, and other of Cather's earlier characters. (Marian, we
note, is often associated with eating, making love, travelling,
and other such hedonistic pursuits.) But Niel represents the
quintessential Cather. He lives vicariously through books and
the observed lives of others, recording but seldom participating.
He is an androgynous self, male attired, conservative, nonsexual, acceptable to the prairie society whose influence Cather
could not move beyond. There certainly is no flash to Niel, but
then again he attracts no fire. What we ultimately ponder in regard to the prostitution motif is the paradox of just which aspect
of self Cather felt she had prostituted. Did she feel that in flirting
with the alternate life style represented by Marian she had jeop-
ardized her rightful place in Nebraska society and ultimately in
Heaven; or more likely perhaps, did she feel that having
espoused Niel and his patriarchal ethic she was whoring for the
crowd and betraying her own moral, sexual ethic? In the chasm
of that paradox may lurk the despair which Woodress records for
Cather.

In Marian Forrester Cather demonstrates that in middle
age she was yet uncertain about the erotic female and thus continues to mull her possibilities, though ultimately she chooses to
deny allegiance to the carnality which Marian personifies. In
short, thoughts of the coital woman seem still to have been an
active part of Cather's creative processes in 1923. That she created out of her imagination the concupiscent Frank Ellinger and

mated him to the historically "real" lady adds credence to such speculation. The overt contemplation of sexuality, however, reaches its zenith with Marian. After *A Lost Lady*, sexuality remains a part of Cather's imagination and of her narratives, but it is not center stage and is subsumed into broader focus. In the post-1923 novels, Cather either avoids erotic relationships altogether for her main characters or demonstrates that such unions are unmitigated disasters. Thus, for example, we have the terrible consequences (but not the close scrutiny) of erotic love in *My Mortal Enemy* and *Lucy Gayheart* and the near total absence of erotic love from the narrative surfaces of *Death Comes for the Archbishop* and *Shadows on the Rock* (subtextually, however, it is still present). In the later novels, Cather's handling of her psychosexuality becomes progressively more sublimated or "buried" beneath other topics and concerns, until she herself seems unaware of the extent of her fictive revelations of authorial self.

With this thought in mind, we need to elucidate a point raised earlier about Frank Ellinger and Ivy Peters, the only two significant characters in *A Lost Lady* who originate solely in Cather's imagination. In interviews concerning the novel, Cather talks at some length about Marian Forrester and to a less degree about Niel Herbert. Yet she does not discuss Ellinger or Peters, though both are essential to the narrative and are the most purely imaginative of the dramatis personae. While the dramatic function which both serve is readily discernible—each precipitates erotic and thus moral conflicts—precisely how they took shape in Cather's imagination is far less clear. Niel himself (projecting Cather's thinking) gives us a clue when he expresses very early his antipathy for Ivy Peters, whom he "hated to look at" (21), and soon thereafter senses "something evil" in Ellinger (46). Niel distrusts them because they personify lust and greed—two "sins" which Cather feared in herself and which she here transposes or reifies in masculine guise. Ellinger especially epitomizes physicality—a characteristic which Bernice Slote is considering when she concludes that *A Lost Lady* demonstrates the "dualities we have been finding in Willa Cather herself as early as 1896—the high secret snows of the ideal, the blood and wine of the body" (*Kingdom of Art* 103). In other words, the novel stands as a portrayal of the debate between body and soul, the oldest of conflicts and one upon which Cather builds her narrative.

Cather professed great love for Marian's prototype, and she identified with the better qualities of that woman. Why, therefore, does she choose to bracket her with Ellinger and Peters, two of the least admirable of her male creations? They may well be transmutations of the destructive male self, especially as that masculine portion of the psyche is identified with lust and money and subsequently power. Ellinger and Peters are each powerful men, the first especially in the physical sense and the latter in the economic; and through them sex and money become so closely joined as to be indistinguishable (a connection Freud had made earlier in his essay "Character and Anal Eroticism.") The prostitution motif we have just analyzed extends and solidifes the sex-money equation. Money simultaneously seduces and debases the finer emotions of individual freedom, compassion, and natural responses to stimuli—"the high secret snows of the ideal," as Slote puts it. Ivy Peter's blinding of the female woodpecker symbolizes the death of these natural responses and, significantly, originates in or echoes Cather's own early fascination with "slicing toads" as a "hobby" and "amputating limbs" as a "perfect happiness" (Woodress 55)—acts which she associated with maleness and with her own desire at the time to become a physician. Peters emanates from what Woodress calls the "dark underside of romanticism, the world of the grotesque" which Cather evinces from the earliest days of her writing (146). Ellinger originates also in the male persona she adopted in her adolescent years—big, strong, self-assured, charismatic, the idealized male personality we see throughout Cather's fiction and to whom she frequently makes her females subservient. He is the reification of that "mightiest of all lovers" of whom Alexandra Bergson fantasizes in *O Pioneers!* In all his various possibilities, Ellinger is the male self Cather sought to express. Put on stage with his counterpart Ivy Peters, however, he demonstrates that ultimately the male self threatens the creative impulses, seduces one into callousness, crudeness, and abandonment of principles. In other words, he makes a lady into a whore and is best left to the field of dreams.

As we discussed in *Alexander's Bridge*, Cather literally saw novel writing as a male prerogative; in *The Song of the Lark*, she transferred that literalness into the image of the male eagle as the soaring spirit of Art. What seems to be occurring by the time of *A Lost Lady*, therefore, is that with such characters as Ellinger and Peters she is drawing away from the early belief that the creative impulses were masculine and is discovering (in staggering steps rather than smooth transitions) that the male self may be the enemy within. The effort to come to terms with the masculine-feminine qualities of artistic creation is a conflict that fueled her creativity and gave it timbre, just as Marian Forrester's refusal to deny her desire for Ellinger and Peters defines her personality and keeps her from being a nonentity, no matter how easy and simple her life could have been had she repressed that desire.

Works Cited

Brunauer, Dalma H. "The Problem of Point of View in *A Lost Lady*." *Renasence* 28 (Autumn 1975): 47-52.

Burch, Beth. "Willa Cather's *A Lost Lady*: The Woodpecker and Marian Forrester." *Notes on Contemporary Literature* 11 (Sept. 1981): 7-10.

Cather, Willa. *A Lost Lady* (1923). New York: Knopf, 1966.

—. *The Kingdom of Art: Willa Cather's First Principles and Critical Statements: 1893-1896*. Ed. Bernice Slote. Lincoln: U of Nebraska P, 1966.

—. *My Mortal Enemy* (1926). New York: Knopf, 1967.

—. *The Professor's House*. New York: Knopf, 1925.

—. *Willa Cather in Person: Interviews, Speeches, and Letters*. Ed. L. Brent Bohlke. Lincoln: U of Nebraska P, 1986.

Cousineau, Diane. "Division and Difference in *A Lost Lady*." *Women's Studies* 3 (1984): 305-322.

Fairbanks, Carol. *Prarie Women: Images in American and Canadian Fiction*. New Haven: Yale U P, 1986.

Gay, Peter. *Freud: A Life for Our Time*. New York: Norton, 1988.

Morrow, Nancy. "Willa Cather's *A Lost Lady* and the Nineteenth Century Novel of Adultery." *Women's Studies* 2 (1984): 287-303.

Nichols, Kathleen L. "The Celibate Male in *A Lost Lady*: The Unreliable Center of Consciousness." *Critical Essays on Willa Cather*. Ed. John J. Murphy. Boston: G. K. Hall, 1984.

Rosowski, Susan J. "Willa Cather's *A Lost Lady*: The Paradoxes of Change." *Novel: A Forum on Fiction* 11 (Fall 1977): 51-62.

Weisstein, Naomi. "Psychology Constructs the Female: Or, the Fantasy Life of the Male Psychologist" in *Radical Psychology*. Ed. Phil Brown. New York: Harper & Row, 1973. 390-420.

Woodress, James. *Willa Cather: A Literary Life*. Lincoln: U of Nebraska P, 1987.

5
The Professor's House:
Poetic Genius Vs. Literary Structure

If we approach *The Professor's House* from the perspective of the conventional, traditional novel formulations, it is not a "good" novel. By conventional and traditional formulations, I am thinking in terms of the structural definitions of the novel genre, the view which Philip Stevick summarizes as being the arrangement of actions "with beginning, middle, and end, with the materials . . . deployed in such a way as to give the image of coherence, continuity, and wholeness, and with certain tensions and anticipations regarding the central characters carried through the entire length of the works, to be resolved only at their ends" (4). *The Professor's House* fails in most of these particulars, and is far more irresolute than resolute in closure. Viewed, however, as a manifestation of authorial processes or creative impulses, it is one of the most important of Cather's narratives. Coming as it does just prior to *My Mortal Enemy*, in which her creativity lapses into near incoherence, *The Professor's House* demonstrates the fragmentation of the artistic self at war with itself. The psychological conflict which overrides the narrative formulations simultaneously obscures the "meaning" of the resultant narrative text and makes difficult any reconciliation of the disjointed style and point of view which are the hallmarks of *The Professor's House*. The text is therefore a technical failure as a representative of the genre in which tradition necessitates our discussing it. Seen in broader focus, however, and recognized as an emotional formulation of artistic processes, the text is a successful document attesting to Cather's refusal to allow traditional structure and critical expectations to dictate poetic genius. She has come a long way from the structural conformity and artistic dishonesty of *Alexander's Bridge*.

No longer can she allow the conscious Artist to have dominion over the human emotions which are the fundamental source of the very genre which she sought to master. This paradox in part explains the momentary lapse into creative dysfunction which we will see in *My Mortal Enemy*; but it explains also the creative power and subtlety offered by the numerous textual and subtextual tensions that fuel her masterpiece, *Death Comes for the Archbishop*, which comes immediately after *My Mortal Enemy*.

Cather began *The Professor's House* before finishing *A Lost Lady*, and the circumstances of her personal life at the time apply as much to explaining the provenance of one novel as to the other. In retrospect, she called *The Professor's House* a "nasty, grim little tale" (Woodress 367), and wondered at its popularity—apparently never suspecting the doors she had opened to her own psychology nor how intriguing the openings were to an inquisitive audience. In *The Professor's House* she continues to concentrate on the dilemma facing an aging artist caught in a modernist society which has no special regard for moral or artistic integrity; and again she transposes her artistic self into male protagonists. The tone of *The Professor's House* is pessimistic, and if Cather had found any solace in her recent conversion to Episcopalianism, it acquires no narrative ambience. Her own brief and frequently quoted explanation of how she wrote the novel is interesting, but seems more quaint than revelatory and adds little to an explanation of the conflicted narrative. She explained that in writing *The Professor's House* she was experimenting with the *Nouvelle* and the *Roman* and that she was also influenced by Dutch painting. In such paintings the main scene is usually of a warmly furnished room, but with a square window through which ships and the sea are visible. The Tom Outland story is the window in Professor St. Peter's conventional room (*WC in Person* 192-193).

One of the most insightful and articulate evaluations of *The Professor's House* remains Leon Edel's assessment from 1959, in *Stuff of Sleep and Dreams: Experiments in Literary Psychology*. Edel emphasizes that "the novel is not a fully realized work" (202) and that with the awkwardly inserted Tom Outland tale the narrative "is a stitching together of two inconclusive fragments about a professor, his family, and his wish for death and the adventures of a young man alone with the past on a mesa and briefly in touch with the modern urban life of Washington" (205). The episodes "hardly constitute a novel; they convey a picture of [the professor's] deep depression, which

nothing in the book really explains" (205). Having recorded the
stylistic limitations of *A Professor's House,* Edel then focuses on
the titular house and ranges outward and inward from that focus to look into the recesses of Cather's imagination. His theorizing from narrative fact and Cather's biography constitutes
"quite admirably literary criticism"—a term he applies to E. K.
Brown (206). All subsequent critical analysis of *The Professor's
House* is indebted to Edel, especially my own. I will focus less on
the house symbology and more on the romantic-realistic or po-
etic-scientific dichotomy which is the basis of narrative design
and which shows Cather's continued dependence upon conflict
as a major element in her imagination.

That Cather bifurcates her artististic self in the fictive personae of St. Peter and Tom Outland epitomizes the conflict
between romanticism and reality which causes much of the narrative tension that is fundamental to Cather's creative processes.
Prior to his disillusionment and subsequent conversion to tech-
nology, Outland personifies the romantic or idealistic self, now
dead. At Blue Mesa he experiences a "religious emotion" (251)
among the artifacts of the ancient Indians and their "little city of
stone" (201), which he propitiously discovers on Chrismas Eve.
Superficially one of the most idealistic and tragic of Cather's
male protagonists (if indeed that is the proper term for a character who technically never appears in the text), he is actually one
of her most ironic characters. With echoes of Tom Swift and his
fabulous contrivances and adventures, Tom Outland is too un-
bendingly idealistic. His later inventing a "vacuum" which en-
riches others suggests the emptiness of his idealism and is the
key symbol in the romantic-scientific or artistic-materialistic polarity of the narrative structure. The romantic view of the Indians holds them in wonderment, just as Outland does; but the
scientific view, less kind and expressed in early writings about
the Mesa Verde cultures available in the 1920s, showed that the
Anasazi did not transcend the harsh reality of their environment nor were as ethereal as Cather presents them on the narrative surface. Some of the turn-of-the-century journal writings of
Albert Ernest Jenks and studies such as Jesse Walter Fewkes'
*Prehistoric Villages, Castles, and Towers of Southwestern Col-
orado* (1919) offer the realistic view of the Anasazi. Cather of
course visited Mesa Verde and no doubt had read some information about it (at least that distributed by park attendants). She
based Tom Outland's story on the actual explorations of the
Wetherill brothers, who were the first non-Indian discoverers of

Mesa Verde and who were themselves accused of vandalism—
and with whom she talked briefly. She also may have known
some of the scientific writings which dealt with the ancient Indians, though substantiation for such reading is problematic. She
does, however, make her other artist-self an authority on the
Spanish presence in the Southwest, and St. Peter in his defini-
tive studies would certainly have to account for the Spanish contact with the aborigines, the pueblo revolts, the harsh reprisals
against the Indians, and the general subsistence quality of the Indian life. While these Indians were not the Anasazi, they were
often their descendants, and indicators of what the Ancient
One's lives were actually like. A more recent writer, Thomas Y.
Canby, summaries the unromanticized daily life of an Anasazi:

> The fact that you [as an Anasazi] are alive means
> you are beating the odds: A third of your brothers and
> sisters died before age five. . . .
> If you are a woman, you probably own all the fam-
> ily's personal property. One of your possessions is a
> metate, a large troughed stone used for mealing corn and
> other seeds. You are its slave. Day after day you bend
> over it, grinding, grinding, grinding. . . .
> You reach your 40s, and you groan under the accel-
> erating disrepair of old age. Arthritis torments your
> joints. Your teeth, worn to the gums by grit from the
> metate, pain intolerably from abscesses that are eating
> deep into your jawbones. (568, 570)

The point is that the context of the narrative itself and the
availability of extratextual information suggest that Cather could
have been aware of at least enough of the historical or scientific
facts of the Anasazi civilizations to realize that the Indian life
was at best marginal. Moreover, anyone having visited Mesa
Verde, as Cather did, would quickly deduce how treacherous life
in the cliffs must have been. Played out against such possible authorial knowledge, Tom Outland's idyll among the ruins and
his naive, benign interpretation of the Ancient Ones certainly
conveys irony. Moreover, the contrast between what the author
knows and the knowledge she is willing to impart to her fictive
persona enhances our understanding of the conflictive point of
view with which Cather is directing the narrative and which is
geared directly to the irony she wishes to impart. That is,
Cather's irony is marked by the "disparity of understanding"
with which Robert Scholes defines irony (240), for what we as
audience originally think Cather is saying and what on closer ex-

amination we learn she may in fact be saying are quite different.

This ironic disparity is perhaps best demonstrated in Out-land's visit to Washington, D. C., an episode which draws from Cather's own brief working stint in the Capitol (Woodress 147). Outland is depressed by the petty lives of the workers streaming in and out of the offices, "like people in slavery, who ought to be free" (234). The reader's first response to this scene is probably to interpret the comparison between the Washington ciphers and the ancient Indians as Cather's admonition that citizens of the modern world should learn to avoid the demeaning life of the oppressed capitalists and return to the primitive harmony Out-land sees in the extinct basket- and pottery-making Indians. In this particular instance Outland himself is conveying the infor-mation to us as first-person narrator (or perhaps more exactly, as St. Peter superimposing himself as Tom the first-person narra-tor); and even if we do not distrust first-person narrators generi-cally (as we well should), in light of what we know of Outland's intense idealism, we should distrust his narration specifically. Thus, the Washington scenario can convey the opposite message from the one we first assume—a de-romanticized message: the contemporary Washington life is the true reality and is a mod-ern version of the Indian existence which has been distorted via mythologizing and which is conveyed by a biased narrator. By inserting Outland's account of Blue Mesa and his "little city of stone" (201) Cather seems not to idealize the past but to put yes-terday in focus by pointing up a modern analog. The point she makes with such an analogy is that there was no idealistic past and the harsh present is the reality with which we must come to terms. The Indians of Blue Mesa did not survive, and they did not survive because they could not adapt. The workers in Washington may not impress the idealistic Outland with their insectile comings and goings, but they have adapted to an envi-ronment (sometimes harsh) and are enduring if not thriving. We cannot say the same for Outland and the Anasazi. Cather's message is that humans must learn to deal with a considerable amount of unhappiness without making much ado about it.

The "scientific" fact is that the ancient people were terri-fied of unidentified enemies and clung to precipitous cliff faces in continual dread. The beauty of the art they created and which Outland so idealizes did not save them from the "catastrophe [which] had overwhelmed them" (213). Their beautiful water jars, bowls, and yucca-fiber mats still exist only because they are made of tougher stuff than human flesh. The survival of the ar-

tifacts into the twentieth century—the result of their being abandoned on the spot—proves how little faith the Indians placed in
them when disaster came. The reality of the Indians' life is personified less by artistic bowls and more by the mummified
young Indian woman Mother Eve, who epitomizes how unlike
"Paradise" was the Ancient Ones' domain. Eve could have been
one of the women who in the distant past created the beautiful
vessels; but she herself is more emblematic of the canyon terrors.
Speculation is she was caught flagrante delicto by her husband,
who immediately claimed his right of uxoricide and ripped open
her chest, in a grim reversal of the Adamic rib creation myth.
Hundreds of years later "Her mouth [is still] open as if she were
screaming, and her face, through all those years, had kept a look
of terrible agony" (214). That terrified countenance, not the
beautiful bowls, "speaks" for Eve's people, whose hazardous
lives froze their psyches into a scream. As anthropologist Al-
fonso Ortiz says of the Mesa Verdeans, the construction of their
Sun Temple "represents a last great effort, born of despair, to
read the heavens, to fathom the reasons for the ordeal" their
gods were inflicting upon them (Canby 589). In short, the Ancient Ones' temples were the stone equivalent of a prehistoric
theodicy, a stone-age *Paradise Lost*, and the ways of the gods the
temples sought to explain were cruel.

Outland is unaware of how little credence his romanticiz-
ing of the Ancient Ones retains in light of logical scrutiny, but
Cather puts the knowledge into the thoughts of her other artist-
self when Professor St. Peter sadly tells his class that humans can
no longer believe "in the mystery and importance of their own
little individual lives" (68) because science has removed the
potential for miracles from human thinking. In contrast to Outland, St. Peter survives this lost paradise because he has modi-
fied the very idealism which motivates his young counterpart.
St. Peter's idealism has turned sour and he wishes to die.
Though he has consciously given less thought to suicide than to
"embezzling," when "he was confronted by accidental extinction,
he had felt no will to resist" (282). He who writes volumes about
the dead past does not (perhaps cannot) articulate his ability to
survive; but it emanates from his willingness to compromise his
idealism—that is, to adapt. As he says after his near asphyxia-
tion, he had never before "learned to live without delight," but
now he would have to learn how to do so. He compares his realization topically to Prohibition, and takes some comfort in
knowing that if he found himself in a Prohibition country, he

could forsake what small pleasure life still affords him and "learn to live with sherry" (282). His major compromise is seen in the two houses which stand as the metaphorical poles of his spiritual quandary: St. Peter manages to make the transition from the past to the present by living with his family in the new house while keeping his work room and garden at the old house. That is, he separates his spiritual or artistic self from his quotidian roles of husband and father without having to destory either. We do not know how long this particular compromise will succeed, since he may have to relinquish the old house once Lillian returns and reestablishes life in the new house; but evidence suggests that St. Peter is capable of making necessary adjustments, exploring (like his beloved Spanish adventurers) new modes of survival. Cather does not try to pretend St. Peter's compromises will bring happiness, but at least he survives with the belief (illusory perhaps) that he can face tomorrow with "the ground under his feet" (283). In this respect St. Peter is the true modern "hero" of the narrative, for he endures and tries to define himself by the process of acting. Tom Outland, on the contrary, is dead because he could not make similar compromises, although his combined scientific ability and artistic sensitivity should have made him ideally suited for similar adaptation. He is Cather's personification of how technical formulations and conventional expectations must not be allowed to dominate instinctive, emotional responses.

The Spanish adventurers to whom St. Peter has devoted eight long volumes were looking for Cibola—the fabled cities of gold and other riches. Yet before the explorations concluded, the explorers themselves valued sanctuaries more than wealth. We do not know much about St. Peter's adventurers, since Cather is careful to keep the contents of his narrative a literal "hidden" text within her own. Other Spanish/Indian histories of the Southwest, however, such as Paul Horgan's *Great River* (1954), detail the cultures along the Rio Grande and give us glimpses of what St. Peter must have included in his own history. St. Peter emulates the Spanish explorers both in physical appearance and psychic questing. He has symbolically traced the path the Spanish soldiers hoped for, leaving the prairie emptiness to which he had been sent against his will and dwelling in the golden city, there to find fame and monetary awards. He discovers, however, that "sanctuary" and the domestic, spiritual peace which the term suggests are lost to him. The "house" which once connoted repose and contemplation is now associated instead with deadly gases, domestic turmoil, invasion by philistines. The clash of domestic expectations with the harsh reality of domiciles remains unresolved within the narrative, and from this irresolution comes the depression that Edel notes. Novels of the past might have manipulated reality to resolve such conflicts, a point which Susan Lanser makes when she discusses how the traditional prescriptive point of view required that narrative technique be evaluated according to preconceived moral and aesthetic criteria (19). The modern narrative, however, is not obligated to such resolution. As Keith May and others have noted, modern fiction is marked by action and choice, which in turn defines self, as opposed to the previous modes which tried to define self from external or socially prescribed values. In posing the question of selfhood, modern novelists such as Cather, according to May, ask "How can I know what I am until I see what I do?" (88). This attitude explains the closure of *The Professor's House* when St. Peter reveals that he has undergone some change which the reader (and St. Peter's family) does not comprehend; but the reason for that lack of understanding is that St. Peter himself is still in the process of defining his future actions. Those actions in turn will define St. Peter, outside the audience's view and beyond its knowing. He is still exploring.

We might well suspect another level of irony beneath the one just outlined, an irony lurking in the deep structure of the narrative. Cather emphasizes how the beautiful vessels of the Ancient Ones belie the harshness of the culture which created those vessels and how the pottery ultimately fell victim to modern commercialism. The art of writing which St. Peter holds in such high esteem may be equally vulnerable, and her deployment of the ancient art smacks of Catherean self mockery. The artistic idealism we see in the earlier works such as *Song of the Lark* and Thea Kronborg's devotion to her music is now tinged with despair and is itself suspect as a personal religion. As James Woodress says, "Throughout her life [Cather] gave art her highest priority, preferring her work to society, to family, to friends" and "sublimated her sexual impulses in her work" (125). In *The Professor's House* she is reexamining that commitment. St. Peter says—rather forlornly echoing Cather's own equation of Art with God—that "Art and religion (they are the same thing, in the end, of course) have given man the only happiness he has ever had" (69). Yet evidence all about him proves that this sentiment is at best problematic: Outland's Indians are dead, gone, and their beautiful bowls and pots desecrated; and St. Peter's own life has deteriorated into routine misery. Not only does Cather express sympathy for Lillian St. Peter in light of her husband's monomaniacal devotion to his art (a point we will explore later), but she shows that his Oxford Award brings him academic renown and respect but no domestic peace or personal happiness. (Cather, we recall, won the Pulitzer Prize in 1923.) Nowhere in the narrative, for instance, do his children express any abiding interest in his Spanish studies or praise his accomplishments. The pragmatic or scientific value of art is more nearly seen in his daughter Kathleen's amateurish dabbling in painting and in her husband Scott McGregor's asinine "prose poems," which Cather borrows from Sinclair Lewis's *Babbitt*. The drivel McGregor writes is the same type which the fool Babbitt deems the highest possible art form, the ultimate marriage of aesthetics and capitalistic boosterism: "When your pocket is under-moneyed and your fancy is over-girled, you'll have to admit while you're cursing it, it's a mighty darned good old world" (44). Just such philistinism may well have been what Cather had in mind when in a December, 1924, interview with the *New York Times* she uncharacteristically launched a bitter attack against Americans' attitude toward art. The novel has deteriorated into trash, she said, because in their desire for profits publishers need to supply the prosperous middle class with something to "fill up commuting boredom every morning" (*WC in Person* 68). All her emphasis upon prostitution, compromise, and lost art offers evidence that much of this distress over the state of the American novel reflects Cather's own doubts about the art of fiction and her place as a well-paid practitioner of that art in a society more concerned with taking "off the edge of boredom" and filling "empty leisure" than with culture (68).

On this same plane with authorial self-doubt we find the unexpected irony. Hayden White once noted that "a trope can be seen as the linguistic equivalent of a psychological mechanism of defense" (2); and *The Professor's House* witnesses White's observation. Beneath its basic imagery of the romantic-scientific conflict and the other elements just discussed lie the dilemmas that troubled Cather. No matter how much she tried to repress them, they insinuated themselves into the deep structure of the narrative. By unconsciously emblematizing her doubts and fears, her tropes become psychological defense mechanisms. Three such tropes are especially important: the socioeconomic, the erotic, and the artistic metaphors.

In the discord which marks the relationship between St. Peter and his wife, daughters, and sons-in-law, the socioeconomic conflict is played out microcosmically. The prairie frontier in which St. Peter spent his formative years is moribund if not dead, its values inexorably replaced by capitalistic greed and mindless boosterism that cultivate neither creativity nor the intrepidity necessary for exploration. None of St. Peter's family creates or actively explores new areas, either geographically or intellectually. All are dedicated to generating money or, as in the case of Scott McGregor, to prostituting art for money. The explanatory cliché is that one cannot serve the god Art and mammon too, and Cather regrets a lost state of innocence symbolized by St. Peter's Kansas childhood (and her own Nebraska childhood). *My Ántonia* and its children have already demonstrated how the Imagination is fueled by the "child" that lives in the artist's psyche. The open freedom of the prairie and the rural economy it suggests have been replaced by houses that constrict space and by capitalistic enterprises that produce neither essential goods nor aesthetic satisfaction. St. Peter tries to deny responsibility for the changes. As he tells himself, with noticeable rationalization, "His career, his wife, his family, were not his life at all, but a chain of events which had happened to him. All these things had nothing to do with the person he was in the beginning" (264). The irony of the comment is that St. Peter's present state has everything to do with his origins, even if he could somehow be exonerated from responsibility for the moves and decisions which have led to his current fame, fortune and despair. Moreover, in St. Peter's comment there seems to be not only a desire to escape responsibility for the monetary rewards he has received and the subsequent emblems of financial success but an apologia too for his efforts to find happiness in the conventionally defined relationships, for his writing, and for his career. If his books, his wife, his family are not his "life," then the obvious question becomes "what is his life?" There is no logical answer, of course, because *The Professor's House* as novel is the "history" of that life in which art and money are inextricably combined; and unless Cather herself as artist is "lying" to us, then we as readers of her text know rather precisely what constitutes St. Peter's life, just as the readers of his history of the Spanish explorers would know about those lives. The text reveals that St. Peter's thinking is involuted, and suggests the dilemma which Cather was facing relative to her own career.

In the much-discussed symbols of the two sewing forms,

which St. Peter associates with a natural linguistic example of
metonymy (17-18), we see the continuation of Cather's psychosexual conflict, something which causes Leon Edel to ponder if
perhaps we as audience are "being offered a virtually meaning-
less diagram, highly speculative, of the unconscious fantasies of
the professor, derived though it may be from the manifest material placed in the book by the author" (209). The forms are con-
fusing images at best, witnessing, as Edel says, "Freud's ideas
about infantile sexuality" that pervade the narrative (209). They
suggest that one can assume the physical shape of the female
without possessing the essence of femininity; and paradoxically,
that dichotomy explains their appeal to St. Peter, who suffers
from "lingering infantile needs" (Edel 209) and whose death
wish they help to define. In their mindless, immobile lack of
essence, they are safe. They are "dead" and are in that sense a
projection of his sexuality into the more encompassing realm of
death which his suicidal impulses entail. In death all things are
safe. Moreover, through the forms he can endorse conventional
male-female sexuality without having to confront the private
realities which such relationships demand and which his wife
and daughters personify. Even when he transfers his interest in
the forms to their caretaker Augusta, the relationship does not
move beyond minor titillations and inconsequential jests. Augusta in many respects is less erotic than the buxom forms, for
she is an aging, "methodical spinster, a German Catholic and
very devout" (16). His manuscripts and her patterns
"interpenetrated" on the work table (22), but only in that linguistic pun is there any sexuality.

To be sure, fetishism or perhaps even iconolagny attach to
St. Peter's fixation on the wire-ribbed "ladies," and emanating as
they do from Cather's creative impulses they suggest how she
may have viewed her own homoeroticism as she approached
her fiftieth year. Though much has been made of Cather's anti-
feminism in the novel, her sentiments seem less anti-feminine
and more the sublimated disappointments of a woman whose
erotic relationships had not proven gratifying. The "real"
women in the narrative (with the possible exception of Augusta)
are collectively unappealing, given to superficialities, jealousy
and greed, thereby suggesting the values for which natural human affections have been bartered. Not only may women such
as Lillian and her daughters serve to personify similar traits
which she feared in herself, but they may serve also to personify
the disappointments Cather had experienced in other females.

The sewing forms with their domestic, traditional female connotations are therefore convenient and appropriate emblems of these corporeal women. In this light, the forms stand as the objective correlatives of psychic fears reified via the creative process, and are thus not simply satirical icons of insensitive, mindless feminine types in general.

Cather personifies in Lillian St. Peter an image of what she feared she herself might become and more generally an image of the pathos which results when a dynamic young woman falls victim to romance and the matrimonial, maternal trap. In *A Lost Lady* Cather identifies with Marian Forrester and therefore constructs the prostitution motif around her so that she might then have just cause for rejecting the emblem she has created. Cather uses a similar technique with Lillian St. Peter. Lillian is "a woman who would grow always more exacting" (261), and serves as another example of how Cather used her imagination to reify psychic elements in order to evaluate them as part of her potential being. That Lillian and St. Peter met in Paris while each was studying there suggests that like Cather she appreciated French culture, once led the "bohemian" existence, and was once devoted to the life of the imagination which her husband personifies. (Though Cather never joined the Left Bank lesbian community, a number of her female characters are associated with Paris). Once a vibrant "pink and gold," Lillian is now tarnished, a "little gray" (36). Herself a lost lady, she has converted from the religion of art and aesthetics to the worship of the dollar, a god to which the new house is the shrine and for which St. Peter's creative energy has paid the price. In the Paris days she was a loving, exciting companion to St. Peter; but now she has deteriorated into coy lusting after her son-in-law Marsellus, who personifies money. (More-sell-us the name suggests.) For him she dons the anachronistic virginal "white silk crêpe that had been the most successful of her summer dresses, and an orchid velvet ribbon about her shining hair" (77). Her "coquetry" merely amuses St. Peter, now the objective observer, and leads him to conclude sardonically that "She was less intelligent and more sensible than he had thought her" (79). As he is to other facets of his life, he seems insensitive to the fact that his wife's progressive dependency upon money as a source of gratification symbolizes his own failure as husband, both erotically and otherwise.

Echoing the prostitution motif and the money-eroticism equations in *A Lost Lady*, Lillian's attraction to the philistine

Marsellus symbolizes the selling of one's soul and body for money. Perhaps expressing Cather's own concern at having to encounter her imago, St. Peter must repress "a feeling of nervous dread" when he learns Lillian is returning to him from Europe (273). Herself recently returned from visiting Isabelle McClung Hambourg in Paris, flush with the large royalties and Pulitzer money just received from *One of Ours,* and planning to build a new cottage soon on Grand Manan island, Cather no doubt was ironically cognizant of how much more than double I's were shared by Lillian and Willa. Had she not recently left her long time publisher Houghton Mifflin because Knopf could make more money for her? While such economic success was deserved and while the conflict between Art and Lucre is classic, Cather may well have perceived her late-arriving rewards as threatening to taint the artistic integrity which had sustained her from the first days of her writing. Bernice Slote, for instance, recognizes the "natural nobility" which Cather saw in Art, her intense devotion to "the aristocracy of genius in all its bewildering variety, color, and degree; genius (which is of God) made complete through human achievement, in the particular human accent of body, voice, hand, or word" (*Kingdom of Art* 115). When that "aristocracy" commenced to look a bit like a "plutocracy," Cather worried.

To lessen the impact of such threats to her integrity, Cather therefore tries to distance herself as much as possible from Lillian and the other female personas who reflect similar values. Aside from using them as personifications of the worst traits that she wished to avoid in herself (greed, jealousy, disloyalty), Cather does not use any of the women as a projection of her artist self. She grants that important (one might even say sacred) role once again to the male persona, dividing the persona this time between her aging, disillusioned self (St. Peter) and her young idealistic self (Tom Outland).

We might note, however, that despite her rejection of Lillian as her artist self, Cather has noticeable compassion for Mrs. St. Peter. The "unsaid" part of the text, that part which Lanser rightfully recognizes as being as crucial as what is literally on the page (42), is Lillian's emotional response to the inordinate amount of time which St. Peter has devoted to those volumes and volumes of Spanish American history. St. Peter over the years of their marriage has shifted his allegiance from his wife to his work, secondarily to his teaching and to Outland. The lack of attention—sexually, spiritually, and otherwise—which Lillian has experienced is easily imagined. Little wonder she is jealous of Outland, that she feels justified in having her husband use his prize money to purchase the new house as a kind of monetary reparation for emotional debts, and that she sublimates her own erotic impulses into coy flirtations with the sons-in-law who offer her the attention she desires. Her resentment, overall, is less than it justifiably might be, for we will see in *Sapphira and the Slave Girl* how retaliatory a vindictive mate can become. In Lillian's emotional deprivation and St. Peter's devotion to his art, we glimpse Cather's own dichotomized self and again hear the questions about whether Art is worth the sacrifice of conventional human relationships. "Art of every kind," she noted at the age of seventeen, "is an exacting master, more so than even Jehovah" (Woodress 74). It was not a master with whom she was totally at ease.

In the divided images of the aging writer-professor and the idealistic young Tom Outland we see once again some of the mental tensions that drove Cather's creativity. St. Peter is the dedicated interpreter of history, the creator of images and narratives which both preserve the past and help satisfy the creative impulses of the recorder. Tom Outland, on the other hand, is the active "doer," the individual about whom history is written, the man whose life is already moving toward mythology. In fact, within the narrative it is often difficult to ascertain where the actuality of Outland's life leaves off and recollected fictions begin. (As James Woodress has noted, Cather "often treats her own life as though it were fiction" [42].) St. Peter's transforming Outland into values which must not be "translated into the vulgar tongue" (62) is a case in point, since in reality Outland consciously chooses to spend much time and energy in developing a mechanical contrivance which he surely knows will "translate" quite readily into "vulgar" applications. Having been outraged by the commercializing of his precious Indian artifacts, Outland sets out to prove that he can be more commercial than anyone else—a somewhat immature "if you can't defeat them, join them" philosophy. The unflattering reality of Outland's life is that he fails in most actions he undertakes, even though the actions themselves later become the stuff of tales and romance. He fails in his mission to Washington, he fails to preserve the Indian artifacts, he fails to patent his invention, and he fails (perhaps intentionally) to preserve himself as a soldier. His falling down the stairs at St. Peter's house upon first visit foreshadows subsequent failures. Instead of saving and preserving humanity,

Outland creates a device which when used maliciously can imperil humanity; then he runs to his death to avoid the moral consequences. Therefore, St. Peter's unrealistic view of Outland raises the question of whether such distortion of fact is beneficial or detrimental—a quandary which has a number of corollary questions relative to the fictionalizing process, since fiction, more so than history, is a premeditated distortion of reality.

Such tension between the passive recorder of events (St. Peter) and the active shaper of events (Outland) suggests the fear of unbalanced values which perplexed Cather, who continued to quest after answers concerning the ultimate purpose and value of the artistic process in a dynamic universe. The dynamics of her universe, however, rather than being Christian or even Darwinian, seem not to tend toward heaven or perfection but toward extinction—as witnessed by the ancient Indians and Outland and previously by the genocidal madness of World War I and Claude Wheeler's personal death. Art, Cather shows in her narrative, does not preserve the life of the artist or of the civilizations he or she seeks to explore, no matter what Keats and other of the Romantics may have taught. As Keith May notes in contemplating psychology and the modern novel, "each action, mental or physical, is an attempt at self-realization, at constituting oneself as a solid being" (84). Art only leaves behind a relatively imprecise record of the creative processes of individuals who have sought to make the abstract perceivable—and who in that process try to perceive themselves. Like her artist self in his nebulous state, Cather is in the process of definition, with her psyche still dynamic and not static.

The narrative structure of *The Professor's House* is determined as much by Cather's desire to explain and cope with these socioeconomic, erotic, and artistic dilemmas as by her technical concern for the conventions of narrative form. While the refusal to be dictated to by traditional expectations is itself admirable and would soon lead to the greatness of *Death Comes for the Archbishop*, in *The Professor's House* the results are unsatisfying. Cather's overriding "defense" mechanism explains, therefore, the "stitching together" structure which Leon Edel saw as a major factor in *The Professor's House* not being fully realized. As Woodress notes, "Nothing can hide the spiritual malaise of Professor St. Peter/Willa Cather" (367). Indeed, the malaise continues and becomes even more pronounced in her next novel, *My Mortal Enemy*.

Works Cited

Canby, Thomas Y. "The Anasazi: Riddles of the Ruins." *National Geographic* 5 (November 1982): 562-592.

Cather, Willa. *A Lost Lady* (1923). New York: Knopf, 1966.

—. *The Kingdom of Art: Willa Cather's First Principles and Critical Statements: 1893-1896.* Ed. Bernice Slote. Lincoln: U of Nebraska P, 1966.

—. *My Mortal Enemy* (1926). New York: Knopf, 1967.

—. *The Professor's House.* New York: Knopf, 1925.

—. *Willa Cather in Person: Interviews, Speeches, and Letters.* Ed. L. Brent Bohlke. Lincoln: U of Nebraska P, 1986.

Edel, Leon. *Stuff of Sleep and Dreams: Experiments in Literary Psychology.* New York: Harper & Row, 1959. Rpt. in part in *Critical Essays on Willa Cather,* Ed. John J. Murphy. Boston: Hall, 1984. 200-217.

Fewkes, Jesse Walter. *Prehistoric Villages, Castles, and Towers of Southwestern Colorado.* Smithsonian Institute, Bureau of American Ethnology, Bulletin 70. Washington, DC: Government Printing Office, 1919.

Gay, Peter. *Freud: A Life for Our Time.* New York: Norton, 1988.

Lanser, Susan Sniader. *The Narrative Act: Point of View in Prose Fiction.* Princeton: Princeton U P, 1981.

May, Keith. *Out of the Maelstrom: Psychology and the Novel in the Twentieth Century.* New York: St. Martin's, 1977.

Scholes, Robert and Robert Kellogg. *The Nature of Narrative.* New York: Ocford U P, 1966.

Stevick, Philip. "Introduction." *The Theory of the Novel.* New York: Free Press, 1967.

White, Hayden. *Topics of Discourse: Essays in Cultural Criticism.* Baltimore: John Hopkins U P, 1978.

Wooddress, James. *Willa Cather: A Literary Life.* Lincoln: U of Nebraska P, 1987.

6
My Mortal Enemy: Struggle of the Artistic Self
Against Nothingness

Using the American female poets of the 1950s and 1960s as criteria, we could argue that female writers a generation or two younger than Cather were characterized by the creative impulse to leave nothing private in their personal lives. Their art was the conduit through which their lifeblood flowed into the public domain. Their abortions, menstrual cycles, fornications (both homo- and heterosexual), suicide attempts, and the most intimate apertures of their bodies and souls were their poems. Having lost contact with the old Calvinist God and abandoned faith in costly psychoanalysts (usually male), writers such as Sylvia Plath, Ann Sexton, and Adrienne Rich confessed everything to an audience fascinated by the sanguineous spectacle and willing to invest considerable psychic capital in the free verse lamentations. As Sylvia Plath suggests in "Lady Lazarus," the audience came as if to a carnival freak show. These confessional poets make a point about Cather's *My Mortal Enemy* (1926): as an expression of the authorial self, it is the diametrical opposite of the poems typical of the confessional poets. Whereas the confessionals attempt to expose everything to the audience, try to eliminate the barriers between author, fictive self, and external audience, Cather in *My Mortal Enemy* tries (with noticeable success) to conceal totally the authorial self and still put text on the page. Shortly after *My Mortal Enemy* was published, Cather asked Elizabeth Sergeant if she thought psychoanalysis would help her (Sergeant 238). There is no record of exactly what events precipitated the question or that Cather followed up by visiting a psychoanalyst, but considering Cather's distrust of anything Freudian, her asking does suggest that at the time she was writing *My Mortal Enemy* she had reached a point of desperation. But rather than finding release through confession, Cather suppressed. The novel is like a psychic tomb into which Cather has retreated. Aside from the tone that is morbid and depressing (we have seen the suicidal tendencies already in her work, and in that respect she is much like Plath and Sexton), Cather represses her creative self so thoroughly that few reliable indications escape to tell us where the audience-author contact is supposed to commence in our effort to understand her text and the characters she sequesters therein. David Daiches was correct when he recognized years ago that "the change from adventurous generosity to bitter resentment" which we see in Myra Henshawe "is the product of poisons working within the character, and these we are never allowed to see" (103).

Yet, regardless of how repressed and obscure the text, *My Mortal Enemy* is proof that Cather's imagination, no matter how conflicted, never permitted her to lapse into the final despair of artistic silence—a silence which for Plath, Sexton, and non-confessionals such as Hemingway and Hart Crane was but a momentary stay against the ultimate silence. We know that suicide was part of Cather's creative self, and no doubt part of her somatic self as well, but we cannot logically speculate that her choices in 1925-26 were either write or die. There does seem to be, however, buried so deep in the subtext of *My Mortal Enemy* as to be almost imperceptible, a near epic struggle of the psyche against Nothingness. The text proves little about the art of fiction, but it does prove that in midst of the most traumatic of conflicts, Cather's art sustained her, even when pain and suffering were its wage.

Edith Lewis barely mentions *My Mortal Enemy*, though she talks at length about the creation of the other works. As James Woodress notes, it has the "most obscure provenance" of any of Cather's novels (379). Cather, still suppressing and always quick to mislead the unwary about her private world (even to lie at times, as she did about her birth date) stated years after she had worked herself out of the darkness which *My Mortal Enemy* epitomizes that she knew Myra's prototype "very well, and the portrait drawn in the story was much as she remembered her" (380). Moreover, Cather added, many friends readily recognized the model, who had been dead fifteen years when the story was written. Ever since, biographers have speculated about the mysterious lost lady but have never been able positively to identify her. One plausible speculation is the most obvious: Cather was referring to herself. The woman she knew "very well" is Willa

Cather from an earlier time. What private jest she may have had in mind when she mentioned fifteen years dead is unknowable, but we may assume that it was just that—a joke—or that something happened about 1910-12 which ultimately drove her near to despair and which she looked back upon as having altered the course of her life. She would have been about forty at the time, a typical period of biochemical, psychic alterations and reconsiderations. A time for visions and revisions.

Moreover, the 1910-12 period was a crowded time in her life. Her close friend and mentor Sarah Orne Jewett died; she first met Elizabeth Sergeant and Zoë Akins, both who would become her intimate friends; *McClure's* magazine folded; she moved to Bank Street in Greenwich Village; and her health—which was never before a problem—commenced to deteriorate rapidly. She spent weeks in the hospital from an operation to cure acute mastoiditis in February of 1910 and was back in the hospital again for most of January 1912 recuperating from a mysterious ailment, which may well have been a hysterectomy or similar "female disorder" that she was especially secretive about. And she published her first novel, thereby publicly challenging the male world that dominated long prose fiction.   James Woodress says that about 1910 Cather tried to escape "the sour, ill-tempered, fussy woman she feared she was becoming" (213). What cause-effect relationships, points-counterpoints we can make of these events is uncertain; but the fact remains that the characters in *My Mortal Enemy* collectively portray a soul in some torment. That fact, coupled with the sense of the unrevealed that permeates the novel, suggests that Cather is offering a very personal statement, one she could not have easily borrowed from another, and one she probably would have repressed entirely if the compulsion to translate her emotions into art had not been so overwhelming.

T. S. Eliot's convenient term "objective correlative" might help explain the audience-author problem in *My Mortal Enemy* more thoroughly. Eliot uses the phrase to express the way in which an author indirectly conveys emotions or psychological states to the audience. The vehicle of conveyance can be objects or images or just about any perceivable "thing" that will cause the desired response in the audience. Implied in the concept of "objective correlative" is a contract between audience and author: once the author has formulated the images or objects or whatever for a particular emotion, the relationship between the objects and the anticipated response will remain consistent—not rigid, but consistent. The audience expects and even demands a certain degree of opacity from the author. That is, the objects, series of events, or other literary devices that correlate to our specific psychological reaction cannot be too simplistic or pellucid. Otherwise, we are merely going through a Pavlovian exercise, not an intellectual, emotional experience. So simplemindedness we do not want. The intended destinies for *My Mortal Enemy*, however, are very obscure. Cather gives an inadequate number of objective correlatives, and does not always fulfill the implied contract for those which she does give us. We are left, therefore, with minimal emotional responses and feel in turn that the novel itself has no directing soul or psyche. What we have instead are items such as houses, literary allusions, fragments of construction from which to hypothesize a culture. Borrowing an image from Tom Outland, we are left with shards but no recognizable bowl; no holistic design. The technique is untypical of Cather, an anomaly; but it is all we have to go on.

Myra Driscoll Henshawe of Parthia, Illinois, exhibits many of the personality traits of Willa Cather. If nothing else, we have once again the duplicated l's which weld Cather to her fictive imago: Willa, Driscoll-Nellie, and later "Molly" when Oswald reverts to using Myra's nickname. Biographers offer more substantial parallels. Woodress, for instance, points out Cather's deep hatreds, her tendency to cynicism, and her desperate turning to religion for solace (386). Moreover, Nellie Birdseye is also Cather's observing self. Psychologically, therefore, the novel seems an attempt by the objective Cather to stand apart and watch herself deteriorate into bitchiness and misery and then find salvation in peaceful death. It is not a pretty scenario, especially since one of the sharpest ironies of the narrative is that even with the fragments of Catholic theology which Cather gives her aging heroine, Myra seems more hell bent than heaven bound. Aside from the fact that she exhibits precious few "Christian" traits, the sacraments she receives prior to her death are symbolically and literally nullified by her being cremated. Oswald's scattering her mortal ashes in the vast frigid waters around Alaska is distinctly pagan, and suggests a revenge which the long-suffering husband enjoys. Even if Myra somehow drifted into Purgatory, nobody remains behind to pray for her immortal soul. Oswald has happily died pursuing the free wilderness life he should have been pursuing all along (according to Nellie) and Nellie is too fascinated by the evil string of amethysts and too dulled by her pedagogical routine to consider such theological subtleties. If Marian Forrester is merely a lost lady, Myra Driscoll Henshawe is a damned lost one.

Conscious of this heaven-hell motif, Cather tries to objectify it—tries, that is, to give us the objective correlative. Thus, like a fragment of a broken Indian bowl, we have the black-white symbology. First seen in Illinois, Myra wears "black velvet," has black hair with streaks of "glistening white" in it (12). The snow in New York is "a line of white upon a line of black" (34). And in California Myra has "an ebony crucifix with an ivory Christ" (109). The image progression is easy enough to theorize about: the image is sexual or profane in Illinois, where Myra looks like a "Persian goat" (12) and is suggestively "playing on cousin Bert's guitar" (11); it suggests innocence forewarned by impending evil in New York, where the naive Nellie imagines the trees and shrubs looking like sociable people but then ironically notes the black lines formed by the white snow on the limbs; and it is both innocent and evil in California where the purity of the white Christ is stark against the black cross on which He died. In discussing *My Ántonia*, we noted that Cather avoids the singular good-evil parallels which the black-white symbology immediately connotes, using such objects as the black and white badger to expand meaning far beyond the conventional responses and to inculcate in the text chronological, moral, and psychological implications. Knowing that she has set that precedent and that she was revising *My Ántonia* in the same year she published *My Mortal Enemy*, we might naturally look for deployment of similar imagery. In the later novel, however, the imagery seems more superimposed than integral and does not expand outward to encompass cousin images such as light-dark, day-night, or seasonal variations. Even in stating such frustrations, however, we are forced back to the audience-author contract we noted earlier. Expecting a certain object or motif to function in any preconceived fashion is audience presumptuousness. The author may have entirely different intent in mind from that which we are assuming. Just because she puts us on the Burlington train and takes us to Denver in one novel does not mean we can safely assume the Burlington train will deliver us to Denver in the next—even though the train, like the black-white image, is familiar to all who see it. Sidetracking and derailing are always possibilities. As audience, therefore, we are left with some awkward responses. We first feel that the paucity of articulated meaning is Cather's fault, a narrative shortcoming; but then we must entertain the possibility that we are obtuse and that the fault lies in our own failure to uncover and decipher the clues which Cather supplies. In this broad sense the contract of the objective correlative fails and we are left ill at ease with *My Mortal Enemy*.

An explanatory hypothetical syllogism might be derived from the black-white images: profane love (heterosexual lust) kills innocence; with innocence dead, we seek salvation in spiritual love or grace; the modern world (epitomized by San Francisco) renders such grace impossible and we are left holding and being mocked by a dead savior on a crucifix purchased by ten-dollar gold pieces. Such theorizing requires much extrapolation, the putting together of a lot of scattered fragments, for Cather neither invites such connections in the narrative construct nor offers adequate subtextual clues to validate hypothetical ethics. Nellie, for instance, is the one associated with the black lines on white snow early in the novel; but Myra is the one who clings to the ivory Jesus; and apart from our own unilateral extrapolating there is little transference one to the other which joins the two black-white images in the theological unity our syllogism implies. Nellie has few discernible religious impulses, seems more sympathetic to the "free thinker" Oswald than to Myra, and closes her narrative with superstitious remarks about unlucky amethysts and romantic love stories. Since the purple amethysts once belonged to Myra, and since they connote hedonism and not spirituality as does the crucifix, the black-white symbology is not carried through to a logical conclusion. That is, the image which puts the audience in final simultaneous contact with Myra and Nellie is the amethysts, not the black-white objects. In *A Lost Lady*, as we recall, Cather ironically over-emphasizes the sexuality, makes it so conspicuous we cannot help but discover and ponder it. Ultimately the prostitution motif is cohesive and informative, and functions effectively as the objective correlative between audience and author, Yet, here in *My Mortal Enemy*, she goes to the opposite extreme, becomes so sparse and obscure that very little is objectified.

One clue to intent which she does give is a geographical progression. She constructs an erratic journey which moves from Illinois to New York and ends in California, a state that for Cather epitomized Strange Land and for which, we recall, she also used as the place of origin for Marian Forrester. She knew little about California in 1926 but would return a few years later to tend her dying mother. Her opinion of it did not alter. She loathed the state, viewing it as one of the most hideous places on earth and feeling constantly out of place while there (Woodress 419). For Cather to send her fictive self into such exile implies an impulse to punish that exceeds the guilts and moments of self disgust we have witnessed in the earlier novels. In disregarding her uncle's pronouncements about sex and marriage, Myra rebels against the patriarchal hegemony—much as Cather herself had done in Red Cloud with her cross-dressing and her homoeroticism. As we have seen, however, Cather's attitudes toward the prevailing social dynamics were very ambiguous, in keeping with the ambiguousness of her own sexuality. Thus, Myra flagrantly breaks too many of the laws Cather had constructed for herself: she foolishly rejects wealth and social status; she publicly proclaims her sexual preferences by running away with Oswald; she lets her emotions overcome her reason; and she flaunts the Catholic dogma which masquerades as tradition by marrying a Protestant German "free thinker."

Such overt rebellion against the status quo was uncharacteristic of Cather. As early as *O Pioneer!*, she severely punishes Myra's psychic prototype, Marie Tovesky Shabata. Marie too is a head-strong girl who runs away with a man who, like Oswald, does not have her parents' blessings and who turns out to be vastly different from the image constructed in the young wife's imagination. In this instance, ironically, Mr. Tovesky relents and ultimately buys his daughter and her new husband a farm. His tolerance, however, proves unwise, for Marie's sexual impulses have not been quelled by marriage and the husband of choice. She dares entertain erotic thoughts of another. Thus, since the father has failed to punish his daughter, Cather intercedes and shows the consequence of such socially unapproved eroticism: she murders Marie. The scene offers a trauma-laden instance of psychological surgery, a bloody removal of the sexual self (Marie) from the nonsexual self (Alexandra). The surgery, however, is not totally successful, and the sexual self somehow remains viable. Thus in Myra Henshawe, we see the reappearance of the type woman which Marie Shabata personifies (the name similarity is self-evident). Myra's and Marie's fate indicate how determined Cather was to purge the sexually active female from her psyche, how determined she was to eradicate marriage from her thoughts. Simply "killing" the impulses no longer suffices, as it does symbolically when she has Myra die; now she wants also to punish severely the fictive self who exhibits the impulses. Even in the brutal killing of Marie, cather allows death to come within minutes. With Myra, however, Cather gives us a protracted disease-ridden and miserable death scene. Taking Marie and Myra collectively, we see a reflection of the irony Cather constructs for Claude Wheeler: it is better to die young, no matter how violently, than to live too long until the cancers of both body and soul come to punish and consume us. In this light, and after considering Myra's prolonged suffering, Cather's eradication of the young Marie may be seen as a blessing unaware.

Another possible theory is that Cather is attempting to say something about the dangers of separating artistic or intellectual existence from the sometimes awful but nonetheless vital quotidian reality—a warning Thomas Mann conveyed eloquently in *The Magic Mountain*, a novel which Cather read but claimed not to have liked and which was published 1924, translated 1927 (Butcher 361). The dedication to art versus devotion to friends, and things of this world was a battle which raged in Cather from first to last, and its presence in *My Mortal Enemy* would not be surprising. However, textual evidence does not offer adequate support for such assumptions. No one in the novel successfully leads a life of the intellect. The poetress Anne Aylward tries, but is dying of tuberculosis and seems more an exotic hothouse flower than a viable thinker. The narrator is certainly no intellect. Nellie is a pedagogue but no thinker. She is as obtuse in the last lines as in the first, a fact which Cather does succeed in conveying objectively: Upon first meeting Myra, Nellie stares at her "necklace of carved amethysts," causing Myra sarcastically to tell her she will remove it if it bothers her so much (13). Oswald later gives the necklace to Nellie, and the last time we hear from her she tells us she refuses to wear the necklace because she superstitiously believes the amethysts to be unlucky (122). Then she immediately begins to comment about "the bright beginning of a love story" (122), thereby naively juxtaposing her belief in two literally unreasonable systems—superstition and romantic love. And as for art in the novel, it appears only indirectly, primarily in the operatic allusions. The artist whom we hear or see most is one Ewan Gray, a love-struck young Scotch actor who is about to marry Myra's friend Esther Sinclair. The puns on the names here (wan and gray; clear sin), indicate how little credence we can give to Gray as one meant to personify art, at least an art with dynamics. On a larger scale, the ineptness of Nellie's own narrative suggests her lack of artistic or creative essence. Because Nellie is the first-person narrator of the tale, any quarrels we have with its design must be directed at her. Cather may well have intended to make Nellie a narrator whose reporting style is too sparse, too beside the point, too superficial to communicate in the traditional author-audience fashion. If that were her purpose, she succeeded admirably, though the ultimate motive for offering such a narrator remains obscure. The point is that while some clues suggest Cather may have had a rather encompassing idea in mind relative to the conflict between the artistic life and the quotidian life, she does not realize the concept in this particular narrative.

The same incompleteness haunts Myra as a fictive persona. Of her suffering, Myra cries out like Job: "I have not deserved it" (113). She claims, but only in whispers to herself, that she has "faithfully nursed others in sickness" and "been true in friendship" (113). Her claims may well be valid, but the audience has not been witness to such noble deeds. If we are meant to respond with compassion, pathos, even disgust at what sounds like self pity, we do not have adequate motivations for doing so. Again the objective correlatives which transmit Myra's deeds to our emotions are not present; and we cannot accept Myra's rhetoric and brief catalog of good service as adequate stimuli for psychological response—especially since Myra's words are conveyed to us by a narrator who has proven to be less than articulate. In short, the narrative lacks convincing scenarios, dramatic set pieces, instances of concreteness—the very factors which make Cather's next novel, *Death Comes for the Archbishop*, so successful as an example of narrative fiction.

My Mortal Enemy is one of the house and marriage novels. The houses are rather self-evident. One notable thing about them, however, is that we rarely see Myra outside a house until her death beneath the tree in California. We meet her in Aunt Lydia's house, go with Nellie to visit her in the small New York apartment, then see her ten years later in the shabby apartment in California. Always lurking behind these houses is the huge mansion in Parthia which she left to elope with Oswald. The houses dictate meaning and act as objective correlates as well as any other single element in the narrative, though in one of the more intelligent essays on *My Mortal Enemy* Harry B. Eichorn (in "A Falling Out With Love: *My Mortal Enemy*") argues well for the Shakespearean and operatic allusions as the conveyors of authorial intent. Such high profile literary allusions represent a narrative trait which did not grow organically out of Cather's stylistic methodology, an argument elucidated in discussing *One of Ours*, where she consciously exaggerates the allusions. The presence of similar allusions in *My Mortal Enemy* suggests Cather's effort (less consciously this time, it seems) to obscure rather than clarify her intent. Thus the houses offer more reliable symbolic possibilities.

The houses are conventional symbols and they do track Myra's economic decline, much in the same way that her geographical movement east to west tracks her emotional dissociation. The state-to-state movement gives us horizontal progression, whereas the movement from house to house gives us vertical progression: Myra moves from the top floors of uncle John's mansion, to the second-floor apartment in New York, to the California apartment with the "palavery" Southerners tromping above her (82). We earlier noted the ironic "house" motif in *A Lost Lady* and reviewed Leon Edel's perceptive analysis of *The Professor's House*, an exegesis made possible by Cather's symbolic, psychological deployment of domiciles. We cannot derive such subtlety of meaning from the houses in *My Mortal Enemy*, however—at least not with the safety net of textual facts beneath us. Obviously the houses trace the Henshawes' economic decline, as the vertical descent suggests, but they reveal little about the Henshawes' psyches. We do not know precisely why Oswald's income declines so precipitously and steadily to force the various changes in address, though we have a clue to the low opinion employers have of him when Cather (actually Nellie) tells us that the new owners offer him only a "small position" (75). We also do not know whether Oswald ever violates the houses with his adultery; what unrevealed "house" goes with the suggestive key Myra finds him secreting; or why she decides finally to abjure the "house" of the Lord and die a paganish death beneath the tree. One possible explanation: the "houses" equate with the Freudian womb—as Edel suggests for the professor's houses—and their progressive deterioration reflects the commensurate deterioration of Cather's own biological femaleness, the deterioration of her own womb and of all the maternal potential affliliated with it. The idea takes us back to the hysterectomy we hypothesized earlier, and while it is a fascinating theory, it remains inadequately substantiated by text.

In fact, the theoretical association of physical, literal houses to subtextual or psychological equivalents is clouded by Cather's having Nellie inhabit the same space as the Henshawes in the crucial California episodes: any speculating we might risk about the jerry-built apartments as being symbolic of psychosexual states for Myra or Oswald is compromised by Nellie's presence in those same cheap dwellings. We can safely infer that Nellie is there because she is young and poor and that the Henshawes are there because they are old and poor and on opposite paths on the capitalist ladder; but the observation strands us on the economic level and offers no real revelations beyond that. We surmise also that Nellie must be in the house to facilitate her role as first-person narrator, but even that narrative requirement does not quite justify the awkward arrangement. The arrangement makes it necessary for Nellie to be present at several arguments and private conversations which an outsider ordinarily would not be permitted to share, such as the bitter scene in which Myra bluntly tells Oswald that "I should have stayed with my Uncle. It was money I needed" (91). Had Cather been more committed to Nellie as reporter and placed her as resident in the same apartment with Myra and Oswald instead of just within the same building, then her being privy to such intimate conversations would be more likely and numerous psychosexual translations would be possible. But the fact remains that Cather did not make such living arrangements, leaving Nellie instead as a kind of resident alien who happens to be present at the most (in)opportune moments.

Several critics have noted the problems which accrue to Nellie's being the conveyor of information, generally concluding as do Dalma H. Brunauer and June D. Klamecki in "Myra Henshawe's Mortal Enemy" that Nellie is unreliable. The trouble with Nellie is not so much that she is unreliable but that Cather puts her into "houses" in which terribly embarrassing scenes occur and for which she subsequently looks the fool for reporting. In this repect she is too much the puppet, not enough the discreet intelligent reflector; and the unrealiability cannot fairly be attributed to her but to the author who manipulates her.

That the mansion in Parthia is now a convent suggests much, but again does not stand up to scrutiny. It is ironic, of course, that Myra deserts the dwelling that later houses the Catholic religion she turns to when moribund, but again the mansion functions more as a symbol of economic shifting than as an indicator of spiritual movement. There is ironic suggestion too that Myra might have fared better if she herself had become a "nun," as her Uncle seems to have wanted. To contemplate the "nunnery" motif underlying the narrative surface of *My Mortal Enemy* is admittedly intriguing because it correlates with the fact that as Cather grew older, celibacy seems more and more to have been her solution to the sexual dilemmas that plagued her. As Woodress puts it, "All the evidence suggests that Cather too avoided sex in her private life" and "Throughout her work there is a fear of sex, as character after character is destroyed by it or survives by escaping it" (127). In Cather's fiction sexual conduct, be it homosexual, heterosexual, marital, adulterous, or even unrequited, is deadly. It exiles one from tranquility and the heart's homeland. If only—Cather seems to imply— Myra had listened to the voice of reason, remained loyal to her Catholicism, denied eroticism, she might have been saved. She might not have ended up tied to a Satyr like Oswald and dying in a hedonistic land that is falling into the ocean. Such a nun motif would correlate nicely with the counterpoint prostitution motif we discussed in *A Lost Lady*, and would substantiate the thesis that Cather's conflicted sexuality continued as a recognizable source of her creative impulses. Such reasoning could indeed lead away from the strictly economic level and on to the realm of the psychosexual, thus emulating some of the transferences Edel manages for *The Professor's House*; but it is a line too tenuous to hold the kind of mass Edel loads into his essay.

Some commentators claim that with the utterly horrible marriage which Cather sketches in *My Mortal Enemy* she purged herself of her demons and moved to the placidity and psychological tranquility symbolized by *Death Comes for the Archbishop*— from nightmare to daydream. James Woodress, the best summarizer of the conventional wisdom on Cather, states that *My Mortal Enemy*'s "astringent portrayal of defeat and death marks the end of Cather's own bitter years" and is her "final comment on the destructive power of money" (386). David Stouck argues that it "moves towards a final Christian reckoning" (121). Neither comment is totally accurate. Aside from the fact that Cather at the end of her life in *Lucy Gayheart* and *Sapphira and the Slave Girl* reexamines the devastation caused by marriage and the destructive fickleness of romantic love, the bitterness which she so overtly expresses in *My Mortal Enemy* is also covertly present in *Death Comes for the Archbishop*. Instead of marking the pinnacle of her peace of mind and the realization of psychic unity, *Death Comes for the Archbishop* is more an interlude—a lull between storms. Especially if we recognize it in its proper sequence, between the three novels we have just discussed and the three which follow it, we see that the dominant authorial mood which it conveys clearly distinguishes it from its neighbors. *A Lost Lady*, *The Professor's House*, and *My Mortal Enemy* are progressively bleak novels, the chronicles of an individual losing contact with sustaining ideas and beliefs and questioning faith in self. Traditional social institutions are disparaged, contemporary mores are rejected, and personal worth is minimized. *Shadows on the Rock, Lucy Gayheart*, and *Sapphira and the Slave Girl* repeat the cycle. And in the middle of these six novels is *Death Comes for the Archbishop*.

Supeficially it is indeed an anomaly—if for no other reason than that it is notably superior to any one of the six as an example of narrative fiction. Coming as it does on the heels of *My Mortal Enemy*, it seems almost miraculous. Yet, if we look closely, we realize that it is not as anamalous as it may first seem. Cather did not resolve any emotional, religious dilemmas in writing *My Mortal Enemy*. She did not purge herself of her "own bitter years," as Woodress believes. She retained the same conflicts and stresses which we have witnessed in all of her novels. She merely used them to produce a different kind of narrative. Beneath the placidity of *Death Comes for the Archbishop*, the great respect for the Catholic priests, and the awe-inspiring landscape, behind the quietly powerful style and subtle narrative management, the angry woman and the conflicted artist we see in the other novels still endures.

Works Cited

Brunauer, Dalma H. and Klamecki, June Davis. "Myra Henshawe's Mortal Enemy." *Christianity and Literature* 25 (Fall 1975): 7-40.

Butcher, Fanny. *Many-Lives—One Love*. New York: Harper & Row, 1972.

Cather, Willa. *A Lost Lady* (1923). New York: Knopf, 1966.

—. *My Mortal Enemy* (1926). New York: Knopf, 1967.

—. *The Professor's House*. New York: Knopf, 1925.

—. *Willa Cather in Person: Interviews, Speeches, and Letters*. Ed. L. Brent Bohlke. Lincoln: U of Nebraska P, 1986.

Daiches, David. *Willa Cather: A Critical Introduction*. Ithaca: Cornell U P, 1951.

Edel, Leon. *Stuff of Sleep and Dreams: Experiments in Literary Psychology*. New York: Harper & Row, 1959. Rpt. in part in *Critical Essays on Willa Cather*, Ed. John J. Murphy. Boston: Hall, 1984. 200-217.

Eichorn, Harry B. "A Falling Out With Love: *My Mortal Enemy*" *Colby Library Quarterly* 10 (Sept. 1973), 121-38. In *Critical Essays on Willa Cather*, ed. John J. Murphy. Boston: Hall, 1984, 230-243.

Gay, Peter. *Freud: A Life for Our Time.* New York: Norton, 1988.

Lathrop, Joanna. Response in "Symposium: Women and Tragedy." *Prairie Schooner* 49 (Fall 1975): 232-34.

Sergeant, Elizabeth Shepley. *Willa Cather: A Memoir* (1953). Lincoln: U of Nebraska P, 1963.

Stouck, David. *Willa Cather's Imagination.* Lincoln: U of Nebraska P, 1976.

Woodress, James. *Willa Cather: A Literary Life.* Lincoln: U of Nebraska P, 1987.

7
Death Comes for the Archbishop:
Guerrilla War of the Female Self

There are a number of reasons why Cather focused so sharply upon the mortal or corporeal manifestations of selfhood in the novels immediately preceding *Death Comes for the Archbishop*: conflicts arising from her calling as artist, especially as female artist; the physiological deterioration of her own body; and her suicidal tendencies. She came to know intimately the brevity and vulnerability of the somatic self; and by the time she finished the most morbid of the novels—*My Mortal Enemy*—she had rather thoroughly explored the traumatic realization of what Robert Frost in another context terms God's big joke on us: our own mortality. With Myra Henshawe, therefore, Cather records her anger at the inescapable, biological fact that she must "die like this, alone with my mortal enemy!" The process of writing about that venerable debate between body and soul, however, purged her of much of the anger, so by the time she came to write *Death Comes for the Archbishop* she had made a separate peace with her mortality. It was not a permanent treaty, as the post-*Archbishop* novels will show; but it was a significant step toward inner calm, a psychic moratorium. It helped her move from concentrating on the decaying body to contemplating the death that sets the spirit free from that body. Obviously the self-destructive impulse remains in that wish to liberate soul from body, but now in *Death Comes for the Archbishop* it has a noticeably less violent or bitter tone than that which we see in Marie Shabata or Claude Wheeler of Myra Henshawe. In short, she seems rather peacefully resigned to death, seems to have decided to see life through to its biologically determined conclusion rather than attempt to wrench free a psyche trapped in a failing body—to sit, like the aged Latour, contemplatively in the middle of her own consciousness. What better place to explore this new awareness than in a strange land, long ago, dominated by men, and governed by a credo that sets its hand so strongly against self-slaughter and promises life everlasting?

Cather appears bemused by the emotional transitions which came with accepting the inevitability of death; and it is the glow of her amazement, propitiously merged with the aura of the New Mexico landscape, which seems in turn to illuminate her thoughts of Father Latour. The novel, therefore, is the near perfect joining of time, place, and authorial psyche. Ironically, however, it is a dangerous narrative. Dangerous because of its success. It remains the most popular of Cather's novels and perhaps the most widely analyzed by academics. Yet, many who read it have read little else by Cather. It is often praised, seldom examined in context of the eleven other novels which surround it, and exists in a kind of literary vacuum. When William Faulkner had the temerity to place Cather with himself as one of America's great novelists, it was *Death Comes for the Archbishop* he most likely had in mind. There is nothing amiss about such singularity, since even in a world of new-wave criticism a work still has to stand or fall on its own unique merit. Yet, especially for Cather as much as for Faulkner, there is continuity to her fiction; and while the "meaning" of any one of her novels is separate from the meaning of any other, the meaning of them all is enhanced by interdependence. Unless we know, therefore, the tensions and conflicts that permeate the pre-*Archbishop* narratives, we less appreciate the fact that those same tensions and conflicts remain as motivating energies in a novel which is superficially a tale of spiritual questing. Like the subterranean river beneath the New Mexican mountains, these tensions and conflicts carve their paths invisibly. Thus the apparently radical change from *My Mortal Enemy* to *Death Comes for the Archbishop* is one of perception rather than essence. While the shift from Myra Henshawe's depressing, concentrated decadence to Father Jean Latour's boundless spirituality may appear abrupt and unannounced, it is in fact a rather logical progression when seen in light of the holistic unity of Cather's fiction.

Thinking she had rid herself of troublesome women such as Marian Forrester and Myra Henshawe, with their perplexing sexuality, Cather happily announced that with *Death Comes for the Archbishop* she had written "a story with no woman in it but the Virgin Mary" (Butcher 358). It is an interesting mis-

statement of fact, and because it is incorrect it suggests something
about Cather's subconscious desire to find solace by consciously
de-emphasizing the feminine self. She did not do what she
thought she was doing, however, because the discontented female which we see throughout her earlier fiction remains to
fight a kind of psychic guerrilla warfare for autonomy. We
therefore see her fragmented into three ostensibly minor
women characters who quietly come and go among the pomp
and circumstance of Father Latour's epic, all subservient and
causing no trouble and hardly noticed in their passing. If we
doubt, however, that Cather's confusions and angers transfer
from the early novels to this one, we need only look closely at
these three inconspicuous women whom Cather herself forgot
to acknowledge. Despite the considerable attention that the
"gender" question in Cather's fiction has received, the actual
role which these three women play in *Death Comes for the
Archbishop* has been overlooked. Far from being the insignificant, supportive good girls meant to swell a progress, they are
more like insurrectionists in the Archbishop's French legion.

How, therefore, do we account for such women in a narrative James Woodress calls "a modern saint's life" (406) which
depicts an archbishop whom John J. Murphy in turn extols as a
nonpareil "father, uncle, husbandman, cook, builder, scholar
and teacher, artist and historian" (54)? More apropos, perhaps,
one might justifiably ask why the women must be explained at
all since they so readily pale to insignificance against the bril-
liance of Latour? They need to be explained first because
although she later slighted them, Cather did carefully place them
in her narrative design, which either consciously or unconsciously she meant for them to serve. More pragmatically, the
women need to be explained because they act as a major correc-
tive to the prevailing foreground image of Archbishop Latour
and because their provenance is the psychological tension which
was the energy source for Cather's creativity. Such tension,
especially that associated with her sexual ambiguity, elucidates
Cather's overall narrative concept and effectively balances the
recent argument presented by critics such as Sharon O'Brien,
who believes that Cather realized a kind of erotic equilibrium,
resolved her sexual dilemmas, and by 1913 "had discovered her
authentic, essential identity" as a female (7). Actually, the crisis
of gender identity which Cather suffered as a child and which is
most overtly identifiable in her patronymic "William Cather"
years of cross-dressing foreshadowed a sexual dichotomy that in

the words of Susan Gubar "was profound enough to inform not
only the themes but even the structure of her mature fiction"
(465). This erotic uncertainty is important because of its influence on the narrative structure of *Death Comes for the Archbishop*. The women who are the focus of my discussion and
who at first seem so insignificant in comparison to the priests,
ultimately determine narrative form and substance.

Magdalena Scales is the first of the women to appear.
Prior to Magdalena's introduction (page 68), Cather portrays
priests in general and Latour especially as determined, devout,
and persevering. She uses garden and sanctuary images to
accentuate Latour's holiness. Once she has accustomed the audience to this particular mode of perception, however, she introduces Magdalena in contrasting desert squalor to mark an entirely different angle of vision—she literally dichotomizes the
view, as it were. Existing in primitive survival conditions,
Magdalena has silently witnessed her husband Buck Scales murder travelers and even her own infants. Because of her devotion
to the Church, however, she cannot ignore the imminent murder of priests who have been driven by the storm to her hovel.
Jeopardizing her own life, she mimes a warning to Latour and
Vaillant that Scales intends to kill them. Untypical of clerics and
more in keeping with western tough guy heroes such as Kit Carson who will soon help bring Scales to justice, Latour carries a
pistol with which he could easily control the unarmed miscreant
and save the woman in distress. John J. Murphy places Latour
in the same western tradition with Leatherstocking and Owen
Wister's Virginian, seeing the priest as a Christian knight-errant
or Palladin charged with bringing law and order to a disordered
land. Murphy, however, sees no irony in this conflict of mission
and method. In any event, Latour places little credence in any
chivalric code, apparently finding no flesh sweeter than that
which sticks to his own bones. Instead of protecting the hapless
Magdalena, the priests flee on their precious white mules; and
only when they are out of range of being "shot in the back" (70)
does Latour ironically lament Magdalena's fate: "Poor woman!
[Scales] will suspect her and abuse her, I am afraid" (70). They
then ride on into Mora, where Cather reemphasizes their self-
serving by having two refugees from the storm "put out of a bed
in order that the Bishop and his Vicar could get into it" (70).
While the priests sleep comfortably, Magdalena eludes death and
reaches Mora so battered and dirty "that the priests could scarcely
recognize the woman who had saved their lives the night be-

fore" (70-71). Just prior to Magdalena's episode, Latour has spoken eloquently about his religion and the Church. He concludes that "The Miracle" of the Church is that it makes our perceptions finer "so that for a moment our eyes can see and our ears can hear what is there about us always (50). The contradiction of Latour's perceptions being so quickly clouded by self-absorption that he fails to recognize his "savior" in Magdalena is acutely ironic, and diagnostic of the entire episode.

To perpetuate this altered and far less flattering view of Latour, Cather makes the second of the three women the diametrical opposite of the poor Spanish peasant. Magdalena is characterized as "half-witted" and "stupid" (68), a characterization which later proves imprecise but which helps excuse her blind devotion to the Church and to priests who are willing to sacrifice her life to save their own. Isabella Olivares, however, is a blonde "Kentucky girl" (176), multilingual, wealthy, urbane, and sexually active. A girlhood education in a French convent has failed to inhibit her, so as an adult she has no logical excuse for her theological gullibility or for allowing herself to fall prey to patriarchal control. As we recall, Isabella has recently been widowed; and to claim her late husband's estate, she must admit to being old enough to be the mother of their aging daughter Inez. Utilizing spatial irony, Cather locates Doña Isabella's chapter immediately after the episode of the miserly priest Lucero, who dies a terrible death because of his greed in accumulating $20,000. Don Antonio Olivares's estate is worth exactly ten times this amount. With this numerical "coincidence" and spatial proximity, Cather emphasizes the irony of Doña Isabella's being torn between rapacious brothers-in-law and Latour, who insists that she claim her inheritance so that he may collect his promised share and thus realize his "one very keen worldly ambition; to build in Santa Fé a cathedral (175). In passing, we might record that the traditional view of Latour's cathedral is that its traditional design and communal intent expresses altruistic motives and emblematizes Latour's moral excellence (Stouck, "Art and Religion" 293-302); but a less flattering appraisal is that Father Lamy was in fact a money-oriented Archbishop who alienated the people of New Mexico with his tithing demands and whose French cathedral thus stands more as a symbol of his French distaste for the Spanish adobe structures preferred by the populace. E. A. Mares refers to *Death Comes for the Archbishop* as "a historical and social anachronism tragically flawed by the narrowness of its ethnic and cultural biases" (60).

Unlike Lucero who sublimates his erotic desires into the accumulation of gold, Doña Isabella—with her lovers in El Paso, New Orleans, and among the household staff—is explictly sexual and perfectly willing to sacrifice the money to maintain the secret of her true birth date. In seeking to preserve her erotic self, she but follows the preservation instincts of the biological being, an impulse certainly as legitimate as the greed which compels Latour and which makes him uncomfortably akin to Lucero, as the similar names suggest. Even Latour admits that forcing her publicly to proclaim her fifty-three years is "cruel" (193), but he nonetheless prevails in his demand that Isabella do what she must do to get the money. Though Doña Isabella—like Magdalena—accepts the treatment without rancor and graciously acquiesces to the priest's wishes, the laughter which concludes the episode may be as much in mockery as in joy.

Cather does not, however, want to paint Latour as a man without conscience or integrity. He has these qualities in large measure, and that he too often compromises both is part of the reason why he increasingly experiences "periods of coldness and doubt" that leave his soul "a barren field" (211)—a despair reflecting Cather's own coincidental spiritual crisis which E. K. Brown and others have discussed (227) and which led to her joining of the Episcopal Church in 1922 in an unsuccessful effort to alleviate the problem. Appropriately, it is a woman who intercedes to restore Latour's faith; but once again in his dealings with her, Latour proves himself more selfish than altruistic. Magdalen has saved Latour's body, literally; Doña Isabella has saved his church; and now old Sada will save his soul. Unlike Isabella, Sada's physical self is totally enslaved. Only her spirit is free to soar. As in the Magdalena episode, wherein the priest's cowardice is overlooked in the glare of Buck Scales's excessive brutality, and in the Doña Isabella episode, wherein the brothers-in-law's avarice overshadows Latour's more subtle acquisitiveness, Cather ironically masks Latour's subsequent "cruelty" by exaggerating the villainy of the Smiths, to whom Sada is enslaved. The Smith family objects to Sada's Catholicism, forbids her contact with the church, and makes her sleep "in a woodshed" (212) in the winter. Typical of the attitude already established in his relations with the previous two women, Latour acts cowardly or at least indifferently toward Sada. Informed by a "pious neighbour woman" (215) that action should be taken to help Sada, he replies that "it was inexpedient to antagonize" (216) the Smiths, whom he fears will make additional trouble for the Church.   Though the Church has ignored her problem for years, Sada has remained devout, maintaining the "pure goodness" that shines from her "countenance" (212). When she finally visits Latour in the Church, an ironic reversal of roles occurs, for Latour draws from the bond woman "the holy joy of religion" (217) he has been unable to reinstate in himself and unwilling to cultivate in her.   Sada redeems him spiritually, and perhaps even prevents his suicide; and the sharpest irony of the episode is that after she has restored his faith, he sends her back to the terrible Smiths while he remains in the church secure in "the peace in his own soul" (219).   The Sada story was Cather's preferred episode from the novel, the only one she allowed to be excerpted and printed as a separate "Christmas" book. (This small book is entitled *December Night. A Scene from Willa Cather's Novel "Death Comes for the Archbishop"* and was published by Knopf in 1933.) Isolated from the total characterization of Latour, which adumbrates the portrait we get from his treatment of the women, the anticlerical ironies of the Sada story are especially pronounced. Cather's allowing the publication may well have been one of her little jokes on an audience too ready to sentimentalize and oversimplify her art and purpose.   Marilee Lindemann puts interesting nomenclature to this problem of sentimenal/oversimplified approaches when she refers to the "Convent Critics" and the "Postcard Critics" who insist on placing Cather into psychical and physical landscapes which do not do justice to the "vast and varied terrain of her fiction" (15).   F. K. Stanzel complains generally that such narrow approaches "schematize the narrative action in a way which fails to do justice to the particularity and complexity of the individual narrative work" (46).

Recognizing the ironic way in which Cather uses the women for one apparent purpose when actually she is using them for quite another is crucial in that it forces a re-evaluation of the dominant priests who traditionally have been viewed as sacrosanct by evaluators of Cather's fiction. David Stouck, for example, epitomizes the traditional view when he says in *Willa Cather's Imagination* that "all events [in the novel] are simply aspects of a divine drama" (132) and that the world of the priests "is circumscribed by a divine order" (131). Once acknowledged, however, the irony raises an equally important question concerning the origin of the women in Cather's imagination. We know that Latour and Vaillant have their factual coordinates in Archbishop Jean Baptiste Lamy and Reverend Joseph P.

Machebeuf, prototypes commonly acknowledged and long since analyzed by Edward A. and Lillian D. Bloom in "The Genesis of *Death Comes for the Archbishop*." However, no similar coordinates have yet been found for the three women, though the biographical elements of Cather's fiction have been scrutinized. James Woodress, for instance, after discussing the various historical records from which Cather borrowed to create Latour, Vaillant, and many of the other males such as Kit Carson, concludes that the rest of the novel "came from Cather's invention" (401). Especially in light of our previous discussions of Cather's tendency to combine biography and other elements into fiction, this juxtaposition of real or historical men with women who have no factual provenance seems a simple enough point of stylistic continuity; but in *Death Comes for the Archbishop* the juxtaposition conceals complex artistic processes which suggest that the ironic power of the three women lay even deeper in her imagination than perhaps Cather herself knew.

By placing these "invented" women in the same environment with the factual churchmen, Cather realizes a metonymic transfer between poetic and scientific realism. Kenneth Burke, seeking to explain the creative process generally, differentiates between those things which emanate from situations that are sensorially verifiable (scientific) and those things which emanate from the imagination (poetic)—the difference, for example, between a literal Grecian urn and the imaginative pictorials which Keats affixes to such an urn. In "poetic realism," Burke explains, "states of the mind as the motives of action are not reducible to materialistic terms," as they are in scientific realism. Therefore, because the workings of the imagination cannot be quantified, as can the sizes and shapes of vases or the comings and goings of real priests, some method must be found by which the abstract can be made visible. Thus we have metonymic conveyance or transfer. The basic intent of metonymy, in Burke's words, is "to convey some incorporeal or intangible state in terms of the corporeal or tangible" (Grammar 506-507). In short, Latour and his life are historically verifiable and therefore offer preexisting corporeality or tangibility. By locating the imaginary women in such a way that they share this tangibility, Cather gives them immediate validity or tangibility of their own, a process which in turn allows them to act as "corporeal" representatives of her "intangible" psychological state. Though never extant in the "scientific" or extratextual reality as are the priests, within the fictive or "poetic" world of the narrative the women are as historically, biologically, socially valid. Since they have no provenance outside the fictive world, they therefore stand as projected images of Cather's creative self. This process is certainly similar to Eliot's "objective correlative" concept which we used in discussing *My Mortal Enemy*; but Burke is trying to clarify the process by which acts are conveyed from the author's imagination into representational forms, whereas Eliot is more focused on how those forms in turn convey meaning to the audience. Each concept concerns the ultimate goal of transmitting ideas from author to audience, but different stages of that process are involved. Because we have already seen the ironic complexities which the women convey to us as audience, Burke's idea seems more apropos at this point in explaining what was taking place in Cather's creative processes when she intermingled the men of fact and the women of imagination.

Because the traditional patriarchal males originate in history or "scientific reality," they in turn emanate more from Cather's imitative or mimetic impulses than from her creative impulses and perhaps convey less complex levels of her response to the world. We might even venture to say that they are representative images of what Cather had been conditioned by various kinds of schooling to think the world should be. Ironically, therefore, the "poetic" women who occupy such a minor portion of the narrative surface are actually more valid spokespersons for the authorial self than the highly visible priests, even though such disproportion may not have been what Cather intended. The women and the symbology that attaches to them can therefore plausibly be interpreted as the "corporeal" manifestation of the sociosexual conflict Cather continued to experience.

Such conflict was in part why Cather consciously and premeditatedly selected the nineteenth-century, frontier milieu for the priests and the women. She was attempting to relocate her sexuality—as Loretta Wasserman notes—"in a kind of time apart, where actions have no particular cause or consequence" (356). With such spatiotemporal distancing she could alleviate the painful dilemma which we have discussed relative to earlier novels and just glimpsed in discussing her metonymic transference in terms of Burke's phraseology. This radical opposition between her poetic self and an external reality incompatible with that self is the conflict Cather exploits in the most subtle of ways in *Death Comes for the Archbishop*. With the historically-based Latour she comes as close as anywhere else in her fiction to recreating a viable equilibrium in the tensions posed by her same-sex eroticism amidst a frontier society which may never have heard of Freud, but which adhered to his basic assumption that the only "normal" mode of sexual behavior was penis-in-vagina, procreative intercourse. Freud is unequivocal on this point: "The union of the genitals in the characteristic act of copulation is taken as the normal sexual aim. It serves to diminish the sexual tension and to quench temporarily the sexual desire . . . " (563). Unable to accept such limited, patriarchal definitions of eroticism, and not choosing to emigrate geographically toward freedom as Gertrude Stein and the Left Bank group did, Cather turned her quest inward.

She dreamed of escaping—as E. K. Brown notes—to such a life as the chronicles told her Lamy/Latour led. She fantasized such escape not only because her reading convinced her that Lamy/Latour was a "personality extraordinarily fine and cultivated" (Brown 254) but also because Latour's intimacy with Vaillant is freed from the heterosexual lifestyle which Cather was constitutionally unsuited to follow and artistically unable to replicate. By identifying with the priests' relationship, Cather is therefore afforded a safe method by which the preferred homoeroticism can be depicted without incurring the ire of a shocked public. Removed to the long ago and far away and blessed both by history and the authoritative if not infallible church, "Jean Marie" and "Joseph" can sleep together, eat together, argue and discuss without having to apologize for the lack of heterosexual contact and the absence of progeny. It is the ideal relationship Cather envisioned, free from intersexual conflicts and maternal obligations; and though we can hardly ignore the irony of her turning to the super-patriarchal Catholic Church for her models, we nonetheless can appreciate the emotions that led her to displace her homoeroticism with the priestly "marriage." We must also acknowledge, however, the commensurate guilt Cather could have experienced as a result of the sexual unorthodoxy which she sublimated and unconsciously objectified in Latour-Vaillant, for out of such unconscious motivations the iconoclastic women and their accompanying irony also arise to mock the haughty clerics whom Cather wanted sincerely to promote as models of ideal behavior.

In this respect, the women testify to a peculiar way in which the novel failed Cather. Had she been successful in making her fiction the instrument of the sociosexual reconciliation, we as audience probably would find manifested in that fiction a counter image of the non-regenerative sexuality depicted in the priests. This counter image would function as Cather's version of the "anti-poetic" or public self which Roy Harvey Pearce notes in defining "that radical opposition which has obsessed so many major American poets. It is the opposition between the poetic and the anti-poetic—between the self . . . and a reality which is not part of that self but must be brought into its purview, composed, and so (as it were) re-recreated" (380). Such a public mask would be intended as a shield to protect her private homoerotic self from calumny, and would logically be personified not in ironic/satiric female rebels but in archetypal characterizations of womanhood: the conventional passive, obedient, sexually orthodox "good girl," content in her roles as wife, mother, nurturer of family, or whatever other roles the prairie fathers assigned her—and with which Cather tried publicly to identify. As witness to this, we have first the obvious facts of her biography, which show her efforts to suppress practically all information about her personal life and thus obviously her eroticism. To her death, she feared being exposed as an "invert"—that peculiar Freudian term which implied upside-downness. As James Woodress notes, "As Cather grew older, her high regard for traditional values, her strong sense of decorum, and her close ties to family would have been strong deterrents to anything she regarded as deviant behavior" (42). Further, we have the testimony of writers such as E. K. Brown that Cather took a protective (if not maternal) interest in her younger sibling and established a vicarious familial association with the traditionally constituted Menuhin family in the 1930s. And most convincingly, we have Cather's own indirect testimony in her earlier fiction, which we have examined. We find such testimony especially in Ántonia, the quintessential earth mother with all her loving children who expiates her past sins via a distinctly heterosexual marriage full of maternal devotion and amazing fecundity (and who paradoxically in that overabundance negates herself as a valid portrait of the traditional maternal female). So the desire to project the image of the orthodox female was clearly a conscious part of Cather's weltanschauung.

　　Yet, in her unconscious where the true impulses lurked and where Magdalena, Isabella, and Sada originated, she could not fabricate the conventional mother-wife-servant female. As Kenneth Burke argues in another context, addressing the creative process generally but not Cather specifically, if traditional heterosexual women were within Cather's creative power, ei-

ther positively or negatively, they would be "objectively, struc-
turally, there" as part of the narrative design (Philosophy 279).
That is, if Cather had given us fictive examples of such heterosexual, maternal women (a kind of mirrored reversal of her true
psyche as Oscar Wilde and others managed to do) we could plausibly argue that she had worked through her erotic conflicts to
fashion in her imagination a "public" feminine model which
conformed to what parents, siblings, friends, and townspeople
expected her to be. She would be saying, in effect, "this is the
image of the conventional self you wish me to be and with
which you feel most comfortable, and I have thus compromised
my true self in order to coexist peacefully with you." In other
words, if she could have made the traditional heterosexual,
childbearing female "corporeal," if she could have exhibited her
own mode of negative capability and convincingly produced the
type of female that she herself was not, we would have some evidence that her private self had made peace with her public self.
Psychosexual balance between the feminine and masculine impulses would be feasible if not verifiable, and the subsequent argument that Cather resolved her gender conflict prior to the
mid-1920s might well be defensible.

Indeed, on the superficial level, she tries to give us these
traditionally obedient women in Magdalena, Isabella, and Sada.
Yet, as we have seen by viewing the three women and their relationships with the priests from a less traditional perspective,
they are not the conventional, heterosexual woman. On the
contrary, they are "traditional" only in their passivity in the face
of masculine authority; and even that acquiesence, as we have
also seen, is a guise which ironically reforms our view of the
righteous clerics. As for being mothers and nurturers, though
Cather grants at least two of them verifiable heterosexualism,
the women distinguish themselves by the degree to which they
reject those roles. In each case of the three liberal women and
even with the omnipresent "Mary," children are dead, denied,
or nonexistent. Magdalena's babies have been murdered by their
biological father, with no significant protest from a mother who
will later risk death to save priests she does not know; Doña
Isabella, to protect her true age and erotic appeal, refuses to admit
she has a child; and Sada is childless. This failed motherhood is,
in fact, one of the few common factors uniting females who are
erotically, economically, and ethnically disparate. A plausible
explanation for this absence of the traditional, maternal female
and the presence of the rebellious female clothed in traditional

garb is that in the mid-1920s Cather still had not come to terms with the numerous contradictions and tensions arising from her conflicted eroticism. On one level she is able to offer us priests who personify the archetypal father-male, and whom she genuinely admires; but against that historical masculine image she is unsuccessful in trying to develop and project out of pure imagination a traditional feminine counterpart.

Certainly Cather was not unique in suffering from the dilemma which the conflict between the women and the priests implies. Although she wanted to define herself uniquely through her own art—apart from sexuality of any type, hetero or otherwise—she was instead defined by what people and their mutual environment dictated she should be. And that environment was severely limited by sexually determined strictures. Jane Gallop, for instance, in *The Daughter's Seduction: Feminism and Psychoanalysis*, discusses at length the traditional patriarchal or phallocentric attitudes which determine that creativity and intelligence in females are sins which must be punished. She analyzes too the subsequent conflictive effects of those attitudes upon creative women such as Cather. The emotions Cather was experiencing, therefore, were not unusual, though her super-private life may suggest that she thought they were. In any event, they were no less troublesome because of their familiarity and effectively motivated Cather to seek some form of psychosexual rapprochement. That is, she needed a method by which to reconcile her homoeroticism and its implicit rejection of childbearing with the reality of her society, which valued females almost solely on the basis of how successful they were in childbearing and child rearing. It is hardly surprising that she would look for that method of reconciliation in the fiction-making processes—her art. In this particular instance, however, her art failed her.

Illustrating the fact they are endemic to the fundamental artistic process which determined the novel's form and substance, tensions and ambiguities commence from the woman-priest paradox and permeate the entire narrative construct of *Death Comes for the Archbishop*. We see them in elements ranging from simple double entendres to elaborate image clusters. The most obvious (and humorous) of several double entendres occurs when the promiscuous Isabella Olivares becomes enthralled by a banjo-playing house boy who is "a magician with his instrument" (178); and the somewhat less overt sexual imagery of the landscape is typified by ambiguous hills which are

"conical" like breasts yet which "thrust out of the ground," and
by "naked" juniper trees which are distinctly phallic but have
feminine "cleavage" (18).   Even the Virgin Mary has a certain
androgyny. One statue of her is described as "long and stiff and
severe, very long" (28). The most noticeable instance of contradictions and tensions associated with her conflicted eroticism,
however, is the cave-snake imagery in Book IV.

As she does by interspersing the three women in the tale
of Latour and Vaillant, Cather once again uses spatial irony by si-
tuating the cave as the central image of a section entitled "Snake
Root," where the dominant concern is the Pecos Indians's sacrificing babies to a monstrous rattlesnake:

> There was also the snake story, reported by the early
> explorers, both Spanish and American, and believed
> ever since: that this tribe was peculiarly addicted to
> snake worship, that they kept rattlesnakes concealed
> in their houses, and somewhere in the mountain
> guarded an enormous serpent which they brought to the
> pueblo for certain feasts. It was said that they sacri-
> ficed young babies to the great snake, and thus dimin-
> ished their numbers. (123)

The cave episode then immediately follows in a sub-chapter entitled "Stone Lips." Though the connection between the snake
and the cave initially appears tenuous, the two are related in that
both emanate from the paradoxical birth-infanticide motif and
the ritualistic eating motif previously established in the narrative by the Buck Scales's story and by numerous scenes involv-
ing the eucharistic taking of food. The serpent and its devouring
of the infants comprise an image which is simultaneously phallocentric and connotative of large mouths and ingestion. Then,
in a clever if somewhat gruesome transference and reversal of
the image, Cather describes the cave in distinctly reptilian terms:
a "mouth-like opening" consisting of "two great stone lips,
slightly parted and thrust outward," an "orifice" with a "throat"
(127). When Latour and Jacinto enter the cave, the cave symbolically swallows them like the snake and the image of the infants
being swallowed by the serpent is thus duplicated. The background symbology of the infanticide (the Indians sacrificing infants to the huge rattlesnake) and the foreground and more
specified image of the men entering the cave thus function in
coherent but nonetheless ambiguous, conflictive fashion.

The ambiguity does not end with the serpent-phallic-
ingestion symbology, however. Cather extends it into the

mouth-vulva, homoerotic symbology of the "great stone lips thrust . . . outward." This imagery connotes oral sex, both oscu- lation and cunnilingus, and is thus predominantly associated with female eroticism. Freud, fixing the traditional view which Cather simultaneously feared and hated, is quite explicit in dis- cussing the lips-to-vulva preference of homoerotic females. He points out that while "the sexual aims" of female homosexuals are diverse, "contact with the mucous membrane of the mouth seems to be preferred." When this preference is transferred to the genitalia, Freud judges it "perverse" (562). Conditioned by prairie ethics which condemned same-sex eroticism, a bias Freud upholds, Cather's unconscious or creative self does not entertain this lips/vulva association for long, and quickly diverts it. With the entrance of Latour and Jacinto into the cave, the lips-vulva symbology dissolves and reshapes itself into a more traditional heterosexual form: penetration of the vagina and reentrance into the womb. Apparently Cather is equally ill at ease with this image, which is foreign to her psychic orientation, for she soon alters the images once again and gives us a traditional symbolic rebirth when Latour and Jacinto "crawled out through the stone lips, and dropped into a gleaming white world" (132).

That Latour and Jacinto enter the cave together in the first place suggests the schizophrenic self trying to reunite, while the schism between the two selves is signified by Jacinto's reverence for and Latour's fear of the cave. Though it literally gives him life (as do Magadalena and the other women), Latour views everything about the cave with "extreme distaste" (127). The powerful subterranean river, an extended symbol of the life force or passion suggested by the symbolically feminine cave, especial- ly horrifies him. Jacinto, on the other hand, is at ease with the cave and stays awake to listen at the "curious hole" that opens in the wall of the cavern and that conveys the mysterious sounds of the river (131). In this particular instance, Jacinto with his pa- tience in tending the fire, feeding Latour, and generally catering to his needs represents maternal elements. In light of our theory that Latour is a reification of major elements in Cather's homo- erotic but suppressed self, this response to the cave and the flow- ing water may feasibly suggest that Cather was perplexed by those menstrual functions which marked her irrevocably as female and which reminded her of the biological, maternal imperative. Jacinto, on the contrary, with his traditional maternal concerns, personifies the conflicting reverence she felt for or the respect she had been conditioned to show to those same biological processes.   We remember the same dichotomy represented in somewhat different form in the Claude-Evangeline imagery of *One of Ours*.

Somewhat paradoxically, the rebirth motif we see with Latour and Jacinto is related to that suicidal tendency previously noted in Cather. Woodress, for one, discusses the "dark mood" that possessed Cather during the time of *The Professor's House* and *My Mortal Enemy* (380f).   Suicides appear throughout her fiction, with "Paul's Case" being perhaps the best known.   We also have the tramp in *The Song of the Lark* who drowns himself in Moonstone's standpipe; the wandering field hand in *My Ántonia* who throws himself into the thresher; and of course Mr. Shimerda.   A less well known example is Carrie Hensen in *O Pioneers!* who gets so depressed with life on the Divide that she attempts suicide, but saves herself by leaving Nebraska. Both Freud and Burke discuss symbolic rebirth and trace it to childhood sexual ambivalence, when the child cannot identify clearly with either parent and consequently develops no distinct male or female identity.   The child thinks the dilemma can be solved by becoming both father and mother, something which in turn entails destruction of the old self in order to be born in a new form.   If the child's efforts to resolve the dilemma are translated into literal actions, the results can be suicide.   However, if the child transfers the dilemma into imaginative or creative actions, the results quite often will be manifested in the kinds of poetic or symbolic suicide we note in Cather.   Symbolically, therefore, the destruction-rebirth cycle represents an act of psychic emancipation which is precipitated by sexual ambivalence such as Cather overtly evidenced in her cross-dressing and which may indicate a desire to be reborn as a member of the opposite sex.   Burke feels that such "assigning of a new lineage to one's self" can be realized only if it is accompanied by both symbolic matricide and symbolic patricide (*Philosophy*, 275f), a symbology which Cather projects in Latour's demise, in the pervasive death-of-Christ motif, and in not offering traditional maternal females.   In many respects, therefore, the images associated with the cave connect us again to the self-destruction motif we have noted all along but which certainly is not as pronounced in the textural surface of *Death Comes for the Archbishop* as it is in the novels immediately preceding and in those following.   The relative weakness of the suicide motif may reflect the momentary phase of comparative inner peace which Cather experienced while composing *Archbishop* and which we previously noted.

Yet the entire complex of contradictory, ambiguous symbology surrounding the cave episode is a notable example of the
cognitive dissonance that marked Cather's thinking as she composed the novel. Out of the complexity, one clear point emerges:
the literal process of birthing and maternity perplexed Cather.
We see this disturbance in her choice of such negative terms as
"glacial" and "fetid" (127) to describe so obvious a womb symbol
as the cave and in her making her alter-ego Latour so fearful of
the fallopian image suggested by the curious opening in the cave
wall. This opening connects the world of the living to the tran-
scendental life force implied by the dark, subterranean river. On
the other hand—reiterating a point we made earlier about
Cather's inability to project traditionally maternal females—a
homoerotic writer who had come to terms with her nontradi-
tional sexuality and who was free from the guilts attached to
homoerticism would probably not be so squeamish as Cather
about the oral sexuality implied by the cave-vulva-mouth image
cluster. The absence of that freedom from guilt is in many respects a key to Cather's thinking as she created the imagery. Surrounded by social pressures which denied non-regenerative sexuality and relegated females to subservient roles as breeders and
caretakers, and no doubt acutely influenced by her adoration of
her own father (Woodress 413-414), Cather could not bring herself to advocate any action which flagrantly opposed patriarchal
standards. In one image she denies the maternal role with a
"glacial" cave that implies a barren womb, an image which—if
my thinking about her hysterectomy is correct—is especially
poignant. Yet she must quickly compensate for that betrayal of
the feminine obligation as defined by patriarchal standards.
Consequently we have the paradox of the frigid womb giving
birth to Latour and Jacinto, the children of her unconscious who
embody the very patriarchal-matriarchal battle that bedevils her.
They are the extraordinary twins of her psychic confusion: one of
the emissary of arch-patriarchal tradition, the other a pagan free
as the New Mexico snow, but both absolved via their masculine
gender from literal maternal obligations.

As we noted earlier, the snake-cave symbol begins with
ingestion or eating. The cave imagery thus interconnects with
the extensive use of food images which Cather also employs. In
using the Catholic Church and its sacramental ritualism as the
controlling image cluster in her narrative, she depends upon a
pure instance of ritualistic eating and manifests the matriarchal-
patriarchal conflict that lay at the heart of much of her personal,

artistic confusion. In *Totem and Taboo*, especially chapter 4, Freud discusses the "feast" qualities of the totemic syndrome (909-914). His term for ritualistic eating is "totemism" and he links it specifically to the patriarchal heritage. On the other hand, and more logically it seems, Burke associates such eating with the matriarchal because it emphasizes nourishment and nurturing (*Philosophy* 274). Cather had no regard for Freud, especially disparaging in *Not Under Forty* young men who had been "inoculated with Freud" (93); and she probably would have responded similarly to Burke had she read him. Thus we do not want to overemphasize either in trying to decipher what Cather was about. Yet their disagreement over the source and meaning of ritualistic eating offers a convenient platform for furthering our point about Cather. The fact is, she agrees with neither and both. First of all, she is fascinated by the ritualistic feeding of babies to snakes, as we have seen. This peculiar image fuses the maternal reproductive instinct (manifested in the infants) with the patriarchal demand for control (manifested in the sacrifice). The masculine urge to dominance obviously prevails over the feminine urge to feed and protect. The image is a sophisticated extension of the barbaric infanticide we see in the Buck and Magdalena Scales episode. Such bifurcated impulses—first to produce children then to destroy them in masculine ritual—correlate with the denial of motherhood we see in Magdalena, Isabella, and Sada. Further still, by surrounding the corporeal women with the mythic Virgin Mary, whose child is also glorified in totemic or ritualistic eating, Cather poetizes a real desire to find a woman who fulfills the maternal obligation while remaining free of the penis-in-vagina syndrome. By emphasizing the Virgin Mary as quintessential mother, Cather shows her awareness that the primordial impulse to bear children is both biologically and mythically validated. Moreover, the metaphorical use of the Virgin shows also that Cather was acutely aware of the fact that maternal affection is an essential adjunct to the childbearing impulse, else the species disappears just as the infanticidal Pecos Indians disappeared.

Nonetheless, Cather cannot easily accede to that predistined feminine obligation of motherhood. Consequently her females—who otherwise have admirable traits—are forbidden the motherly affection that accompanies the unfettered maternal instinct. We have already seen how Magdalena, Isabella, and Sada all in one way or another fail to fulfill their motherly duties. Interestingly enough, none of the three women is ever depicted as giving food directly to her child, though Vaillant dines lavishly on under-cooked mutton and in turn feeds Latour on several occasions. In short, the women of *Death Comes for the Archbishop* appear as a later manifestation of those impulses Cather was repressing when as a child she adopted the masculine persona. As Susan Gubar notes, such cross-dressing can mask a feminine self-hatred, "for the male facade or persona may be an attempt born of shame to deny, hide, or disgrace the female self" (485). Cather's (in)famous "William" period, therefore, was considerably more than a child's rebellious charade. At its most fundamental, it was an early sign of the masculine self pondering its existence in a feminine body. In essence, however, it epitomized a psychic dichotomy incompatible with psychological integration—the catalyst that lay at the heart of Cather's novels.

The society upon which Cather depended for sustenance and camaraderie had limited respect for feminine art and less tolerance of sexual ambiguity, and even as a child, she "was already beginning to feel that the conventionalism of Red Cloud was a denial of life itself, a network of caution, evasion and negation" (Brown 47). During the final years of her life, sick and inactive, she retreated into the past, where like Latour awaiting the release of death, she "sat in the center of [her] own consciousness" (290). Damned to be both artistic and sexually unorthodox in a society suspicious of both, and refusing to leave it, Cather was perplexed from first to last by the tricks biology and environment had sprung on her by giving her ambiguous erotic drives and by locating her in a society not amenable to ambiguity. Her resultant dilemma manifests itself in interesting psychoanalytic coordinates, some as overt as the post-pubescent transvestism and others as subtle as the iconoclastic women we encounter in *Death Comes for the Archbishop*.

With the three female characters, the cave, the totemism, and other narrative elements we have a synecdochic representation of Cather's own fragmented sexuality. Collectively, they illustrate a point Ed Cohen explores in discussing the homo-eroticism of Oscar Wilde and the ways in which he transformed his same-sex orientation into acceptable heterosexual fiction. Cohen points out that even if a text does not explicitly depict same-sex behavior or use homoerotic terminology, it nonetheless can function quite adequately to depict the conflict between the heterosocial demands and the artist at odds with the conventional hegemony (803). Cather probably would not like the comparison with Wilde, having herself written a scathing review of *Lady Windemere's Fan* a year before Wilde was put on trial for going against the prevailing moral codes (*World and Parish*, I, 89-92); but ironically Cohen's point holds true for her text as well as Wilde's.

Works Cited

Bloom, Edward A. and Lillian D. "The Genesis of *Death Comes for the Archbishop*." *American Literature* 26 (January 1955): 479-506.

Brown, E. K. *Willa Cather: A Critical Biography*. New York: Knopf, 1953.

Burke, Kenneth. *A Grammar of Motives and a Rhetoric of Motives*, Cleveland: Meridian Books, 1962.

—. *The Philosophy of Literary Form*, Baton Rouge: LSU P, 1941.

Butcher, Fanny. *Many Lives—One Love*. New York: Harper, 1972.

Cather, Willa. *Death Comes for the Archbishop*. (1927). New York: Vintage, 1971.

—. *Not Under Forty* (1936). Lincoln: U of Nebraska P, 1988.

—. *The World and The Parish: Willa Cather's Articles and Reviews, 1893-1902*. Ed. William M. Curtin. Lincoln: U of Nebraska P, 1970.

Cohen, Ed. "Writing Gone Wilde: Homoerotic Desire in the Closet of Representation." *PMLA* 102 (1987): 801-813.

Freud, Sigmund. *The Basic Writings of Sigmund Freud*. Ed. and trans. A. A. Brill. New York: Modern Library, 1966.

Gallop, Jane. *The Daugther's Seduction: Feminism and Psychoanalysis*. Ithaca: Cornell U P, 1982.

Gubar, Susan. "Blessings in Disguise: Cross-Dressing as Re-Dressing for Female Modernists." *Massachusetts Review* (Autumn 1981): 477-508.

Lindemann, Marilee. "Con-Quest or In-Quest? Cather's Mythic Impulse in *Death Comes for the Archbishop*." *Willa Cather Pioneer Memorial Newsletter* XXXI, 3, (Summer 1987): 15-18.

Mares, E. A. "Padre Martinez, Defender of the People." *New Mexico Magazine* (June 1985): 57-60.

Murphy, John J. "Willa Cather's Archbishop: A Western and Classical Perspective." *Western American Literature* 13 (1978): 141-150.

—. "Willa Cather and Catholic Themes." *Western American Literature* 17 (1982): 53-60.

O'Brien, Sharon. *Willa Cather: The Emerging Voice*. New York: Oxford U P, 1987.

Pearce, Roy Harvey. *The Continuity of American Poetry*. Princeton: Princeton U P, 1961.

Stanzel, E. K. *A Theory of Narrative*. Trans. Charlotte Goedsche. London: Cambridge U P, 1984.

Stouck, David. *Willa Cather's Imagination*. Lincoln: U of Nebraska P, 1975.

—, and Mary-Ann Stouck. "Art and Religion in *Death Comes for the Archbishop*." *Arizona Quarterly* 29 (1973): 293-302.

Wasserman, Loretta. "The Lovely Storm: Sexual Initiation in Two Early Willa Cather Novels." *Studies in the Novel* 14 (1982): 348-358.

Woodress, James. *Willa Cather: A Literary Life*. Lincoln: U of Nebraska P, 1987.

The Last Three Novels:
Re-Visioning Critical Perspectives

After *Death Comes for the Archbishop*, Cather did not publish another novel for four years—a considerable slowing from the nearly book-a-year pace she set during the 1920s. The events of her life relative to the slowdown are familiar. Her health continued to be a problem, and she suffered from neuritis, influenza, depression, and sprained tendons in her right wrist that literally kept her from writing. She had to leave the security of her Bank Street apartment, which was torn down, and move to the Grosvenor Hotel. Her father died in 1928 and her mother in 1931. The Depression, international unrest, and another impending world war added to her misery (see Woodress 412f). These calamitous events could be cited as basis for an apologia for the drop in quality of the last three novels. As we have seen in previous chapters, however, Cather was facing equally difficult times during the writing of some of the earlier and "greater" narratives. With the possible exception of *Sapphira and the Slave Girl*, the final three novels equal or are superior to the quality of some of the novels written between *My Ántonia* and *Death Comes for the Archbishop* and should be approached with that awareness. Moreover, if we look at what Cather was writing in her late fifties and early sixties vis-à-vis what her contemporaries were writing at the same age, her accomplishments as a durable writer of fiction assay rather high. At comparable ages, for instance, Sinclair Lewis was publishing *Kingsblood Royal* and Hemingway *Across the River and Into the Trees*.

Much of the existing criticism of these last novels argues Cather's continued affirmation of life and adheres to other traditional views of her art. David Stouck, speaking well for the majority in this regard, says Cather's last works illustrate her "most joyful assertion of life's triumph" (299), though the facts and arguments he presents to support this conclusion point to an opposing view. Susan Rosowski, writing specifically about *Shadows on the Rock* in a chapter which offers perhaps the most intelligent compendium of the motifs, symbols, and mechanical workings of the novel, correctly notes that Cather addresses "modern themes of alienation, loss, despair, and annihilation" (176). Rosowski then vitiates her observation by finding resolution and affirmation in Cather's application of domestic ritual and the myth of the Virgin, of whom Cécile Auclair is the apotheosis, as we will see.

Such criticism suggests that while *Shadows on the Rock* and the other late novels have been well explicated, they continue to suffer from a bifurcated critical conscience. That is, for those who see only the peace, calm, and anticipated ascendancy of Father Latour in *Death Comes for the Archbishop*, there is a tendency to expect that same tone and intent from the subsequent narrative. When in fact the final novels give us even more explicitly the fear, darkness, physical and psychological isolation, and symbols of ingestion and cannibalism which lurk subtextually in *Archbishop*, we have a crisis of recognition. On the one hand we perceive the bleakness; on the other we do not wish to acknowledge it. Thus we seek affirmation where in fact an ironic skepticism prevails. Instead of approaching the final three novels with preconceived notions and thus being taken aback by the motifs of alienation, despair, and darkness, we might benefit more from re-visioning our own perspectives: look at the earlier novels—especially *Archbishop*—through the lenses Cather offers in her closing narratives, which in their own right are substantive examples of Cather's art.

The point of view of *Shadows on the Rock* requires first mention because the narrative presenter seems at times to be Cather herself (giving asides in the form of footnotes, for instance) and at other times to be a more traditional omniscient conveyor of information. Being thus neither first person nor third person, the narration comes to us as "psycho-narration," the term Dorrit Cohn uses to describe a narrative wherein a third-person narrator reports other characters's feelings and thoughts, usually keeping to those characters's spatial and temporal perspectives. The language is usually the narrator's, but the characters's words and thoughts may filter through (11f). Such techniques seem at times to emanate from an involved narrative personae and at other times from a reporter who wants to distance herself from that which is reported. This inter-narrational conflict permeates the text.

The artistic processes of *Shadows on the Rock* continue to exhibit the tensions arising from Cather's sociosexual dilemmas which are discernible in her earliest writing and which Bernice Slote in her critical statements introducing *The Kingdom of Art*, Sharon O'Brien in *Willa Cather: The Emerging Voice*, and others elsewhere have traced. Adumbrating the subtextual homoerotic bias found in the earlier narratives, Cather, via the psycho-narration, presents heterosexuality only negatively. She conveys this attitude in a prostitution motif which stands as a pragmatic and ironic counter theme to the purity of Cécile Auclair and the mythic Virgin Mary. One of the prominent female characters is the prostitute Antoinette Gaux and one of the several flashback stories within the narrative concerns a second prostitute, Marie. Together Antoinette and Marie contradict the moral structure of the narrative and contravene the Marian/Catholic theology which the text superficially advocates, or, more precisely, which an element of the narrative consciousness seems to endorse. The text and subtext, consequently, stand in an antithetical relationship, thereby conveying the peculiar dynamics of conflict upon which the philosophical or ontological intent depends.

Antoinette is the mother of Jacques, the angelic boy who is fathered by some sailor from France and whom Cécile mothers (practicing for her own maternity). Whereas Jacques is presented as an orchid growing in a dung heap, Antoinette is admirably unregenerate, a fallen woman without conscience who mistreats her child and makes few concessions to the prevailing patriarchy and no vows to the holy Virgin. While Cather is superficially careful to condemn such a personality, the narrative presenter subtextually exhibits some regard for Antoinette: she lets her cavort on the ice (one of Cather's favorite sports) and characterizes her with a clever double entendre. Antoinette goes dog sledding on the frozen river with several men late at night, thereby abandoning her child Jacques. Context makes clear that even on this coldest of nights Antoinette is out plying her profession with the men; but Cather, passing no judgment and trusting her intent to understatement reminiscent of Hemingway, merely observes: "Dog-sledging by moonlight on that broad marble highway with no wind, was fine sport" (71). Marie, the other prostitute, stands as counterpoint to Antoinette. More fabulous than factual, her story comes to us not directly from the narrative presenter, who is careful throughout the text to report only verifiable events, but indirectly as a story-within-a-story, a narrative device which distances the narrator from the incredible supernaturalism of the embedded tale. The secondary or borrowed narrative voice is Mother Juschereau, who is informing Cécile about Mother Catherine de Saint-Augustin. Mother Juschereau relates that when Catherine was a novice at Bayeaux, she encountered Marie. Like Antoinette, Marie was a life-long sinner; and she ended up living in a cave and dying of a "loathsome disease" (37), probably syphilis. Though Catherine prayed for everybody else, she self-righteously did not pray for poor Marie. Twelve years later, after Catherine has come to Canada, a soul from purgatory appears to her. It is Marie, explaining that she has been saved by "the infinite mercy of the Blessed Virgin" (38) and demanding to know why Catherine has not prayed for her. Feeling herself properly chastised and reminded of God's unending and democratic grace, Catherine sets about to have masses said for Marie so that she can go to Paradise and "sing the mercies of God" (39).

Cather uses the antipodal or contravening device elsewhere in the visible text. For example, she inserts the tale of Jeanne Le Ber, the educated and wealthy girl who gives up a life of luxury to pursue the Blessed Virgin's path, and who (not unlike Marie in the cave) ultimately spends her life as a hermit in an unheated cell. Distancing herself once again from such pietistic episodes, the narrator gives the first version of this story as it forms itself in Cécile's mind while she is half asleep, remembering information she has earlier received from the misshapen vagrant and former executioner Blinker. Conveyed in this form, Jeanne Le Ber's story is a highly romanticized or glorified miracle tale. Later, however, Cather has Pierre Charron (Mademoiselle Le Ber's rejected suitor, Cécile's future husband, and a nononsense, pragmatic woodsman) narrate the counter version. Charron tells how terrible the changes in Jeanne Le Ber have in fact been over the years, how the once beautiful and happy young girl now screams "harsh and hollow like an old crow's [voice]" (180). As in these two contrastive versions of Mademoiselle Le Ber's story, the juxtaposed stories of the two prostitutes Antoinette and Marie establish an irony which neither alone could muster. In other words, they produce a polyphonic story. The irony derives mostly from the contrast set forth first between Antoinette, who is devoted exclusively to the body, and the Auclairs and their circle whose lives center upon theology, heaven, and proper Christian conduct. They are the faithful who would believe that an unregenerate prostitute could, through divine intervention, become holy. The contrast between the "real" Antoinette selling herself on the streets of Quebec and the miraculous Marie who speaks to Catherine from beyond the grave maps a curious reversal between the textual surface and the subtext: a gritty realism and endurance accrue to the prostitute figure which not even superimposed miraculous interpretations can conceal and which force our grudging admiration of the female who rebels in the most radical fashion against the patriarchal hegemony, though she is presented literally as a character to be pitied or scorned. On the other hand, the unrealistic, exaggerated piety and devotion of the persona of primary textual focus (Cécile) cloys. Confronted, for instance, by the rural, sexually-aware Harnois girls with their bleeding legs and blood-stained bed (from mosquito bites), Cécile becomes almost hysterical. She wants only to flee the small island on which the country girls live and return to the sanctuary of the "rock" and her own small room. There she can keep her "white blouse" pure (193).

Cather, by sending the syphilitic Marie to Heaven and despite all her efforts to love Cécile, seems to anticipate a special place in Hell for such pietism and for the artist who might superimpose morality tales over harsh reality. In a radio speech in 1933 (less than two years after *Shadows on the Rock* was published), Cather chastised American novelists who compromise "something true" by fixating on "youth, love, and success" and then falling into a "nervous chill because they knew they weren't always bubbling over with these three desirable things" (*WC in Person* 170). Moreover, in having the virgin Cécile flee rather than sleep with the bloodied Harnois girls, Cather also reveals her hesitancy about manifesting her own eroticism, especially when that eroticism might be categorized as same-sex or "inverted." The term "inversion" is Freud's, and I have used it previously. Freud applied it to male and female homosexuals: "Such *persons* [the emphasis is Freud's] are designated as contrary sexuals, or better, inverts, and the situation of such a relationship is called inversion" (554).

The same conflict between apparent authorial intent and subtextual realization is discernible in the character of Cécile's father. Like Father Latour in *Death Comes for the Archbishop*, another of those Frenchmen who intrude into Indian lands, Euclide Auclair is superficially and sincerely a kind, good man. A fictive version of Cather's own father (Woodress 426), as an apothecary-physician he also recalls the profession to which Cather was drawn as a child and with which she identified during her "William" period of cross-dressing. He is, in short, as much the masculine element in Cather's psyche as he is Cather's father. Amidst all the corruption which surrounds him, the bitter fighting between churchmen and nobles, the turmoil and violence, he never raises his voice in anger or lifts a hand to anyone. Paradoxically, this passivity is also his weakness, for (like Cather's father) there is an ineptness about Auclair that impugns his actions and words. Though several factors testify to this ineptness, one of the most telling occurs with Mother Juschereau de Saint-Ignace, who is one of the most convincing characters in the narrative, perhaps because she reflects the elements in the presenter which are most nearly those of Cather herself. She is described as "a little over forty, a woman of strong frame, tall, upright, with a presence that bespoke force rather than reserve; a handsome face . . . perhaps a trifle masculine" (34). She is cousin to a type common to earlier Cather novels, most notably Alexandra Bergson and Ántonia Shimerda. She speaks with knowledge and assurance. Mother Juschereau is one of Auclair's patients, but she too has doubts about his abilities. She politely questions his practices and tells him that when Indians sprain their legs, they bind them with deer thongs and keep going. "And they recover," she emphasizes (35). Ignoring any advice a woman might give him (even a woman of the Church), and certainly not impressed by Indian folk medicine, Auclair tells her that Indians are savages and thus feel less pain than Europeans. The woman is correct in this particular case, a fact which the modern audience registers. Yet because she is female, her voice carries no authority against the male who is supposed to know about such matters. Mother Juschereau's correctness, however, is secondary to the true irony of the episode: the fact that a man of medicine—primitive though it be—views humanity so narrowly that he excludes Indians from its brotherhood. If we take the dove in its traditional symbolism of peace and Christian understanding, then Auclair's passion for preserving it in lard so that he may feast on its flesh throughout the Canadian winter suggests how inverted Christian ethics have become. Such eating is a parody of the Eucharist. Auclair serves as a key to Cather's intent with the narrative, a warning to consider the parallel view with which the story is presented.

Against the "savagery" of the Indians whom Auclair disparages stands the civilization of the French colonists and their home government. Though Auclair admires it, the narrative presenter (via a process of accretion) characterizes this Gallic civilization with syphilitic prostitutes; government- and church-approved torture of prisoners; bizarre religious fanatics who spend their lives in cells screaming like crows; a king who keeps carp that devour little girls at Fountainbleau; starving people on the streets of Paris, in the shadow from the palace at Versailles. Cather's artistic process may have altered the way she used Indians in her fiction between the writing of *Death Comes for the Archbishop* and *Shadows*, or perhaps she simply came to prefer Southwestern Indians to Northern ones; but an equally plausible argument is that it was not her attitude toward native American culture which had altered but her attitude toward French culture. Most of her life she felt that the French epitomized the best of everything, and her Francophilia is one of the cliches of her biographies—as evidenced by such books as Robert J. Nelson's *Willa Cather and France: In Search of the Lost Language* (Urbana: U of Illinois P, 1988). Yet, in this tale of seventeenth-century Quebec the French are as barbaric as the "savage" aborigines. The explanation which best explains the negative view Cather gives of France and of its projection into the new world is that *Shadows on the Rock* is her farewell to a country and to what it symbolized in her earlier years. Apart from the culture, the elegance, the exotic ideas that France generally and Paris particularly represented for Cather, it symbolized a psychological freedom she did not feel in America—be it Main Street or Park Avenue. Time and again she traveled to France, as she did during the composition of *Shadows on the Rock*. For many years, her great love Isabelle McClung resided in Paris. Paris had always offered symbolic if not literal liberation from the sexual mores back home, a motif she explored in *One of Ours* (1922) when she took Claude Wheeler away from a horrible marriage to fight and die for the Gallic paradise. Even if she never participated in the Left Bank lifestyle of Gertrude Stein and other lesbian writers, it was there with its promised freedoms. Had she chosen, she could have stayed there and become a part of the unorthodox but liberating life style epitomized by Stein and her coterie—a milieu thoroughly analyzed by Shari Benstock in *Women of the Left Bank: Paris 1900-1940* (Austin: U of Texas P, 1986). As Cather aged, however, and as the Twenties' atmosphere of Paris began to alter in the Thirties, the concept of the

French connection became less and less a feasible alternative. The Paris Escape, therefore, was something which she had to eliminate psychologically, just as earlier she had to kill off Claude Wheeler to prevent the psychic reentry into the Nebraskan antithesis of the French ideal. Once she finally realized that America was her fate and that there she would die, France assumed the image of a once beautiful lady now tired and distorted whom she had to purge from her imagination. Cécile is the beautiful French virgin, aglow with great expectations, a creature from the past as unreal as the imagination could make her; but the French prostitutes are both more numerous and more convincing as fictive persona. In that contrast lies an important tropic revelation about Cather as artist and her changing attitude toward Paris.

Despite the fact that Isabelle McClung set aside a special room for Cather in her Paris home, duplicating the working atmosphere they had shared years earlier in the McClung mansion in Pittsburgh, Cather could not productively write there. Her creative forces could not flow in Paris. As she said, she could not "produce my kind of work away from the American idiom" (WC in Person 84). Only back home could she create—though Wharton, Stein, Hemingway and many more of her contemporaries wrote their great novels in France and in many respects were more successful in exploiting the "idiom" when geographically removed from it. Cather could not create in Paris because the very atmosphere which made it so appealing temporarily freed her from the sociosexual tensions and ambiguities which she felt in America and which were the source of her creative energy. Perhaps (and it is an emphasized perhaps) if Cather had taken advantage of the freedom offered by the Left Bank lesbian community, the results might have been palliative for her psyche but disastrous for her art. Without the stresses and contradictions which came from her homoeroticism in the context of a conventional, patriarchal society, her imaging would not have functioned as it did. Quite simply, the tensions of her sociosexual conflicts fueled her creativity. In Paris, especially when Cather was with Isabelle, those tensions lessened—and her creative energies waned commensurately. Either consciously or instinctively, she knew not to sacrifice Art to domestic tranquility.

Trying to recapture the source of those tensions that fueled her creativity, Cather abandoned France and the past and returned to the Nebraskan prairie for the setting of her next novel and to the struggles of the conflicted artist which she had previously examined in *The Song of the Lark*. Not surprisingly, *Lucy Gayheart* is the story of a young woman's fight to escape the quotidian trap of church, marriage, and domesticity, and to be a true Artist. That Lucy fails—or is killed during the struggle—in contrast to her earlier counterpart Thea Kronborg is testament to Cather's changing attitudes toward her artistic processes and to the pessisimism that increased as she continuously battled against the encroachment of philistinism into her Kingdom of Art. Again, the point of view requires some clarification. Though technically first-person, as identified by the first-person personal pronoun of the "we live in the present" (3) opening statement, the entirety of the narrative cannot emanate from the traditional first-person narrative voice. Too often the thoughts and views of characters other than those of a first-person narrator are revealed (especially late in the narrative when Harry Gordon commences to psychoanalyze his actions and to suffer remorse), and no traditional devices such as letters or overheard conversations are presented to explain how the first person narrator would know such personal revelations. Thus, once again Cather creates the narrative ambiguity which Dorrit Cohn terms "psycho-narration"; and once again the technique establishes a conflict between text and subtext which is a major focus of my analysis.

Consensus opinion ranks *Lucy Gayheart* below most other of Cather's novels, a point which Susan Rosowski makes when she says that she does not "regard it as a successful book" (231). In developing its symbology, however, Cather foregoes the artifice which flaws *Shadows on the Rock* and recaptures the natural, organic technique she uses effectively for the emergence motif in *My Ántonia*, with its animals, plants, and seasonal changes, as discussed in Chapter Two. As in *My Ántonia*, the imagery upon which *Lucy Gayheart* depends is so fundamentally ordinary and universal that it is easily overlooked; but it transfers audience awareness efficiently from the surface of the narrative into the subtextual zones of mystery and uncertainty, where author and audience convene for whatever shared meaning is possible. One deceptively simple image cluster stands out: the contrast between hot and cold. It is a contrast which adumbrates the psychosexual conflicts which underlie the narrative and which manifest themselves in the several erotic relationships Cather outlines.

The contrast between heat and coldness pervades the narrative, but a few examples must suffice. The three books of the novel all begin in cold seasons: Book I and III in winter and II in late November. Summer and the warm months are mentioned in contrast, but the narrative action occurs mostly in wintry settings. The two significant "warm" actions are Harry Gordon's visit to Chicago, which is set in April, but which is ruined by Lucy's untruthfully telling him she has had an affair with Sebastian; and Lucy's spending "the long hot evenings" of summer (134) in Chicago waiting for Sebastian's return from Europe, a season terminated by his icy death in September. Both "snowfall" and "summer" (3) make the inhabitants of Haverford remember Lucy Gayheart: "Cold she used to say, made her feel more alive; heat must have had the same effect" (4). The hot-cold imagery carries through in the simplest of narrative detail. From such details, it transfers into more essential elements that illuminate the narrative subtext. For example, Lucy's room in Chicago is located above a bakery, where Mrs. Schneff, the owner, bakes the breads and other German dishes which create the atmosphere of warmth Lucy so enjoys. Yet the room is in a building where "winter winds blew up through the halls" (27). This image of food and domestic warmth which offset the chill is continued in Nebraska when Lucy braves the "deep snow-drifts" to deliver the warm Christmas cakes her sister Pauline has baked for their friends (182) and in Harry's ruminations after Mr. Gayheart's winter death, when he sits for hours before the fire and calls the hotel to "send over some sandwiches" (213). Such scenes are ironic because both Lucy and Harry have sacrificed domestic warmth and because the image itself is belied throughout the narrative by examples of marital turmoil which contravene any apparent domestic happiness. For example, Clement Sebastian's marriage is cold and unhappy and Harry Gordon's rebound marriage to Harriet Arkwright is business-like and barren.

From such irony of situation the hot-cold expands to the characters themselves as a device of psychological characterization. Lucy (the name itself suggesting lucency) is characterized by red, a color exemplified in the scarf which she wears when we first meet her and when she dies and in the red feather which she wears on her hat and which attracts Sebastian (50). This red of passion and fiery spirit contrasts with the snow and ice signifying her death. The white of the snow is parodied on the face of James Mockford, the specter of death whom Lucy hates and who is responsible for drowning Sebastian. His face is so white it looks "like a handful of flour" (39). Later, in her nightmares, Lucy experiences "nights when she lost consciousness only to drop into an ice-cold lake and struggle to free a drowning man from a white thing that clung to him" (157). Mockford's hair, in contrast, is ominously red, a parody of the life force which burns in Lucy. A most notable application of the hot-cold metaphor to convey Lucy's psychological state occurs when she first sees Sebastian perform. She later remembers the experience in terms that suggest hymenal penetration or symbolic loss of virginity. She feels that "a protecting barrier" is gone, "a window had been broken" (32). Her passion paradoxically makes her shiver, and she repeatedly whispers the words of Sebastian's song which has had such an erotic impact upon her and which again foreshadows her death beneath the ice:

> Pale grew thy cheek and cold,
> Colder thy kiss;
> Surely that hour foretold
> Sorrow to this. (32)

The contrastive heat of passion is much on the surface of the narrative. Lucy's suppressed desire for Harry is apparent, and her affair with Clement Sebastian is psychologically if not literally consummated, as we see in the "barrier" and "window" images mentioned above. Sebastian may have no sexual intimacy with his accompanist James Mockford, but innuendoes about Sebastian's interest in "boys" suggest homoerotic relationships. Sebastian's wife, for instance, grows jealous of the rapport her husband establishes with the "charming boy" Marius and demands that he be sent away to Paris (79). At another point Mockford suggestively informs Lucy that "Mrs. Sebastian takes a fancy to a new pianist now and then, and Clément tries him out" (58). Then Mockford and Sebastian drown together in an embrace which symbolizes their affair and simultaneously emblematizes the mutual punishment they must share. Lucy's attachment to Sebastian, though presented textually in conventional heterosexual terms, suggests her devotion to art more than to a literal man, and Mockford represents the insidious forces which counteract things of beauty. In another sense, Mockford personifies yet another bifurcation of Lucy as Cather's artist self: they both play the piano, both are associated with red, both are attached to Sebastian. Mockford, with his etiolated skin, his condescending dislike for Lucy, his innuendoes about his relationship with Sebastian, is one of the most unlikable characters in Cather's fiction—rivaling Ivy Peters of *A Lost Lady* for despicableness. As Lucy exclaims, "he was cowardly, envious, treacherous, and she knew it!" (158). Lucy herself, however, is described in several instances as being "rather boyish" (80) or "like a boy" (26), thus repeating the androgyny we see throughout Cather's female characterizations. Lucy/Cather therefore finds Mockford so repellent because he represents her own homoerotic impulses; and though Cather manifests her erotic self in the socially acceptable heterosexual attraction between Sebastian and Lucy, the homoerotic self is always there in some spectral form, ominously threatening the stability that might otherwise exist.

The abiding image in the novel is the Platte River ice beneath which Lucy drowns, an image which both conveys the understated horror of her silent death beneath the frigid waters and acts as metaphor for the unfathomable mysteries of the human mind. Just prior to the skating accident, Lucy has been preparing for a "warm welcome" (186) back in Chicago, at the home of her teacher Paul Auerbach and his wife. Moreover, she has also had an argument with Pauline about money, a heated quarrel which causes Lucy to grow "red" with anger (191) and which precipitates her temperamental flight to the frozen river. Much earlier in the novel Cather has foreshadowed the river-as-life metaphor which the Platte assumes: the river is described as a "formidable river in flood time" and "it sometimes cuts out a new channel" without warning (7). Moreover, the river freezes over with the coming of winter, the frost and ice assuming the symbology of the mysterious working of time and human thought, as Coleridge notes in "Frost at Midnight": "The frost performs its secret ministry, / Unhelped by any wind." Thus anticipated, the drowning scene is powerful in its understatement, articulating the warmth of spring which brings floods and the coldness of winter which brings the river ice:

> Lucy was more stimulated than frightened; she had got herself into a predicament, and she must keep her wits about her. The water couldn't be very deep. She still had both elbows on the ice; as soon as she touched bottom she could manage. (It never occurred to her that this was the river itself.) She was groping cautiously with her feet when she felt herself gripped from underneath. Her skate had caught in the fork of a submerged tree, half-buried in sand by the spring flood. The ice cake slipped from under her arms and let her down. (199)

Lucy's death ends Book II. Book III opens 25 years later, in the winter of 1927, with the funeral of Lucy's father. Though the death emphasized in Book III is literally the collective death of all the Gayhearts, the death which haunts the subsurface to which the frost symbology helps convey us is the living death of Harry Gordon—the substructure of meaning where the ostensible first-person narrator could not possibly take us. As Harry says to himself, out of context and leaving us to imagine the preceding thoughts which lead him to speak: "Well, it's a life sentence" (221). Made cold by the immediate death of his friend Jacob Gayheart and haunted by Lucy's earlier frigid death, Harry returns to his private retreat to contemplate his existence before "a fireplace where he burned coke when the steam got low after banking hours" (209). The artifical heat warms his body, but cannot duplicate the fire Lucy kindled in his soul. Like his vaults holding the money which cannot buy his peace of mind, he hordes memories of having refused her the ride on the day she drowned and the pervasive guilt of having wed a frigid, unattractive woman to retaliate against Lucy for rejecting his marriage proposal. He never confesses these "sins" but knows that "Life would have been much easier for him" (220) if he could have opened them to the light and warmth of confession. He rationalizes that the guilt "had gradually grown paler" with time (222). He is misled, just as he has been misled in his treatment of Lucy and in his materialistic pursuits. The guilt has not paled so much as it has been sublimated, transferred to the subconscious where it works unbeknownst, like the machinations of frost and freeze—making him seek atonement by acquiring the Gayheart homestead, preserving Lucy's footprints, cherishing her memory. His mind has become like the water flowing beneath the surface ice which disguises the river's course and content. Underlying the ice which is so inviting to skate upon are the tree snags, treacherous sands, and shifting currents into which we may plunge at any turn.

Harry and Lucy personify additional coordinates of Cather's artist-self, and that the two never join reiterates the point that Cather did not reconcile the sexual tensions which marked her life and that they continued as an element in her creative energies. The psycho-narrator is explicit about this connection between Lucy and Harry's sublimated self: "There was a part of himself that Harry was ashamed to live out in the open . . ., but he could live it through Lucy" (107). In Cather's creative imagination, Lucy personifies the uninhibited, fiery emotions that Harry never allows in himself—fiery, at least, compared to the frigid standards set forth by a turn-of-the-century prairie society. Harry epitomizes the traditional male—large, authoritative, successful at sports and business, and not expressly cerebral or artistic. Lucy, on the contrary, epitomizes "feminine" qualities that Harry cannot publicly endorse: creativity, dependency, reckless emotions, willfulness—even human tenderness. For Harry to acknowledge such characteristics is to risk public exposure as an invert, and it is his fear of exhibiting such "feminine" tenderness which motivates his harsh refusal to help Lucy on the night of her death and which later haunts his every thought.

Just as she cannot permit the physical consummation of the Lucy-Sebastian relationship, neither can Cather permit a marriage between Lucy and Harry. Since both are fictive manifestations of her bifurcated self, to allow them nuptial union would be an incestuous acknowledgement of her homoerotic desires. As with Jim Burden in *My Ántonia*, Harry carefully shields his femine sensitivity with success in the masculine world of sports, war, and especially business. Thus safe from accusations of inversion-perversion, he is transformed into an element of Cather's artistic self, careful and premeditative. Trapped in a barren marriage with a woman who has more business acumen than he, Harry has completely sublimated his eroticism. He is therefore a "safe" tangible representative of Cather's psyche. Lucy, however, has no such sublimations. She is full of sexual energy, as her actions and crimson scarf signify, and is thereby "unsafe." Frederick J. Hoffman's use of the term "exogamy" (18) conveniently explains the fear of incest inherited from our primitive ancestors. It clarifies the taboo with which Cather struggled in the Ántonia-Jim situation, and again aids in understanding the Lucy-Harry relationship. Because they emblematize segments of Cather's psyche, the brother-sister of her unconscious, Cather can permit no sexual contact. They must remain celibate in their relationship, else Cather has unconsciously sanctioned the forbidden crime of incest—incest in this case which has strong homoerotic undertones.

Consequently, Cather kills Lucy, thereby summarily guaranteeing that neither heteroerotic nor homoerotic consummation occurs, and incidentally echoing the suicide motif which permeates her fiction. As much a daughter of the Nebraska village in 1935 as she was in 1918, Cather remained very prudent in revealing the painful dichotomy between her private and social selves. Her art continued to be, therefore, both syntomic and asyntonic, just as it proved itself to be in her management of the Jim and Ántonia dilemma in 1918. By 1935, however, she was more tired, more harried, less sympathetic even with that art. Whereas she goes to great lengths to permit Ántonia to expiate her "sins" by reintegrating herself (reingratiating, we might even say) into the prairie hegemony, she no longer demonstrates such patience with Lucy, who is dead almost before she reaches the age of majority. (As she began work on *Lucy Gayheart,* Cather complained of being "very tired" and said Lucy "was a silly young girl and she was losing patience with her." Cather wondered if perhaps she were "too old for this sort of a book" [Woodress 450]).

That Cather chooses to eliminate the female and retain the male persona offers a final paradox. Ostensibly Harry's survival would suggest that Cather's masculine self ultimately dominated her feminine self, thus offering some evidence that the much-discussed gender conflict ended in favor of the male. However, as Harry himself says, and as we have seen with Claude Wheeler especially, one is sometimes blessed by dying young. Lucy, therefore, may be Cather's chosen one. The entire novel, told retrospectively, is a testament to how Lucy lives in the memories of those who knew her. She has attained a modicum of heroic stature she may well never have attained had she lived. She has died virginal, has avoided the disappointments of sexual involvement, marriage, failed art, and all the sorrows flesh is heir to. Her cement footprints remain as her monument, the symbol of eternal youth in movement, escaping the age-inflicted repose and regret which Harry is experiencing. Thus, Cather leaves us with the same conundrum with which we began: we do not know finally whether the masculine or feminine self was dominant. Nor, for that matter, is a resolution demanded. What is inescapable is the realization that she was beset from first to last by perplexities arising from her unorthodox sexuality—and the resultant conflicts shaped her art.

In many respects *Sapphira and the Slave Girl* is an unfortunate finale, demonstrating most of the faults and little of the virtuosity of the preceding novels. The point of view is best described as narrative trickery (or ineptness), for the unexpected appearance of the "I" narrator is not foreshadowed in the previous text; and any number of resultant faults could be documented. There is more incongruity than irony when the five-year-old narrator introduces herself in the final few pages and

injects a tone of naive innocence and nostalgia, when the tale
she claims to have told suggests her ancestress to have been so-
ciopathic and the past to have been nightmarish. As James E.
Miller observes, the novel becomes "eerie" (142) at the point
where we suddenly learn we have been in the mind of a child all
along, when we thought we were listening to an omniscient
narrator. We are shocked that a child's mind could entertain
such malevolence. Miller is correct when he says that with *Sapphira and the Slave Girl* "we are in the presence of an imagination that is flagging, of a talent that has lost its firm grasp on
technique and craft" (142). Yet, Cather could well have been
writing an epigram for *Sapphira and the Slave Girl* when she
records Lucy's first reponse to Clement Sebastian's singing. Lucy
watches Sebastian return for an encore that is perfunctory, and
judges it "a sad, simple old air which required little from the
singer, yet probably no one who heard it that night will ever for-
get it" (31). Sapphira Colbert emerges from the textual rubble as
one of the most fascinating wicked women in American fiction
and as an appropriate valedictory personification of Cather's
conflicted art.

Cather tries with the benevolent Henry Colbert, his compassionate daughter Rachel Blake, and minor characters such as
David Fairhead and Mrs. Bywaters to establish a narrative of
hope. The superficial text has as a major motif people helping
people. Yet such dramatis personae dim in Sapphira's hard
light. Herself characterized by moments of compassion, Sapphira nonetheless materializes to rival Ken Kesey's Big Nurse
Ratched for malevolence disguised as altruism which in turn
disguises sexual repressions. At times she also sounds like
Faulkner's Jason Compson in her acerbic pronouncements about
those who are at her mercy. Near the time she began to create
Sapphira, Cather wrote Sinclair Lewis that "Americans were the
most gullible and easily taken in of all people because they could
not think evil of anyone" (Woodress 479). Though few would
agree with her assessment of the American's capacity for assuming evil, Cather seems to have created Sapphira to show how
foolish and dangerous such naive blindness to evil could be.
Although the traditional, affirmative view is that *Sapphira and
the Slave Girl* is another example of Cather's "affirmation of life
through sympathy and understanding" (Stouck 300), Sapphira's
unsympathetic desire for revenge against both her husband and
his favorite slave girl is clearly what motivates the narrative action. Moreover, Sapphira—not unlike the unregenerate prosti-

tutes of *Shadows on the Rock*—is Cather's final indication that the unapologetic, dark self continued to hold its own if not win against the forces of sweetness and light.

Compared to the dedicated virtue of Henry, Rachel, and Nancy, Sapphira is Satanic. The dropsy which confines her to a wheel chair is simultaneously her mark of Satan and a symbol of her social incapacitation. Ostensibly she is a Virginia lady, an aristocrat of long standing who still owns the mill and the land which was deeded to her ancestors by Thomas, Lord Fairfax in 1747. Trapped in the most patriarchal of societies, Sapphira wars against the forces that would mold her into subservience, that would enslave her as surely as the "darkies" she owns in ironic mockery of the bondage she herself is expected to assume. Far from acquiescing to her predestined role as wife, mother, and servant (as her daughter Rachel has obediently done), Sapphira revolts in the only ways open to her. Legally and conventionally restrained by her gender, she resorts to irony, vitriol, and other forms of verbal retaliation to establish her will or to shield herself from the socio-economic, sexual forces that are more dangerous to her than any other element in the semi-civilized Virginia wilderness. For good measure, she adds jealousy, deviousness and revenge to supplement her verbal arsenal.

Early in the narrative Cather begins Sapphira's innuendoes about Nancy, whose father was a white "painter from Baltimore" (9). Sounding the repressed fury of Jason Compson, Sapphira observes sardonically of the itinerant artist who came to paint family portraits and stayed longer than necessary: "We got the portraits out of him, anyway, and maybe we got a smart yellow girl into the bargain" (9). Henry's superficially good, patient, Christian virtues fold before his wife's dedicated meanness and acerbic wit, a trait which Freud says "is used with special preference as a weapon of attack or criticism of superiors who claim to be in authority" and is "well adapted as a weapon of attack upon what is great, dignified, and mighty, that which is shielded by internal hindrances or external circumstances against direct disparagement" (BW 699). Henry's escape from his wife's attack upon "authority" is in reading John Bunyan's *Holy War*, a book about the Devil's taking up residence in the town of Mansoul—an appropriate allegory, since Henry seems unaware that Diabolus has changed gender and resides in his own house if not his soul. Like Euclide Auclair in *Shadows on the Rock*, Henry consistently sounds more self-righteous and ineffective than strong and well meaning, a moral waffling which accounts in part for Sapphira's delight in goading him. When her daughter tells her that the Baptists are good people, Sapphira quips: "So your father thinks. But then he never did mind to forgather with common people. I suppose that goes with a miller's business" (16). She especially likes to antagonize him with threats to sell or remove Nancy, whom she owns but cannot sell without his agreement. At one point she threatens to send the slave girl Bluebell (whom he hates) instead of Nancy to clean his room, forcing Henry to lose his calculated calm in an outburst of masculine, blustering authority that gives Sapphira another small victory over his patriarchal demeanor. Later Sapphira goads him one more time by casually mentioning a feat which she can accomplish without his permission: she might take Nancy instead of Till with her on her annual extended Easter visit to Winchester. Yet, toward her daughter Rachel, whom she does not have to honor or obey, she can be manifestly unkind. She applauds Rachel's early marriage because it removes her from home, and after Rachel helps Nancy escape to Canada, Sapphira officially bans her from visiting at Mill House.

The apex of Sapphira's capacity for evil is her scheme to set Nancy up for the scoundrel Martin Colbert. For Sapphira, the plan serves three primary purposes: it revenges her against a girl whom she only suspects may have replaced her in her husband's bed but whom she knows has replaced her in his affection; it allows her to retaliate against her husband, a move which law, convention, and even some grudging respect would never let her manage directly; and it serves as a vicarious sexual experience. It is this third element and its attendant metaphors which convey us from surface narrative to the sociosexual implications of the subtext. Book V is entitled "Martin Colbert," and introduces the nephew who stands as the masculine counterpart to Sapphira in her capacity for evil, though his evil is more overt and crude. One of his amusements is rolling turtles onto their backs to see their legs kick (151). (To the relief of the neighborhood, he will be killed in the Civil War.) Sapphira's reasons for inviting Martin to Mill House are not immediately clear, especially since she is conspicuously more subtle and clever than her husband's callow nephew. When she assigns Nancy to be his maid, however, her true intentions take shape, though the vicarious sexual gratification she receives from the plotting of Nancy's ruin is less apparent, even to Sapphira. However, Sapphira is confined to a wheel chair, her husband takes his meals in the big house with Sapphira but sleeps in the

mill, and she is surrounded by slaves who are relatively uninhibited and sexually active. Such textual clues suggest that not
only are Sapphira and Martin wed in their mutual capacity for
hurting others but that Sapphira sees Nancy's imminent seduction as an extension of her own frustrated eroticism, which here
is cast in relatively conventional heterosexual modes but which
(because Martin is her nephew) is tinged with the same incest we
note in earlier Cather novels.

As she does with the prostitute motif in *Shadows on the
Rock*, Cather juxtaposes scenes to convey displaced eroticism and
the conflicts which underlie it. When Henry finally confides to
Sapphira that he is concerned about the scoundrel Martin and
his threat to Nancy, Sapphira (aware of the danger long before
Henry) counsels her husband to understand that his nephew
needs a refuge and that he has a "gentlemanly side" (199).
Moreover, she continues rather coyly, punning on the phallic
dull blade, "I am certainly not very lively company for a young
blade to spend his evenings with, but if he is dull here he never
shows it. Certainly I shall miss him when he is gone" (199). In
other words, if the "darkie" girls must be seduced to keep Martin
content, Sapphira is willing to make that concession. If they
must serve as surrogate sex partners so that he remains to give
her "pleasure in his company" (199) then, in her ironically appropriate choice of words, "it's no affair of mine" (199).

Immediately following this revealing conversation,
Cather echoes the "blade" pun and presents the mowing vi-
gnette in which the Negro Tansy Dave is introduced. Tansy
Dave, like Martin, once developed a sexual passion for a slave
girl and went mad when she was sent away. The connection in
the scenes is that Sapphira had tried to purchase the slave girl
Susanna so that Dave could have her, an instance of her
matchmaking which sets the precedent for the Martin-Nancy
plot. Susanna is a "taking wench" (205) who not only has enthralled Dave but whose erotic dances have also intrigued Sapphira. Sapphira (again living through surrogates) fails in her
efforts to purchase a lover for Dave, but for one who has just re-
nounced any responsibility for the Negroes' affairs, she shows an
untypical interest in him. She is especially fond of the wild
turkey he shoots for her, makes sure he periodically washes
himself "in the creek" when he shows up naked (208), and in
general is very solicitous of him. As Cather says of the situation,
"Colbert often wondered at Sapphira's forbearance with Dave"
(208). The observation is innocent enough superficially, as is the

entire episode about Tansy Dave; but when Sapphira's earlier conversation concerning Martin is examined in conjunction with the Tansy Dave episode, Sapphira's suppressed eroticism becomes a plausible element in explaining not only the narrative placement of the Tansy Dave story but also Sapphira's motivations relative to Martin Colbert. For Cather, the "darkies" onto whom Sapphira displaces her erotic motivations are the objective epitome of the unresolved "dark" conflicts which surrounded her own sexuality. In this respect, *Sapphira and the Slave Girl* is Cather's journey into the heart of darkness and into the primitive, subconscious workings of her own psyche. (I am aware of the racial undertones of Cather's terminology here and of accusations of bigotry directed at her, most of which do not take into account the retrospective fallacy entailed in such judgments. Conrad I use more as metaphor than to imply direct influence, though Cather obviously knew Conrad's works [see Woodress 193]).

Cather offers the child narrator as her historical self, and in divesting herself of the fictive narrative mask she relinquishes the fragile distinction between what Wayne C. Booth terms the "implied author" (151) which the audience assumes the right to construct and the literal author who remains comparatively inviolate. It is an authorial divestiture which to a considerable degree threatens the generic identity of the novel as such, and which in this specific instance significantly compromises narrative integrity in that it tests audience credulity. Yet, more apropos to our immediate purpose, Cather's biographic shift suggests how much of her literal self she embedded in the previous narratives and how finally she wished to move out of the subterfuge which defines fiction and to make a public, historical statement of self. She wanted to document certain elements of her past (both genealogical and mythic) which would to one degree or another define what she had become in her final reckoning. That she does not succeed in making that confession a very convincing narrative is testament to how firm in the audience's mind is that thin but nonetheless distinct barrier between fiction and biography, and testament also to how thick was the shield Cather had erected between herself and the world. Even when she wanted to write fact, she felt compelled to package it as fiction, to offer to the world a form of psychological disingenuousness.

It seems appropriate, however, that the fictionalized manifestations of self which come to dominate the narrative speak most honestly for the tensions which continued to motivate Cather. That the title of the work and its dominant theme designate the enslaved self and the efforts to escape that slavery via flight and subterfuge indicate the degree to which Cather had not freed herself from the psychic battles. The irony of the narrative, certainly, is that whereas the Negro slaves of the pre-Civil War South dominate the surface text, the subtext is dominated by the guerrilla war waged by an aging, physically handicapped woman against those sexual and economic conventions which enslave her more permanently than any laws of indenture. Nancy the slave girl goes free, at least from her slavery; but Sapphira dies while still in mortal combat against servitude, "upright in her [wheel]chair" and alone (294).

I noted in the Introduction that Cather's frequent use of children (as in *My Ántonia*) was less a slavish adherence to nostalgia and more an attempt to attain psychological union with nature, to decrease the culturally imposed strictures of sexual/sexist dogmas. She attempted, somewhat mystically at times and through an imagination grounded in her own childhood and the past, to reenter a preadult time of innocence, thereby to free herself from the complexes that first create and then feed upon guilt and repression. The intrusion of the child-narrator in *Sapphira and the Slave Girl* demonstrates that Cather did not ultimately attain the reconciliation such desired freedom implies. In her final novel, rather than imagining the adult self as existing in a pre-innocent state, Cather brings the child-self forward out of the past into a corrupted present, or at least into a present which the text shows as offering little room for unbridled optimism about the capabilities of the human heart. The consequence is that the reader senses having witnessed a rather startling form of Cesarean birth, a narrative superimposition which is as disturbing as it is improbable. Cather herself may have found some comfort in resurrecting the innocent child, but the reader is unconvinced that this particular child is in fact a valid narrative voice. Sapphira Colbert, dying alone and proudly unregenerate, ultimately connects more with those conflicted authorial personae who precede her, and therefore speaks more convincingly for the author than does the incredible, bumptious child who intervenes in the epilogue and usurps the right of narrator.

Works Cited

Booth, Wayne C. *The Rhetoric of Fiction*. Chicago: U of Chicago P, 1961.

Cather, Willa. *The Kingdom of Art: Willa Cather's First Principles and Critical Statesments 1893-1896*. Ed. Bernice Slote. Lincoln: U of Nebraska P, 1966.

—. *Lucy Gayheart*. New York: Knopf, 1935.

—. *Sapphira and the Slave Girl*. New York: Knopf, 1940.

—. *Shadows on the Rock*. New York: Knopf, 1931.

—. *Willa Cather in Person: Interviews, Speeches, and Letters*. Ed. L. Brent Bohlke. Lincoln: U of Nebraska P, 1986.

Cohn, Dorrit. *Transparent Minds: Narrative Modes for Presenting Consciousness in Fiction*. Princeton: Princeton U P, 1978.

Freud, Sigmund. *The Basic Writings of Sigmund Freud*. 1938. Trans. and ed. A. A. Brill. New York: The Modern Library, 1966.

Fryer, Judith. *Felicitous Space: The Imaginative Structures of Edith Wharton and Willa Cather*. Chapel Hill: U of North Carolina P, 1986.

Hoffman, Frederick J. *Freudianism and the Literary Mind*, 2nd ed. Baton Rouge: LSU P, 1957.

Miller, James E., Jr. "Willa Cather and the Art of Fiction" in *The Art of Willa Cather*. Ed. Bernice Slote and Virginia Faulkner. Lincoln: U of Nebraska P, 1974. 121-148.

Nelson, Robert J. *Willa Cather and France: In Search of the Lost Language*. Urbana: U of Illinois P, 1988.

O'Brien, Sharon. *Willa Cather: The Emerging Voice*. New York: Oxford U P, 1986.

Rosowski, Susan. *The Voyage Perilous: Willa Cather's Romanticism*. Lincoln: U of Nebraska P, 1986.

Stouck, David. "Willa Cather's Last Four Books." *Novel: A Forum on Fiction*, 7 (Fall 1973): 41-53. Rpt. in *Critical Essays on Willa Cather*. Ed. John J. Murphy. Boston: Hall, 1984. 290-304.

Woodress, James. *Willa Cather: A Literary Life*. Lincoln: U of Nebraska P, 1987.

Index